# First World War
## and Army of Occupation
# War Diary
## France, Belgium and Germany

I0311141

50 DIVISION
Headquarters, Branches and Services
Royal Army Veterinary Corps
Deputy Assistant Director Veterinary Services
1 July 1915 - 31 March 1919

WO95/2816/4

The Naval & Military Press Ltd
www.nmarchive.com
**Published in association with The National Archives**

Published by

The Naval & Military Press Ltd

Unit 10 Ridgewood Industrial Park,

Uckfield, East Sussex,

TN22 5QE England

Tel: +44 (0) 1825 749494

www.naval-military-press.com

www.nmarchive.com

*This diary has been reprinted in facsimile from the original. Any imperfections are inevitably reproduced and the quality may fall short of modern type and cartographic standards.*

# Contents

| Document type | Place/Title | Date From | Date To |
|---|---|---|---|
| Heading | WO95/2816/3 | | |
| Heading | 50th Division Asst Dir. Veterinary Services Jly 1915-Mar 1919 | | |
| Heading | 50th Division A.D.V.S. 50th Division Vol I 1-31-7-15 | | |
| War Diary | St Jans Cappel | 01/07/1915 | 21/07/1915 |
| War Diary | Armentieres | 22/07/1915 | 31/07/1915 |
| Heading | 50th Division A.D.V.S. 50th Division Vol II From 1-31.8.15 | | |
| War Diary | Armentieres | 01/08/1915 | 31/08/1915 |
| Heading | A.D.V.S. 50th Division Vol III Sept 15 | | |
| War Diary | Armentieres | 01/09/1915 | 30/09/1915 |
| Heading | A D V S. 50th Division Vol IV Oct 15 | | |
| Miscellaneous | Part Companies By Major F Fail A.V.C. | | |
| War Diary | Armentieres | 01/10/1915 | 31/10/1915 |
| Heading | A.D.V.S. 50th Div. Nov 1915 Vol V | | |
| War Diary | Armentieres | 01/11/1915 | 11/11/1915 |
| War Diary | Menis | 12/11/1915 | 30/11/1915 |
| Heading | A.D.V.S. 50th Div Dec Vol VI | | |
| War Diary | Menis | 01/12/1915 | 20/12/1915 |
| War Diary | Hooggraaf | 21/12/1915 | 31/12/1915 |
| Heading | A.D.V.S. 50 Div Jan Vol VII | | |
| War Diary | Hooggraaf | 01/01/1916 | 31/01/1916 |
| Heading | A D V S 50 Div Vol VIII | | |
| Miscellaneous | D.A.G. 3rd Echelon. Base | 03/05/1916 | 03/05/1916 |
| War Diary | Hooggraaf | 01/02/1916 | 31/03/1916 |
| Heading | A D V S 50 Div Vol | | |
| War Diary | Hooggraaf | 01/04/1916 | 02/04/1916 |
| War Diary | Hestoutre | 03/04/1916 | 25/04/1916 |
| War Diary | Fletre | 26/04/1916 | 01/06/1916 |
| War Diary | Hestoutre | 01/06/1916 | 30/06/1916 |
| Heading | War Diary A.D.V.S. 50 Division From 1st July 1916 To 31st July 1916 Volume X | | |
| War Diary | Hestoutre | 01/07/1916 | 31/07/1916 |
| Heading | War Diary Of A.D.V.S. 50th Division August 1916 Vol XI. | | |
| War Diary | Hestoutre | 01/08/1916 | 08/08/1916 |
| War Diary | Fletre | 09/08/1916 | 11/08/1916 |
| War Diary | Bernaville | 11/08/1916 | 15/08/1916 |
| War Diary | Vignacourt | 16/08/1916 | 16/08/1916 |
| War Diary | Montigny | 17/08/1916 | 09/09/1916 |
| War Diary | Millencourt | 09/09/1916 | 30/09/1916 |
| Heading | War Diary Of A.D. Of V.S. 50th Division From 1st Oct. To 31st Oct. 1916 Volume XIII | | |
| War Diary | Millencourt | 01/10/1916 | 25/10/1916 |
| War Diary | Fricourt Farm | 26/10/1916 | 31/10/1916 |
| Heading | War Diary Of A.D. Of V.S. 50th Division From Nov 1st 1916 To Nov 30th 1916 Vol XIV | | |
| War Diary | Fricourt Farm | 01/11/1916 | 18/11/1916 |
| War Diary | Albert | 19/11/1916 | 30/11/1916 |

| | | | |
|---|---|---|---|
| Heading | War Diary Of A.D.V.S. 50th Division From December 1st To December 31st 1916 Volume XV | | |
| War Diary | Baizieux | 01/12/1916 | 31/12/1916 |
| War Diary | Fricourt | 01/01/1917 | 27/01/1917 |
| War Diary | Ribemont | 28/01/1917 | 31/01/1917 |
| Heading | War Diary Of A.D. Of V.S. 50th Division From February 1st 1917 To February 28th 1917 Volume XVII | | |
| War Diary | Ribemont | 01/02/1917 | 02/02/1917 |
| War Diary | Bois St Martin | 14/02/1917 | 28/02/1917 |
| Heading | War Diary Of A.D.V.S. 50th Division From 1st March 1917 To 31st March 1917 Volume XVIII | | |
| War Diary | St Martin's Wood | 01/03/1917 | 08/03/1917 |
| War Diary | Mericourt Sur Somme | 09/03/1917 | 31/03/1917 |
| Heading | War Diary Of A.D. Of V.S. 50th Division From 1st April 1917 To 30th April 1917 Volume XIX | | |
| War Diary | Molliens Au Bois | 01/05/1917 | 01/05/1917 |
| War Diary | Beauval | 02/05/1917 | 02/05/1917 |
| War Diary | Bouque-Maison | 03/05/1917 | 03/05/1917 |
| War Diary | Ramecourt | 04/05/1917 | 04/05/1917 |
| War Diary | Ramecourt | 05/04/1917 | 06/04/1917 |
| War Diary | Roellecourt | 07/04/1917 | 07/04/1917 |
| War Diary | Le Cauroy | 08/04/1917 | 09/04/1917 |
| War Diary | Berneville | 10/04/1917 | 11/04/1917 |
| War Diary | Arras | 12/04/1917 | 25/04/1917 |
| War Diary | Couturelle | 26/04/1917 | 30/04/1917 |
| Heading | War Diary Of A.D. Of V.S. 50th Division From 1st May 1917 To 31st May 1917 Volume XX | | |
| War Diary | Couturelle | 01/05/1917 | 01/05/1917 |
| War Diary | Basseux | 02/05/1917 | 03/05/1917 |
| War Diary | Couturelle | 04/05/1917 | 18/05/1917 |
| War Diary | Beaumetz | 19/05/1917 | 22/05/1917 |
| War Diary | Couin | 23/05/1917 | 31/05/1917 |
| Heading | War Diary Of A.D.V.S. 50th North In Division From 1 June 1917 To 30 June 1917 Volume XXI | | |
| War Diary | Couin | 01/06/1917 | 17/06/1917 |
| War Diary | Nr Boisleux Au Mont | 18/06/1917 | 30/06/1917 |
| Heading | War Diary Of The D A D V S 50th (N) Division July 1917 | | |
| War Diary | Boisleux Au Mont | 01/07/1917 | 31/07/1917 |
| Heading | War Diary Of D.A. D. V. S. 50th Division From August 1st 1917 To August 31st 1917 Volume XXIII | | |
| War Diary | Boisleux Au Mont | 01/08/1917 | 31/08/1917 |
| Heading | War Diary Of D.A.D.V.S. 50th Division From Sept 1st 1917 To Sept 30th 1917 Volume 24 | | |
| War Diary | Boisleux-Au-Mont | 01/09/1917 | 30/09/1917 |
| War Diary | War Diary Of D.A.D.V.S. 50th Division From 1st Oct. 1917 To 31st Oct 1917 Vol 25 | | |
| War Diary | Boisleux-au-Mont | 01/10/1917 | 05/10/1917 |
| War Diary | Achiet-le-Petit | 06/10/1917 | 16/10/1917 |
| War Diary | Lederzeele | 17/10/1917 | 19/10/1917 |
| War Diary | Proven | 20/10/1917 | 23/10/1917 |
| War Diary | Elverdinge 28/a.18.b.2.8 | 24/10/1917 | 31/10/1917 |
| Heading | War Diary Of D.A.D.V.S. 50th Division From 1.11.17 To 30.11.17 Volume XXVII | | |
| War Diary | Elverdinghe 28/a 18.6.2.8 | 01/11/1917 | 09/11/1917 |

| | | | |
|---|---|---|---|
| War Diary | Eperlecques | 10/11/1917 | 30/11/1917 |
| Heading | War Diary Of D.A.D.V.S. 50th Division From 1st Dec. 1917 To 31st Dec. 1917 Volume XXVII | | |
| War Diary | Eperlecques | 01/12/1917 | 12/12/1917 |
| War Diary | Brandhoek | 13/12/1917 | 31/12/1917 |
| War Diary | War Diary Of D.A.D.V.S. 50th Division From 1.1.18 To 31.1.18 Volume XXVIII | | |
| War Diary | Brandhoek | 01/01/1918 | 05/01/1918 |
| War Diary | Steenvoorde | 06/01/1918 | 18/01/1918 |
| War Diary | Wizernes | 19/01/1918 | 29/01/1918 |
| War Diary | Brandhoek | 30/01/1918 | 31/01/1918 |
| Heading | War Diary Of D.A.D.V.S. 50th Division From 1.2.18 To 28.2.18 Vol XXIX | | |
| War Diary | Brandhoek | 01/02/1918 | 22/02/1918 |
| War Diary | Wizernes | 23/02/1918 | 28/02/1918 |
| Heading | War Diary Of D.A.D.V.S. 50th Division From 1st. March 1918 To 31st March 1918 Volume XXX | | |
| War Diary | Wizernes | 01/03/1918 | 08/03/1918 |
| War Diary | Moreuil | 09/03/1918 | 10/03/1918 |
| War Diary | Harbonnieres | 11/03/1918 | 20/03/1918 |
| War Diary | Beaumetz | 21/03/1918 | 21/03/1918 |
| War Diary | Le Mesnil-Bruntel | 22/03/1918 | 22/03/1918 |
| War Diary | Foucaucourt | 23/03/1918 | 24/03/1918 |
| War Diary | Harbonnieres | 25/03/1918 | 25/03/1918 |
| War Diary | Marcelcave | 26/03/1918 | 26/03/1918 |
| War Diary | Villers Bretonneux. | 27/03/1918 | 27/03/1918 |
| War Diary | Hangard | 28/03/1918 | 28/03/1918 |
| War Diary | Boves | 29/03/1918 | 29/03/1918 |
| War Diary | Sains-an-Amienois | 30/03/1918 | 30/03/1918 |
| War Diary | Douriez | 31/03/1918 | 31/03/1918 |
| Heading | War Diary Of D.A.D.V.S. 50th Division From 1st April 1918 To 30th April 1918 Volume XXXI | | |
| War Diary | Douriez | 01/04/1918 | 03/04/1918 |
| War Diary | Robecq | 04/04/1918 | 07/04/1918 |
| War Diary | Merville | 08/04/1918 | 10/04/1918 |
| War Diary | La Motte Au Bois | 11/04/1918 | 11/04/1918 |
| War Diary | Thiennes | 12/04/1918 | 13/04/1918 |
| War Diary | Wittes | 14/04/1918 | 15/04/1918 |
| War Diary | Rocquetoire | 16/04/1918 | 19/04/1918 |
| War Diary | Aire. | 20/04/1918 | 25/04/1918 |
| War Diary | Fismes Arcis Le Ponsart | 26/04/1918 | 28/04/1918 |
| War Diary | Aras Le Ponsart | 29/04/1918 | 30/04/1918 |
| Heading | War Diary Of D.A.D.V.S. 50th Division From May 1st To May 31st 1918 Volume XXXII | | |
| War Diary | Aras-le-Ponsart | 01/05/1918 | 04/05/1918 |
| War Diary | Beau Rieux | 05/05/1918 | 26/05/1918 |
| War Diary | St Gilles | 27/05/1918 | 27/05/1918 |
| War Diary | Lhery | 28/05/1918 | 28/05/1918 |
| War Diary | Igny Le Jard | 29/05/1918 | 29/05/1918 |
| War Diary | Le Breuil | 30/05/1918 | 30/05/1918 |
| War Diary | Vert-la Gravelle | 31/05/1918 | 31/05/1918 |
| Heading | War Diary Of D.A.D.V.S. 50th Division From 1st June 1918 To 30th June 1918 Volume 33 | | |
| War Diary | Vert-la Gravelle | 01/06/1918 | 08/06/1918 |
| War Diary | Mondement | 09/06/1918 | 15/06/1918 |
| War Diary | La Noue | 17/06/1918 | 30/06/1918 |

| | | | |
|---|---|---|---|
| Heading | War Diary Of D.A.D.V.S. 50th Division From 1st July To 31st July 1918 Volume XXXIV | | |
| War Diary | La Noue | 01/07/1918 | 03/07/1918 |
| War Diary | Pont Rely & Huppy | 04/07/1918 | 10/07/1918 |
| War Diary | Gamaches | 11/07/1918 | 11/07/1918 |
| War Diary | Martin Eglise | 12/07/1918 | 15/07/1918 |
| War Diary | Greges | 16/07/1918 | 31/07/1918 |
| War Diary | War Diary Of D.A.D.V.S. 50th Division From 1st Augt. 1918 To 31st Augt. 1918 Volume XXXV | | |
| War Diary | Greges | 01/08/1918 | 31/08/1918 |
| Heading | War Diary Of D.A.D.V.S. 50th Division From. 1st Sept 1918 To 30th Sept 1918 Volume XXXVI | | |
| War Diary | Greges | 01/09/1918 | 14/09/1918 |
| War Diary | Greges/Lucheux | 15/09/1918 | 16/09/1918 |
| War Diary | Lucheux | 17/09/1918 | 25/09/1918 |
| War Diary | Montigny | 26/09/1918 | 27/09/1918 |
| War Diary | Combles | 28/09/1918 | 30/09/1918 |
| Heading | War Diary Of D.A.D.V.S. 50th Division From 1.10.18 To 31.10.18 Volume XXXVII | | |
| War Diary | Lieramont | 01/10/1918 | 04/10/1918 |
| War Diary | Epehy | 05/10/1918 | 09/10/1918 |
| War Diary | Guisancourt Farm | 10/10/1918 | 11/10/1918 |
| War Diary | Le Trois Aux Soldats | 12/10/1918 | 29/10/1918 |
| War Diary | Le Cateau | 30/10/1918 | 31/10/1918 |
| Heading | War Diary Of D.A.D.V.S. 50th Division From 1st Novr To 30th November 1918 Volume XXXVIII | | |
| War Diary | Le Cateau | 01/11/1918 | 04/11/1918 |
| War Diary | Lannoy | 05/11/1918 | 06/11/1918 |
| War Diary | Noyelles | 07/11/1918 | 07/11/1918 |
| War Diary | Monceau St Waast | 08/11/1918 | 10/11/1918 |
| War Diary | Dourlers | 11/11/1918 | 30/11/1918 |
| Heading | War Diary Of D.A.D.V.S. 50th Division From Dec 1st. To Dec 31st. Vol XXXIX. | | |
| War Diary | Dourlers | 01/12/1918 | 11/12/1918 |
| War Diary | Le Quesnoy | 19/12/1918 | 31/12/1918 |
| Heading | War Diary Of D.A.D.V.S 50th Division From 1st Jan To 31st Jan 1919 Vol 40 | | |
| War Diary | Le Quesnoy | 01/01/1919 | 31/01/1919 |
| Heading | War Diary Of D.A.D.V.S. 50th Division From 1st February 1919 To 28th February 1919 Volume XLI | | |
| War Diary | Le Quesnoy | 01/02/1919 | 28/02/1919 |
| Heading | War Diary Of D.A.D.V.S 50th Division From 1st March 1919 To 31st March 1919 Vol XLII | | |
| War Diary | Le Quesnoy | 01/03/1919 | 31/03/1919 |

<u>50TH DIVISION</u>

ASST DIR. VETERINARY SERVICES

JLY 1915-MAR 1919

50th Division

121/6390

A.D.V.S. 50th Division

Vol I

1-31-4-15

Instructions regarding War Diaries and Intelligence Summaries are contained in F. S. Regs., Part II. and the Staff Manual respectively. Title pages will be prepared in manuscript.

# WAR DIARY
or
~~INTELLIGENCE SUMMARY~~.
(Erase heading not required.)

F. Fail Major. A.V.C

Army Form C. 2118.

A.D.V.S. 50th (North'bn) Division

| Place | Date | Hour | Summary of Events and Information | Remarks and references to Appendices |
|---|---|---|---|---|
| 1. Janus Cappel. | 1 7/15 | | Indented for 8 remounts to complete establishment of the Mobile Veterinary Section - received information from A.D.V.S 46th Division of their having evacuated a mule belonging to 50th Division. A.C - | F.F. |
| | 2 | | Inspected 14 horses prior to their being sent to Base Veterinary Hospital. | F.F. |
| | 3 | | Ordinary Routine | F.F. |
| | 4 | | O.C. M.V. Section reported having collected 7 horses - | F.F. |
| | 5 | | Arranged with O.C. M.V.S. that he give assistance to owner of his farm - to harvest his hay - | F.F. |
| | 6 | | Experimented on horses drinking pool with Kerosine oil and reported to D.D.V.S. 2nd Army | F.F. |
| | 7. | | Inspected 14 horses prior to their being sent to Base Veterinary Hospital - inspected horses of 3rd Battery. 3rd Brigade. R.F.A - A.D.V.S. 46th Division reported having evacuated a horse belonging to 116th Bty. R.G.A. | F.F. |
| | 8. | | Visited Mobile Veterinary Section | F.F. |
| | 9, 10, 11, 12 | | Inspected all animals in the 50th Division on 9th 10th 11th + 12th - also requested 'Q' to issue orders that all government animals must be distinctly branded with ↑ Brand - and that every endeavour should be made by O.C's to get their animals into good big condition pending approach of Winter - | F.F. |

1577 Wt. W10791/1773 500,000 1/15 D. D. & L. A.D.S.S./Forms/C. 2118.

Instructions regarding War Diaries and Intelligence Summaries are contained in F. S. Regs., Part II. and the Staff Manual respectively. Title pages will be prepared in manuscript.

# WAR DIARY
or
# INTELLIGENCE SUMMARY.
(Erase heading not required.)

Army Form C. 2118.

| Place | Date | Hour | Summary of Events and Information | Remarks and references to Appendices |
|---|---|---|---|---|
| St JANS Cappel | 13/1/15 | | Inspected 14 horses at M.V.S. prior to their being sent to Base Veterinary Hospital | f.f. |
| | 14 | | " horses of 2nd Brigade. R.F.A. | |
| | 15 | | Visited Mobile Section | |
| | 16/10 – 21 | | on leave to England. Captain Southall acted for me. M.V.S. moved into new area on 19th. Hd Qrs left St Jans on 21st for ARMENTIERES. | f.f. |
| ARMENTIERES | 22 | | CAPTAIN WILLIAMS. A.V.C. reported for temporary duty from 28th Division. Saw Lt Hobday demonstrate on the intra-dermal palpebral method of Mallein testing | f.f. |
| | 23 | | ordinary routine. Suggested 'Q' that wind-screens and permanent standings be provided for animals in view of the winter. | f.f. |
| | 24 | | Saw C.R.A. with reference to trying to get all artillery horses into bigger condition. impressed on my V.O's that it was part of their duty to stable manage as well as to attend sick animals. All government animals in 50th Division are now distinctly branded | f.f. |
| | 25 | | Visited M.V.S. and inspected 11 horses + 4 mules prior to their dispatch to Base. Captains Southall + Williams proceeded on leave to England | f.f. |
| | 26 | | ordinary routine | f.f. |
| | 27 | | Inspected horses of the 16th Brigade. R.G.A. | f.f. |

1577 Wt. W10791/1773 500,000 1/15 D. D. & L. A.D.S.S./Forms/C. 2118.

Instructions regarding War Diaries and Intelligence Summaries are contained in F. S. Regs., Part II. and the Staff Manual respectively. Title pages will be prepared in manuscript.

# WAR DIARY
*or*
# INTELLIGENCE SUMMARY.
*(Erase heading not required.)*

Army Form C. 2118.

| Place | Date | Hour | Summary of Events and Information | Remarks and references to Appendices |
|---|---|---|---|---|
| [ARM]ENTIERES | 28 7/15 | | Visited M.V.S. and inspected horses of No. 2 Coy. A.S.C. | F.F. |
| | 29. | | CAPTAIN. CRONE returned to duty - inspected 14 horses and 2 mules prior to their departure to the Base. | |
| | 30. | | CAPTAIN. Williams returned from leave and rejoined 28th Division | F.F. |
| | 31. | | " Southall " " " ordinary routine. | F.F. |

1577 Wt. W10791/1773 500,000 1/15 D. D. & L. A.D.S.S./Forms/C. 2118.

50th Division

121/6587

A.D.V.S. 50th Division

Vol II

From 1 - 31. 8. 15

Army Form C. 2118.

# WAR DIARY
*or*
# INTELLIGENCE SUMMARY.
*(Erase heading not required.)*

Instructions regarding War Diaries and Intelligence Summaries are contained in F. S. Regs., Part II. and the Staff Manual respectively. Title pages will be prepared in manuscript.

| Place | Date | Hour | Summary of Events and Information | Remarks and references to Appendices |
|---|---|---|---|---|
| ARMENTIERS | 1 8/15 | | Inspected 15 horses for Base - Applied for the issue of horse clippers for all mounted units - on a scale of 2 per cent - | F.F. |
| " | 2 8/15 | | Issue of 2 lbs maize in lieu 2 lb oats to take effect from to-day. Inspected 4th Howitzer Brigade horses - | F.F. |
| " | 3 8/15 | | Arranged for Classification of all animals in the Division by veterinary Officers i/c - units - | F.F. |
| | 4 8/15 | | Issue of 2% Horse clippers Sanctioned - Visited Mobile Section and A.C. of 1st Brigade R.G.A - Put forward a suggestion that the scale of forage for Shires + Clydesdales might be altered to advantage - viz that the grain ration be reduced to 17 lbs and hay increased to 17 lbs - | F.F. |
| | 5 8/15 | | Inspected horses of the 149th Brigade Infantry | F.F. |
| | 6 8/15 | | Visited Mobile Veterinary Section - | |
| | 7 8/15 | | Wired to Base for 150 doses of mallein - instructed V.O's to be more exact in their remarks on the nature of cases on A.F. 2000 - | F.F. |
| | 8 8/15 | | Inspected A.C. 3rd Brigade R.F.A. Horses looking well | F.F. |

Instructions regarding War Diaries and Intelligence Summaries are contained in F. S. Regs., Part II. and the Staff Manual respectively. Title pages will be prepared in manuscript.

# WAR DIARY
*or*
# INTELLIGENCE SUMMARY.
*(Erase heading not required.)*

Army Form C. 2118.

| Place | Date | Hour | Summary of Events and Information | Remarks and references to Appendices |
|---|---|---|---|---|
| ARMENTIERS | 9 8/15 | | Had a D.O. published forbidding the clipping off the hair from heavy horses heels - Mallein received - visited mobile Section | F.F. |
| " | 10 8/15 | | Inoculated 124 horses - 5th Durham Battery - | |
| " | 11 8/15 | | Visited 5th Durham Bty - 10 A.m. + 5 p.m. with - | F.F. |
| " | 12 8/15 | | " " (one horse showed re-action) | F.F. |
| | | | - Col. Wilson. D.D.V.S. 2nd Army - " " +(one horse suspicious) | F.F. |
| | | | - make the necessary arrangements re disinfection etc. | F.F. |
| | 13. 8/15 | | Sent the horse that re-acted to mobile Section and had it destroyed. The doubtful case to be re-tested - | F.F. |
| | | | informed Q office of action taken etc. | |
| | 14 8/15 | | Impressed on V.O.S the necessity of careful supervision of their units. Inspected animals of 150th Brigade Infantry - | F.F. |
| | 15 8/15 | | Visited mobile Veterinary Section and 3rd Brigade R.F.A. | F.F. |
| | 16 8/15 | | Inspected horses Hd Qrs. A.S.C. - | F.F. |
| | 17 8/15 | | V.O.s instructed to classify all animals in their charge - | F.F. |
| | | | Inspected horses of 1st Brigade. R.F.A | F.F. |

Instructions regarding War Diaries and Intelligence Summaries are contained in F. S. Regs., Part II. and the Staff Manual respectively. Title pages will be prepared in manuscript.

# WAR DIARY
*or*
# INTELLIGENCE SUMMARY.
*(Erase heading not required.)*

Army Form C. 2118.

| Place | Date | Hour | Summary of Events and Information | Remarks and references to Appendices |
|---|---|---|---|---|
| ARMENTIERS | 18 8/15 | | Visited Mobile Section and inspected 14 horses for Base. | F.F. |
| | 19 8/15 | | Wrote C.R.A. reference crowded horse lines. | |
| | | | Wrote D.D.V.S. 2nd Army as follows: "In view of the coming winter I beg to suggest that the question of making horses rugs waterproof over the region of animals' loins - be considered. I think this could be easily done by attaching half a ground sheet (either new or partly worn) to each rug." | F.F. |
| | | | Inspected 2nd Brigade R.F.A. horses & visited Mobile Section | |
| | 20 8/15 | | Wrote 'Q' office as follows: "over 50% of the casualties to animals in the division are due to injuries - mostly kicks - heel rope galls and picked up nails. The latter are more or less unavoidable - but kicks and heel rope galls mostly occur at night & are largely due to stable pickets not doing their duty" - The G.O.C. sent circular memo to all concerned saying he looked to them to remedy this | F.F. |
| | 21 8/15 | | D.D.R. 2nd Army cast three horses for vice at M.V.S. | |
| | | | Captain Southall A.V.C. reported sick & sent to hospital | |

1577 Wt. W10791/1773 500,000 1/15 D. D. & L. A.D.S.S./Forms/C. 2118.

Instructions regarding War Diaries and Intelligence Summaries are contained in F. S. Regs., Part II. and the Staff Manual respectively. Title pages will be prepared in manuscript.

# WAR DIARY
*or*
# INTELLIGENCE SUMMARY.
*(Erase heading not required.)*

Army Form C. 2118.

| Place | Date | Hour | Summary of Events and Information | Remarks and references to Appendices |
|---|---|---|---|---|
| ARMENTIERS | 22.8.15 | | Inspected animals of 2nd Mountain Battery. | [illegible] |
| | 23.8.15 | | Visited M.V.S. and inspected horses of 2nd Brigade R.F.A | [illegible] |
| | 24.8.15 | | ordinary routine. | [illegible] |
| | 25.8.15 | | Inspected animals of 151st Infantry Brigade – wrote to all V.O's requested them to send in weekly report on Skin disease. | [illegible] |
| | 26.8.15 | | Visited M.V. Section and inspected animals of the Divisional Ammunition Column. | [illegible] |
| | 27.8.15 | | Instructed V.O.S as to the disposal of workably sound animals inspected animals of 149th Brigade (Infantry). | [illegible] |
| | 28.8.15 | | Again drew attention to the danger of leaving loose nails about visited M.V. Section. | [illegible] |
| | 29.8.15 | | Visited M.V. Section & saw horses (8) prior to their dispatch to Base | [illegible] |
| | 30.8.15 | | Inspected horses of 1st Coy. A.S.C. | [illegible] |
| | 31.8.15 | | Visited M.V.S. and inspected 4th Brigade R.F.A animals. | [illegible] |

50th Division

121
6994

A.D.V.S. 50th Division

Vol III

Sept. 15

avs

Army Form C. 21[illegible]

Instructions regarding War Diaries and Intelligence Summaries are contained in F. S. Regs., Part II. and the Staff Manual respectively. Title pages will be prepared in manuscript.

# WAR DIARY
*or*
# INTELLIGENCE SUMMARY.
*(Erase heading not required.)*

| Place | Date | Hour | Summary of Events and Information | Remarks and references to Appendices |
|---|---|---|---|---|
| Armentières | 1 9/15 | | Opened Divisional forge with a staff of 1 Sergt and 3 shoeing-smith for the purpose of making up old horse-shoes - visited M.V.S and No. 3 Coy A.S.C. transport. | F.F. |
| | 2 9/15 | | Visited divisional forge & transport of 9th D.L.I. | F.F. |
| | 3 9/15 | | Inspected horses of the M.M.P and Hd Qrs. | |
| | 4 9/15 | | Visited M.V.S. and inspected 7th D.L.I and R.E Transport. | F.F. |
| | 5 9/15 | | Inspected animals of No. 2 Mountain Bty. found excellent stable management. have had only one death in over six months. Saw No. 3 Coy. A.S.C. horses. | F.F. |
| | 6 9/15 | | Inspected animals of the 4th Brigade R.F.A & visited M.V. Section | F.F. |
| | 7 9/15 | | Took over 77 Remounts at Steenwerck Station and issued 50 of them same day. | F.F. |
| | 8 9/15 | | Visited M.V. Section and inspected horses of the 3rd Brigade R.F.A. | F.F. |
| | 9 9/15 | | Visited Field Remount Section with the G.O.C. | F.F. |
| | 10 9/15 | | Visited M.V.S and inspected 13 horses prior to their being sent to Base - inspected transport of the 2/2 Field Ambulance. | F.F. |

Instructions regarding War Diaries and Intelligence Summaries are contained in F. S. Regs., Part II. and the Staff Manual respectively. Title pages will be prepared in manuscript.

# WAR DIARY
*or*
# INTELLIGENCE SUMMARY.
*(Erase heading not required.)*

Army Form C. 2118.

| Place | Date | Hour | Summary of Events and Information | Remarks and references to Appendices |
|---|---|---|---|---|
| Armentiers | 11/9/15 | | G.O.C. visited Mobile Veterinary Section. | F.F. |
| " | 12 | | Lt. Wright A.V.C. reported for duty. Inspected transport animals of 149th Infantry Brigade. Captain Southall left for Base. | F.F. |
| " | 13 | | Weekly reports of V.O's on Infectious Diseases received. Inspected transport animals of the 150th Infantry Brigade. Wrote D.D.V.S. re motor car. Saying I had no difficulty in getting one when required. | F.F. F.F. |
| " | 14 | | Instructed O.C. M.V. Section re disposal of carcases fit for consumption. Inspected 4th Howitzer Brigade Horses. Wrote D.A. & Q.M.G. that I considered heel ropes necessary for all animals picketed in the open. | F.F. |
| " | 15 | | Visited M.V. Section & inspected transport animals of the 151st Infantry Brigade. Visited Divisional Forge. | F.F. |
| " | 16 | | Submitted list of officers & men that I considered worthy of mention in dispatches. Inspected horses of Nos. 1 & 2 Cos. A.S.C. | F.F. |

1577 Wt. W10791/1773 500,000 1/15 D. D. & L. A.D.S.S./Forms/C. 2118.

Army Form C. 2118

Instructions regarding War Diaries and Intelligence Summaries are contained in F. S. Regs., Part II. and the Staff Manual respectively. Title Pages will be prepared in manuscript.

# WAR DIARY
*or*
# INTELLIGENCE SUMMARY
*(Erase heading not required.)*

| Place | Date | Hour | Summary of Events and Information | Remarks and references to Appendices |
|---|---|---|---|---|
| Armentieres | 17/9/15 | | Visited M. V. Section + inspected horses of No 3. Coy A.S.C | J.J. |
| " | 18/9/15 | | Despatched Remount demand - inspected R.E. horses + 1st Field Ambulance transport animals. | J.J. |
| " | 19/9/15 | | Received V.O.S weekly report on Infectious Diseases. visited M.V. Section | J.J. |
| " | 20/9/15 | | Inspected 9th + 14th Btys. R.G.A. + No 2 Mountain Btys animals. | J.J. |
| " | 21/9/15 | | Visited M. V. Section + inspected. 9th D.L.I. transport | J.J. |
| " | 22/9/15 | | Asked by 'Q' Office my opinion on the clipping of horses during the winter - replied as follows - Re the attached I am of opinion that the clipping of horses all over should be forbidden excepting under the orders of V.O.S in the case of Skin Disease + animals affected with Lice - Animals with abnormally heavy coats do better if they are clipped as per attached drawings (behind the elbows and half along belly) otherwise they are in a continual state of moisture and discomfort | J.J. |

1875 Wt. W593/826 1,000,000 4/15 J.B.C. & A. A.D.S.S./Forms/C. 2118.

Instructions regarding War Diaries and Intelligence Summaries are contained in F. S. Regs., Part II. and the Staff Manual respectively. Title Pages will be prepared in manuscript.

# WAR DIARY
*or*
# INTELLIGENCE SUMMARY
*(Erase heading not required.)*

Army Form C. 2118

| Place | Date | Hour | Summary of Events and Information | Remarks and references to Appendices |
|---|---|---|---|---|
| Armentières | 23/9/15 | | Divisional Forge blown up - only one man slightly wounded and two horses injured - removed shoes that had been made to ordinance - visited M.V. Section. | J.J. J.J. |
| " | 24/9/15 | | Inspected 5th N.F. Transport - | |
| " | 25/9/15 | | Eleven horses killed and four wounded by one shell out of a total of 20 standing in the stable. (belonging to Hd Qrs. of the 150th Brigade 3rd Brigade. R.F.A) - inspected horses of the | J.J. J.J. |
| | | | Visited M.V. Section | J.J. |
| " | 26/9/15 | | Inspected transport of 2/2 Field Ambulance. | J.J. |
| " | 27/9/15 | | Motored to Dunkirk and saw some water-proof canvas with a view to getting water-proof corn sheets for animals picketed out in the open - | J.J. |
| " | 28/9/15 | | | |

1875 Wt. W593/826 1,000,000 4/15 J.B.C. & A. A.D.S.S./Forms/C. 2118.

Army Form C. 2118.

Instructions regarding War Diaries and Intelligence Summaries are contained in F. S. Regs., Part II. and the Staff Manual respectively. Title Pages will be prepared in manuscript.

# WAR DIARY
*or*
# INTELLIGENCE SUMMARY
*(Erase heading not required.)*

| Place | Date | Hour | Summary of Events and Information | Remarks and references to Appendices |
|---|---|---|---|---|
| Armentières | 29.9/15 | | Wrote the A. A. & Q. M. G. as follows. Could authority be obtained please for the purchase of 50 Square Yards of water-proof Canvas for the purpose of experimenting in making water-proof loin Sheets for animals picketted out in the open during the winter. The idea is to attach a square yard of this canvas to the ordinary horse rug – as per attached drawing. I have seen some suitable material at Messrs Dickson & Walrave. Dunkirk. It is a stout canvas made water proof by a special process. The price is 4 francs per square 7d. I am of opinion that if animals could be kept dry over the region of the loins it would greatly conduce to their comfort & welfare. Inspected 5 D.L.I. transport. | J.J. |
| " | 30.9/15 | | Visited M. G. Section & inspected transport of 9th D.L.I. | J.J. |

1875 Wt. W593/826 1,000,000 4/15 J.B.C. & A. A.D.S.S./Forms/C. 2118.

121/7429

A.D.V.S. 50th Division

Vol IV

Oct 15

Part compiled by
Major F. Fail. A.V.C.
& part by
Major E. Franklin A.V.C.

Army Form C. 2118

Instructions regarding War Diaries and Intelligence Summaries are contained in F. S. Regs., Part II. and the Staff Manual respectively. Title Pages will be prepared in manuscript.

# WAR DIARY
*or*
# INTELLIGENCE SUMMARY
*(Erase heading not required.)*

| Place | Date | Hour | Summary of Events and Information | Remarks and references to Appendices |
|---|---|---|---|---|
| Armentieres | 1/10/15 | | Visited Mobile Veterinary Section - inspected 5th N.F. transport - | F.F. |
| | 2/10 | | 29 Remounts arrived - and issued to units - inspected 1/1 Nth Field Ambulance transport - and applied Mallein Test to one horse - | F.F. |
| | 3/10/15 | | Visited 1/1 Nth Field Ambulance - horse showing no re-action - | F.F. |
| | 4/10/15 | | " " " " " " | |
| | | | Inspected 3rd Brigade. A.C. horses + visited Mobile Section | F.F. |
| | 5/10/15 | | Reminded all V.O's that only sick animals were to be sent to the Section without authority - | F.F. |
| | 6/10/15 | | Inspected 2nd Mountain Bty animals - stable management perfect - | F.F. |
| | 7/10/15 | | Went to Dunkirk and got 50yds of water-proof canvas - which I intend experimenting with as loin sheets - | F.F. |
| | 8/10/15 | | Remounts arrived + issued - visited Section + inspected Hd Qrs horses | F.F. |
| | 9/10/15 | | Saw C.R.E with reference to water-troughs - visited Section. | F.F. |

1875 Wt. W593/826 1,000,000 4/15 J.B.C. & A. A.D.S.S./Forms/C. 2118.

Instructions regarding War Diaries and Intelligence Summaries are contained in F. S. Regs., Part II. and the Staff Manual respectively. Title Pages will be prepared in manuscript.

# WAR DIARY
*or*
# INTELLIGENCE SUMMARY
*(Erase heading not required.)*

Army Form C. 2118

| Place | Date | Hour | Summary of Events and Information | Remarks and references to Appendices |
|---|---|---|---|---|
| Armentieres | 10/10/15 | | Wrote 'Q' as follows. "I have noticed a slight falling off in condition of a large number of animals in the Division during the last month. I attribute this to bad watering arrangements and indifferent stable management and beg to make the following suggestions. (1) That water-troughs with pumps be constructed at - and -. (2) That transport officers or reliable senior N.C.O.S always attend watering parades." Visited Section | J.J. |
| | 11/10/15 | | Inspected Divisional Cavalry horses. Wrote A.D.V.S. 21st Division saying that units attached temporarily to this division would receive attention. Wrote all V.O.S asking them to take greatest care in diagnosing lameness - and to make careful examination of the foot in all cases. | J.J. |
| | 12/10/15 | | Inspected 150th Infantry Brigade Transport. | J.J. |
| | 13/10/15 | | " 151st " " | J.J. |
| | 14/10/15 | | " 149th " " | J.J. |

Instructions regarding War Diaries and Intelligence Summaries are contained in F. S. Regs., Part II. and the Staff Manual respectively. Title Pages will be prepared in manuscript.

# WAR DIARY
*or*
# INTELLIGENCE SUMMARY
*(Erase heading not required.)*

Army Form C. 2118

| Place | Date | Hour | Summary of Events and Information | Remarks and references to Appendices |
|---|---|---|---|---|
| Armentières | 15/10/15 | | Arranged for veterinary attendance of the 62nd Infantry Brigade att. temporarily | F.F. |
| " | 16/10/15 | | Visited mobile Section. Correspondence on Ringworm received | F.F. |
| " | 17/10/15 | | " " " inspected animals for Base. | F.F. |
| " | 18/10/15 | | Major Franklin. A.V.C. T. reported to relieve me. | F.F. |
| " | 19/10/15 | | Handed over to Major Franklin. | F.F. |
| " | 20/10/15 | | Left for England. | F.F. |

F. Fail Major A.V.C.
A.D.V.S.
50th Division

Army Form C. 2118

Instructions regarding War Diaries and Intelligence Summaries are contained in F. S. Regs., Part II. and the Staff Manual respectively. Title Pages will be prepared in manuscript.

# WAR DIARY
*or*
# INTELLIGENCE SUMMARY
*(Erase heading not required.)*

| Place | Date | Hour | Summary of Events and Information | Remarks and references to Appendices |
|---|---|---|---|---|
| Armentières | 19/10/15 | | Reported for duty with 50th (N) Division | JH. |
| | | | Inspected 14 horses at M. V. Sect for evacuation to B. V. H. | |
| | 20/10/15 | | Informed V. Os of the Division to discontinue sending horses to the M. V. Sect for shoeing. | |
| | 21/10/15 | | Visited 3rd Northd. N. Bg. R. F. A. & Am Col. Visited M. V. S. | JH |
| | | | The attention of the ADVS 21st Div was drawn to an outbreak of Ringworm in a unit of his Division. | JH. |
| | | | Visited & examined a horse suffering with an inflamed eye of the Yorks Hussars. | |
| | 22/10/15 | | Visited horses of 1st N. Fd Co R. E. One was very lame from bullet wound. Ordered two others to be removed to M. V. S. one chronically lame from Navicular Disease, the other suffering from Pneumonia. | JH |
| | | | Visited & Inspected the 149th Inf Bde & Fd Ob horses<br>1504<br>1/2 Fd Amb. R. A. M. C. | |

1875 Wt. W593/826 1,000,000 4/15 J.B.C. & A. A.D.S.S./Forms/C. 2118.

Army Form C. 2118

Instructions regarding War Diaries and Intelligence Summaries are contained in F. S. Regs., Part II. and the Staff Manual respectively. Title Pages will be prepared in manuscript.

# WAR DIARY
*or*
# INTELLIGENCE SUMMARY
*(Erase heading not required.)*

| Place | Date | Hour | Summary of Events and Information | Remarks and references to Appendices |
|---|---|---|---|---|
| | | | 5th Border Regt. Horses | JH |
| Armentières | 22/10/15 | | "Mobile Vet Section" | |
| | | | Inspected horses Hd Qt staff Steenwerck shoeing forge. | JH |
| | 23/10/15 | | Inspected horses Mta Bty R.G.A. & 116th Hy Bty R.G.A. and Mobile Vet Sect in the morning. | JH |
| | | | Again visited 1st Fd Co. R.E. at Gasworks. Found wounded horse slightly improved. | JH |
| | | | Dispatched weekly returns to D.D.V.S. II Army. | JH |
| | | | Inspected horses A.P.M. | JH |
| | | | Informed the I.S. of the arrival of 52 Remounts on 24th & requested O.C. to send collecting party immediately at 7-30am. | JH |
| | 24/10/15 | | Caused to be circulated to V.Os. in the Division the D.D.V.S. II Army Memo V. 1050, d. 13/10/15, dealing with prophylaxis of strike Remounts | |
| | | | Visited & inspected 52 Remounts, Mob Vet Sect. | JH |
| | | | Inspected 14 horses 1 mule at Mob Vet Sect for evacuation to B.V. Hpl. | |

Instructions regarding War Diaries and Intelligence Summaries are contained in F. S. Regs., Part II. and the Staff Manual respectively. Title Pages will be prepared in manuscript.

Army Form C. 2118

# WAR DIARY
*or*
# INTELLIGENCE SUMMARY
*(Erase heading not required.)*

| Place | Date | Hour | Summary of Events and Information | Remarks and references to Appendices |
|---|---|---|---|---|
| Armentières | 25/10/15 | | Visited the 1st (N) Fd Co R.E. Gnr works & inspected the horses. Several horses in this unit are falling off in condition. They are only getting 10 lbs hay, this is not sufficient for draught horses in hard work, their allowance is 12 lbs. The O.C. the unit has been written to on the subject of drawing his proper hay ration, vide Q x 833 d 3/6/15 of which a copy has been sent. This unit are also very short of shoes. Visited & inspected the M.M.P. horses, excepting 3 horses which had been kicked they were all looking well and in good condition. I ordered the wounded horses to be admitted to M.V.S. | JH |
| | 26/10/15 | | Visited & inspected horses at H.Q. suffering from chronic cracked heels, ordered its removal to M.V. Sec. Visited M. Vet Sec. Received instruction from D.D.V.S. II Army re testing horses for glanders by the Intra-dermal palpebral method | JH |

1875 Wt. W593/826 1,000,000 4/15 J.B.C. & A. A.D.S.S./Forms/C. 2118.

Army Form C. 2118.

Instructions regarding War Diaries and Intelligence Summaries are contained in F. S. Regs., Part II. and the Staff Manual respectively. Title Pages will be prepared in manuscript.

# WAR DIARY
*or*
# INTELLIGENCE SUMMARY
*(Erase heading not required.)*

| Place | Date | Hour | Summary of Events and Information | Remarks and references to Appendices |
|---|---|---|---|---|
| Armentières | 26/10/15 | | Instructions have been issued to the V.Os of the Division on this subject, & the tests will be carried out in due course. | JA |
| | 27/10/15 | | Forwarded to the D.D.V.S. a report on the Veterinary Administration of the 50th Division. | |
| | | | Inspected & examined Horses Hd Qrs Horses. | JA |
| | | | Visited 1st Hy Bty of 16th Hy B. R.F.A. The attention of O.C. was drawn to the unnecessary wastage of hay. | |
| | 28/10/15 | | Visited & inspected the horses of the 151st Inf Bde. | |
| | | | Visited & inspected the horses of 2/2 Fd Amb R.A.M.C. | JA |
| | | | Visited & inspected the horses of 1/3 Fd Amb R.A.M.C. | |
| | | | Found the horses lines satisfactory considering the inclement weather. Warned all concerning the importance of husbanding their Hay. | |

1875 Wt. W593/826 1,000,000 4/15 J.B.C. & A. A.D.S.S./Forms/C. 2118.

Instructions regarding War Diaries and Intelligence Summaries are contained in F. S. Regs., Part II, and the Staff Manual respectively. Title Pages will be prepared in manuscript.

# WAR DIARY
*or*
# INTELLIGENCE SUMMARY
*(Erase heading not required.)*

Army Form C. 2118.

| Place | Date | Hour | Summary of Events and Information | Remarks and references to Appendices |
|---|---|---|---|---|
| Armentières | 28/10/15 | | Visited the mobile Vety Section. | JA |
| | 29/10/15 | | Visited M.V.S. & examined 24 horses prior to their evacuation to the B.V.H.Q. Inspected the new position to be taken up by my Mob. Vety Sec. and now occupied by the 21st Div. M.V.S., and considered it suitable. Visited & inspected the 4 sections of the D.A.C. and found everything in order, at least, as far as the weather would permit. Visited & inspected the 1st (N) Fd Amb. R.A.M.C. & York Hussars and as the latter are moving into new area soon I wrote A.D.V.S. 17th Div. to try & arrange temporary Veterinary attendance for the 1st (N) Fd Amb. R.A.M.C. | JA |
| | 30/10/15 | | Visited & inspected 21 horses prior to their evacuation to the B.V.H.Q. and 3 mules. Visited & inspected the 16th H. Bge Am Col horses, and the 14th Bg | JA |

1875 Wt. W593/826 1,000,000 4/15 J.B.C. & A. A.D.S.S./Forms/C. 2118.

Army Form C. 2118.

Instructions regarding War Diaries and Intelligence Summaries are contained in F. S. Regs., Part II. and the Staff Manual respectively. Title Pages will be prepared in manuscript.

# WAR DIARY
*or*
# INTELLIGENCE SUMMARY
*(Erase heading not required.)*

| Place | Date | Hour | Summary of Events and Information | Remarks and references to Appendices |
|---|---|---|---|---|
| Armentières | 30/10/15 | | R.G.A. As they were under orders to move I had to cast the following horses as unfit to travel:- No 36 Br G. H.D. No 71 Bay G. H.D. No 558 Bay G H.D. No 122 Bay G. L.D. No 14 Bay G. This was reported to H. Qrs and authority was obtained from D.D.R. to replace them with others which the O.C. of the unit was to collect from the Field Remount Section. | S.H. |
| | 31/10/15 | | Routine work. | S.H. |

A. D. V. S. 50th Dn.

Nov 1915

Vol V

Army Form C. 2118

Instructions regarding War Diaries and Intelligence Summaries are contained in F. S. Regs., Part II. and the Staff Manual respectively. Title Pages will be prepared in manuscript.

# WAR DIARY
or
# INTELLIGENCE SUMMARY
(Erase heading not required.)

| Place | Date | Hour | Summary of Events and Information | Remarks and references to Appendices |
|---|---|---|---|---|
| Armentières | 1/11/15 | | Visited Mobile Vety Section. There are no ashes used in Horse Lines of the 50th Div. Nails must be picked up at the Dumps or on the road. | J.A. |
| | 2/11/15 | | Visited & inspected horses of the 1st & 2nd Bge. R.F.A. & Am Cols. Considering the adverse conditions, the horses were looking well. Impressed on several officers that hay nets must be used to prevent wastage of hay. | J.A. |
| | 3/11/15 | | Visited the Mobile Section | J.A. |
| | 4/11/15 | | Visited & inspected the 150th Inf Bge. 4th E. Yorks horse lines were very dirty. The Transport Officer attention was drawn to this. Visited & inspected No 3 & 4 Co. A.S.C. Horses were looking well. Inspected 12 horses at Mob Vety Sect prior to their evacuation to Base Vety Hpl. | J.A. |

1875 Wt. W593/826 1,000,000 4/15 J.B.C. & A. A.D.S.S./Forms/C. 2118.

Instructions regarding War Diaries and Intelligence Summaries are contained in F. S. Regs., Part II. and the Staff Manual respectively. Title Pages will be prepared in manuscript.

# WAR DIARY
*or*
# INTELLIGENCE SUMMARY
*(Erase heading not required.)*

Army Form C. 2118

| Place | Date | Hour | Summary of Events and Information | Remarks and references to Appendices |
|---|---|---|---|---|
| Armentières | 5/11/15 | | Visited & inspected 1st (R) Fd Amb. R.A.M.C. (St James Cattell). Found the horses in good condition. Visited the Mobile Vety Section | J.F. |
| | 6/11/15 | | Visited & inspected 14 horses at Mob Vety Sect prior to evacuation to Base Vety Hpl. | J.F. |
| | 7/11/15 | | Visited the Mob Vety Section, and 1st & 2nd Fd Co. R.E. to reclassify the draught horses. Several animals of the 1st Sect were in poor condition, due in my opinion to the shortage of forage, from information received they had only been drawing hay 12 lbs & Oats 10 lbs. These horses are used for drawing heavy Pontoons and require more food. | J.F. |
| | 8/11/15 | | Visited & inspected 8 horses at Mob. Vety. Sect. prior to evacuation to Base Vety Hpl. Visited & inspected 263 mules at Div. Am. Col. that are to be transferred to other units. In my opinion they are all fit for service, and free from Contagious Disease | J.F. |
| | 9/11/15 | | Visited Mobile Vety Section & gave the O.C. his movement orders for the 11th inst. | J.F. |

Army Form C. 2118

# WAR DIARY
*or*
# INTELLIGENCE SUMMARY
*(Erase heading not required.)*

Instructions regarding War Diaries and Intelligence Summaries are contained in F. S. Regs., Part II. and the Staff Manual respectively. Title Pages will be prepared in manuscript.

| Place | Date | Hour | Summary of Events and Information | Remarks and references to Appendices |
|---|---|---|---|---|
| Armentières | 10 11/15 | | Visited ~~& inspected~~ 8 horses at Mob. Vet. Sect previous to their being ~~[illegible]~~ evacuating to Base Vet Hpl. | J.T. |
| | 11 11/15 | | Visited Mobile Vety Section before moving to their new position. | J.T. |
| Merris | 12 11/15 | | Visited the Mobile Vety Section, consulted the O.C. with a view to occupying a new position. Inspected the Hd Qrs Stables & Sheds. | J.T. |
| | 13 11/15 | | Visited & Inspected 1st & 2nd Durham Bty. 3 Bge R.F.A in the morning. Visited Div. Am. Col. at Borre in the afternoon. In No 3 Sect there were 16 sick horses suffering from lameness & debility. 1 was affected with suspicious mange & three with Ringworm. No 2 Sect horses were in a poor condition. | J.T. |
| | 14 11/15 | | Inspected several farm buildings round Merris for a position for Mob Vety Section. Found a suitable place at Sheet 36A, f 7 a 2·3 | J.T. |

1875 Wt. W593/826 1,000,000 4/15 J.B.C. & A. A.D.S.S./Forms/C. 2118.

Instructions regarding War Diaries and Intelligence Summaries are contained in F. S. Regs., Part II. and the Staff Manual respectively. Title Pages will be prepared in manuscript.

# WAR DIARY
*or*
# INTELLIGENCE SUMMARY
*(Erase heading not required.)*

Army Form C. 2118

| Place | Date | Hour | Summary of Events and Information | Remarks and references to Appendices |
|---|---|---|---|---|
| Merris | 15/11/15 | | Visited & Inspected Horses No 3 Sect, 3rd F. Amb. Visited 1/4 Yorks Btl, & 1/4 E. Yorks Btl. The Transport Officers attention was drawn to D.R.O. No 24 d 24/4/15. re the use of hay nets. Visited 1/2 F. Amb. Strazeele, & A. & B. Sects at Pradelles. Visited 8th Irish Horse (21st Div) [illegible] Veterinary Inspection. | J.H. |
| | 16/11/15 | | Visited & Inspected No 3 Signal Sect & No 4 Sect A.S.C. At H.Q. horses 150th Inf Bde, & Transport lines of 5th Yorks & 5 D.L.I. & Yorks Hussars at Strazeele. Visited 50 Div Signal Co. R.E. Merris & Mobile Vety Section in the new position. | J.H. |
| | 17/11/15 | | Visited & Inspected horses in company with D.D.R. at Pradelles. Visited & Inspected the 7th North'd Fusiliers transport lines. & 5th Border Regt. Transport lines | J.H. |
| | 18/11/15 | | Visited Mobile Vety Section & examined sick horses before being evacuated to Base Vety Hptl. | J.H. |

1875 Wt. W593/826 1,000,000 4/15 J.B.C. & A. A.D.S.S./Forms/C. 2118.

Army Form C. 2118

Instructions regarding War Diaries and Intelligence Summaries are contained in F. S. Regs., Part II. and the Staff Manual respectively. Title Pages will be prepared in manuscript.

# WAR DIARY
*or*
# INTELLIGENCE SUMMARY
*(Erase heading not required.)*

| Place | Date | Hour | Summary of Events and Information | Remarks and references to Appendices |
|---|---|---|---|---|
| Meris | 19/11/15 | | Visited Mobile Vety Section. Had a conference with the Vety Officers of the 50th Northern Division. | J.F. |
| | 20/11/15 | | Visited Mobile Vety Section & examined 16 horses before being evacuated to Base Vety Hpl. Visited C.R.A. H.Q. Caestre & inspected 4th Howtz Bge Aty, & 4th (N) Transport Lines. Lines very dirty, too much hay being wasted in consequence of not using hay nets. | J.F. |
| | 21/11/15 | | Visited Mobile Vety Section, & examined 10 sick horses before being evacuated to Base Vety Hpl. | J.F. |
| | 22/11/15 | | Visited & Inspected 48 Remounts at Div Am Col, found them a very useful lot. Visited & Inspected 1/2 Fd Amb. Raielle. Chaff [illegible] losses in this unit were being fed off the ground in consequence of not having nose bags, reported this matter to Div H.Q. | J.F. |
| | 23/11/15 | | Visited & Inspected 5th (N) Fusiliers, & 6th (N) Fusiliers Transport | J.F. |

1875 Wt. W593/826 1,000,000 4/15 J.B.C. & A. A.D.S.S./Forms/C. 2118.

Instructions regarding War Diaries and Intelligence Summaries are contained in F. S. Regs., Part II. and the Staff Manual respectively. Title Pages will be prepared in manuscript.

# WAR DIARY
*or*
# INTELLIGENCE SUMMARY
*(Erase heading not required.)*

Army Form C. 2118

| Place | Date | Hour | Summary of Events and Information | Remarks and references to Appendices |
|---|---|---|---|---|
| Menis | 23/4/15 | Ct | Lines. | S.A. |
| | 24/4/15 | | Visited the 151st Inf Bge, 1/3rd Fd Amb R.A.M.C., No 3 Co A.S.C. 8th D.L.I. lines very clean. 9th D.L.I. have neither hay nets or nose bags. 7th D.L.I lines good. 5th Loyal Nth Lancs have neither hay nets or nose bags, 6th D.L.I. are the same. I was informed that Hay nets & nose bags have been indented for, without success. | S.A. S.A. |
| | 25/4/15 | | Visited & Inspected the Mobile Vety Section & examined 16 horses before being evacuated to Base Vety Hpl. Visited & inspected 3rd N. Bge R.F.A. Horse Room & 3rd N Bge Am Col. The attention of the Vety Officer i/c was drawn to the fact that there are too many sick horses in this Bge, principally Kicks. Visited & Inspected the Yorks Hussars. | S.A. |
| | 26/4/15 | | Visited & Inspected the Mobile Vety Section in company with D.D.V.S. 2nd Army. Had a conference with the | S.A. |

Army Form C. 2118

Instructions regarding War Diaries and Intelligence Summaries are contained in F. S. Regs., Part II. and the Staff Manual respectively. Title Pages will be prepared in manuscript.

# WAR DIARY
*or*
# INTELLIGENCE SUMMARY
*(Erase heading not required.)*

| Place | Date | Hour | Summary of Events and Information | Remarks and references to Appendices |
|---|---|---|---|---|
| Merris | 26/11/15 | A. | Vety Officer of the 50th (N) Division. | J.F. |
| | 27/11/15 | | Visited & examined 16 sick horses at Mobile Vety Section before evacuation to Base Vety Hpl. Visited Yorks Hussar lines and issued 33 remounts to various units. 34 were sent to Railhead but one was too lame for issue, This one was sent into Mobile Vety Section & evacuated to Base Vety Hpl. | J.F. |
| | 28/11/15 | | Visited Mobile Vety Section. Visited Cyclist Co & issued a L.D. to them. | J.F. |
| | 29/11/15 | | Visited the Mobile Vety Section with the D.D.R. Submitted a report to "Q" Office on the issue of maize in too large a quantity, which from reports of two V.O's in the Division had caused serious +fatal intestinal troubles. | J.F. |
| | 30/11/15 | | Visited & examined 8 sick horses at Mobile Vety Section before evacuation to Base Vety Hpl. Visited & inspected 39 horses of the 3rd Bty 2nd Bde R.F.A. which have been inoculated today by the Intra Dermal Palpebral method of testing for glanders. | J.F. |

Instructions regarding War Diaries and Intelligence Summaries are contained in F. S. Regs., Part II. and the Staff Manual respectively. Title Pages will be prepared in manuscript.

# WAR DIARY
*or*
# INTELLIGENCE SUMMARY
*(Erase heading not required.)*

Army Form C. 2118

| Place | Date | Hour | Summary of Events and Information | Remarks and references to Appendices |
|---|---|---|---|---|
| Amiens | 30/11/15 | | The health & condition of the horses of the 50th (N) Division on the whole is satisfactory. There has not been any outbreak of a Contagious or Infectious Disease during the month, excepting two cases of mange. Six horses have had to be destroyed, one for an open hock joint, two for incised hocks, one for lacerated Cornet, two for fractures. Seven have died, two from Valvular disease of the heart, three from Colic, one from Pneumonia, one from Septicaemia. | J.F. |

1875 Wt. W593/826 1,000,000 4/15 J.B.C. & A. A.D.S.S./Forms/C. 2118.

A.D.V.S. 50th Divn.

Dec

Vol. VI

121
7929

Instructions regarding War Diaries and Intelligence Summaries are contained in F. S. Regs., Part II. and the Staff Manual respectively. Title Pages will be prepared in manuscript.

# WAR DIARY
*or*
# INTELLIGENCE SUMMARY
*(Erase heading not required.)*

Army Form C. 2118

| Place | Date | Hour | Summary of Events and Information | Remarks and references to Appendices |
|---|---|---|---|---|
| Merris | 1/12/15 | | Visited & inspected 8 horses at Mobile Vety Sect before being evacuated to Base Vety Hospital. Visited & inspected horses at No 3 Bty. 2 Bge which had been inoculated the previous day. These horses did not show any reaction to the test. | J.T. |
| | 2/12/15 | | Visited & inspected horses at 3rd Bty. 2nd Bge in company with D.D.V.S. 2nd Army. none had reacted to the test. Visited & examined a horse at Mobile Vety Section suspected of mange, belonging to Army Commander. I did not consider it had mange, altho' there was a bare patch on each shoulder. | J.T. |
| | 3/12/15 | | Visited & inspected 8 horses at Mobile Vety Section before being evacuated to Base Vety Hpl. Visited & inspected 4th Howtz Bge R.F.A. at Caestre in company of Vety Officer. One Bty was very good indeed | J.T. |

1875 Wt. W593/826 1,000,000 4/15 J.B.C. & A. A.D.S.S./Forms/C. 2118.

Instructions regarding War Diaries and Intelligence Summaries are contained in F. S. Regs., Part II. and the Staff Manual respectively. Title Pages will be prepared in manuscript.

# WAR DIARY
*or*
# INTELLIGENCE SUMMARY
*(Erase heading not required.)*

Army Form C. 2118

| Place | Date | Hour | Summary of Events and Information | Remarks and references to Appendices |
|---|---|---|---|---|
| Menin | 4 12/15 | | Visited several farms in the 50th Div area which were reported as suffering from Foot & Mouth Disease. I failed in my examination to find any symptoms of the Disease. In my opinion it ~~does~~ not present any of the symptoms of the Disease as one has seen in England. The Cattle all looked well & natural in every way. | J.T. |
| | 5 12/15 | | Acting under instructions received from D.D.V.S. II Army I visited & inspected two horses at the Field Remount Section reported as suffering from Skin Disease. They presented every Clinical symptom of mange. Advised them to be moved to Mobile Vety Section. Inspected more farms to examine Cattle, in my opinion not anything in the nature of Foot & mouth Disease affecting them. The Cattle all look in too good condition for such a Complaint. | J.T.<br>J.T. |

1875 Wt. W593/826 1,000,000 4/15 J.B.C. & A. A.D.S.S./Forms/C. 2118.

Instructions regarding War Diaries and Intelligence Summaries are contained in F. S. Regs., Part II. and the Staff Manual respectively. Title Pages will be prepared in manuscript.

# WAR DIARY
*or*
# INTELLIGENCE SUMMARY
*(Erase heading not required.)*

Army Form C. 2118

| Place | Date | Hour | Summary of Events and Information | Remarks and references to Appendices |
|---|---|---|---|---|
| Menin | 6/12/15 | | Visited & inspected 14 horses at Mobile Vety Section before evacuation to Base Vety Hospital. Visited & inspected the Units in the 150th (N) Inf Bde. | J.A. |
| | 7/12/15 | | Visited Transport Lines 5th Bord Regt, I found three horses affected with suspicious Mange, moved them to Mobile Vety Section | J.A. |
| | 8/12/15 | | Visited Mobile Vety Section & examined 15 horses before evacuation to Base Vety Hpl. Visited D.D.V.S. 2nd Army who gave me instructions ~~about~~ 6 horses & 2 mules left behind by other units which he wished the 50th Mob Vety Section to collect. Visited the French Vety Officer & Prefect of Police to obtain information about Farms affected with Foot & mouth Disease. | J.A. |
| | 9/12/15 | | Visited Flêtre, Becke, & Steenvoorde with O.C. 50th Mob Vety Section & examined horses & made arrangements for their removal. | |
| | 10/12/15 | | Visited & examined 8 animals at Mob Vety Section before | J.A. |

1875 Wt. W593/826 1,000,000 4/15 J.B.C. & A. A.D.S.S./Forms/C. 2118.

Instructions regarding War Diaries and Intelligence Summaries are contained in F. S. Regs., Part II. and the Staff Manual respectively. Title Pages will be prepared in manuscript.

# WAR DIARY
*or*
# INTELLIGENCE SUMMARY
*(Erase heading not required.)*

Army Form C. 2118

| Place | Date | Hour | Summary of Events and Information | Remarks and references to Appendices |
|---|---|---|---|---|
| Merris | 10 12/15 | | evacuation to Base Vety Hpl. Visited Transport Lines 5th Bnd Regt & inspected horses. Issued 50 specially made Head ropes to V.Os of the 50th Division for distribution amongst the units under their charge who had horses & mules which destroyed the head ropes by eating them. | J.F. |
| | 11 12/15 | | Visited & examined Head Qrs horses. | R.A. |
| | 12 12/15 | | Visited & inspected horses at Field Remount Sect at the request of D.D.R. Visited & examined my horses at Mobile Vety Section before evacuation to Base Vety Hpl. Visited & examined Div Amm Col horses, ordered two to be sent to Mob. Vety Sect. | |
| | 13 12/15 | | Visited & examined the 151st Inf Bge Horses. | J.F. |
| | 14 12/15 | | Visited Div Amm Col and issued 137 ~~[illegible]~~ remounts to various units. Visited & examined my horses at Mobile Vety Section before evacuation to Base Vety Hptl. | R.A. J.F. |

1875 Wt. W593/826 1,000,000 4/15 J.B.C. & A. A.D.S.S./Forms/C. 2118.

Instructions regarding War Diaries and Intelligence Summaries are contained in F. S. Regs., Part II. and the Staff Manual respectively. Title Pages will be prepared in manuscript.

# WAR DIARY
*or*
# INTELLIGENCE SUMMARY
*(Erase heading not required.)*

Army Form C. 2118

| Place | Date | Hour | Summary of Events and Information | Remarks and references to Appendices |
|---|---|---|---|---|
| Merris | 15/12/15 | | Visited & examined 7 horses at Mobile Vety Section before evacuation to Base Vety Hptl. Arrangements were definitely fixed with A.D.V.S. 9th Division for changing over the Mob Vety Sections. | J.F. |
| | 16/12/15 | | Visited Fd Remount Section & ordered 6 lame horses into the Mob Vety Section. No fresh cases of skin Disease. Visited & examined 7 horses at Mob Vety Section before evacuation to Base Vety Hptl. | J.F. |
| | 17/12/15 | | Visited & examined 8 horses at Mob Vety Sect before evacuation to Base Vety Hpl. Visited Transport lines of the 5th Yorks Btt. | J.F. |
| | 18/12/15 | | Visited 50th Div Train A.S.C. selected 5 horses for exchange for 5 H.D. from Fd. Remount Sect. | J.F. |
| | 19/12/15 | | Visited & examined 16 horses at Mob Vety Sect before evacuation to Base Vety Hptl. | J.F. |

1875 Wt. W593/826 1,000,000 4/15 J.B.C. & A. A.D.S.S./Forms/C. 2118.

Army Form C. 2118

Instructions regarding War Diaries and Intelligence Summaries are contained in F. S. Regs., Part II. and the Staff Manual respectively. Title Pages will be prepared in manuscript.

# WAR DIARY
*or*
# INTELLIGENCE SUMMARY
*(Erase heading not required.)*

| Place | Date | Hour | Summary of Events and Information | Remarks and references to Appendices |
|---|---|---|---|---|
| Amiens | 20/12/15 | | Visited & inspected Mobile Vety Section before leaving for new area. Visited & examined M.M.P. horse reported to me lame & ordered it to Mobile Vety Section, injured in the night. | J.A. |
| Hoofgraaf | 21/12/15 | | Division removed to new area. | J.A. |
| | 22/12/15 | | Visited H.Q. & Mobile Vety Section & inspected 14 horses before evacuation to Base Vety Hpl. | J.A. |
| | 23/12/15 | | Visited H.Q. & Mobile Vety Section. Inspected mens billets, horse lines. Visited 1st (N) Fd Amb. Pointed out to O.C. that horse lines must be kept cleaner, & that greater care must be taken of the forage. Visited 3rd (N) Fd Amb horse lines. | J.A. |
| | 24/12/15 | | Visited & inspected 14 cases of suspected mange at Mobile Vety Section before evacuation to Base Vety Hpl. | J.A. |

# WAR DIARY
*or*
# INTELLIGENCE SUMMARY
*(Erase heading not required.)*

Army Form C. 2118

Instructions regarding War Diaries and Intelligence Summaries are contained in F. S. Regs., Part II. and the Staff Manual respectively. Title Pages will be prepared in manuscript.

| Place | Date | Hour | Summary of Events and Information | Remarks and references to Appendices |
|---|---|---|---|---|
| Hoofgraaf | 25/12/15 | | Visited units round H.Q | S.A. |
| | 26/12/15 | | Visited H.Q. & mobile Vety section. Visited M.M.P. horses. D.D.V.S. II Army called in the afternoon & gave me instructions on the Malleinisation of horses & made arrangements to give a demonstration at the mobile Vety section on the following afternoon. | S.A. |
| | 27/12/15 | | Visited mobile Vety section with the D.D.V.S. II Army who gave a practical demonstration on the new test. Very simple, & in my opinion if reliable, an improvement on the subcutaneous inoculation. 12 horses were tested. | S.A. |
| | 28/12/15 | | Visited mobile Vety section. Visited H.Q. & arranged for some of H.Q. horses to be tested. | |
| | 29/12/15 | | Visited & inspected 5th Bord. Regt Transport lines & found 7 cases of suspected mange. Gave instructions for Horse Reg | S.A. |

Army Form C. 2118

Instructions regarding War Diaries and Intelligence Summaries are contained in F. S. Regs., Part II. and the Staff Manual respectively. Title Pages will be prepared in manuscript.

# WAR DIARY
*or*
# INTELLIGENCE SUMMARY
*(Erase heading not required.)*

| Place | Date | Hour | Summary of Events and Information | Remarks and references to Appendices |
|---|---|---|---|---|
| Hoofgraaf | 29/12/15 | | blankets, cleansing utensils, harness & saddlery to be thoroughly well cleaned & disinfected. Reported the steps I had taken to H.Q of the Division. Visited Mobile Vety Section, and examined horses undergoing the test, no reactions. Inspected 13 horses at the Section before evacuation to the Base Vety Hptl. 10 horses from H.Q's were tested in the morning. | J.Y. |
| | 30/12/15 | | Visited & examined H.Q's horses which were tested the previous day, no reactions. Visited & examined horses at Mobile Section, no reactors. | J.Y. |
| | 31/12/15 | | Visited & examined 66 horses of 1st Bty, 1st (H) Bde R.F.A, which had been tested, no reactions. Visited & examined H.Q's horses no reactors. 10 more H.Q's horses were tested this morning. Visited Mobile Vety Section, scrapings were examined under microscope from horses admitted | J.Y. |

1875 Wt. W593/826 1,000,000 4/15 J.B.C. & A. A.D.S.S./Forms/C. 2118.

Instructions regarding War Diaries and Intelligence Summaries are contained in F. S. Regs., Part II. and the Staff Manual respectively. Title Pages will be prepared in manuscript.

# WAR DIARY
*or*
# INTELLIGENCE SUMMARY
*(Erase heading not required.)*

Army Form C. 2118

| Place | Date | Hour | Summary of Events and Information | Remarks and references to Appendices |
|---|---|---|---|---|
| Hoofgraaf | 31/12/15 | | with suspicious mange by the O.C. of the section & myself but we failed to find the Parasite. | |
| | | | Summary of remarks on the health & condition of horses of the 50th Division. Excepting the outbreak of suspected mange in the Transport lines of the 5th Border Regt, the health & condition of the horses is satisfactory. There has not been any outbreak of an Infectious or Contagious nature, notwithstanding the bad weather & conditions under which they are placed. In many cases to get to their standings they have to go through mud up to their bellies, and taking everything into consideration during the hardships & bad weather which we are experiencing I consider ~~was~~ an increase in ~~this~~ ~~rat~~ of oats should be issued to prevent their losing condition. | |

1875 Wt. W593/826 1,000,000 4/15 J.B.C. & A. A.D.S.S./Forms/C. 2118.

Instructions regarding War Diaries and Intelligence Summaries are contained in F. S. Regs., Part II. and the Staff Manual respectively. Title Pages will be prepared in manuscript.

# WAR DIARY
*or*
# INTELLIGENCE SUMMARY
*(Erase heading not required.)*

Army Form C. 2118

| Place | Date | Hour | Summary of Events and Information | Remarks and references to Appendices |
|---|---|---|---|---|
| Hoffgraaf | 31/12/15 | | The V.O's of this Division have commenced the Mallienisation of the horses. As a practitioner of many years, I consider the Intra Dermal Palpebral method the best. I am not in a position to testify yet whether it is reliable or otherwise. This Division received 50 wire reinforced head ropes for trial with the worst rope eaters. These have proved successful, for in two cases only have the animals managed to eat through the wire, ~~chain~~ head collar chains are in my opinion the only effective means to secure these animals. The Forage has been satisfactory and of good quality. I would like to see greater care exercised with the horses. The way in which some officers & men trot horses on these hard Pavé roads is certain to affect the animals soundness, and only | |

1875 Wt. W593/826 1,000,000 4/15 J.B.C. & A. A.D.S.S./Forms/C. 2118.

Instructions regarding War Diaries and Intelligence Summaries are contained in F. S. Regs., Part II. and the Staff Manual respectively. Title Pages will be prepared in manuscript.

# WAR DIARY
*or*
# INTELLIGENCE SUMMARY
*(Erase heading not required.)*

Army Form C. 2118

| Place | Date | Hour | Summary of Events and Information | Remarks and references to Appendices |
|---|---|---|---|---|
| | | | and only when it is necessary should be prevented. | HJ |

1875 Wt. W593/826 1,000,000 4/15 J.B.C. & A. A.D.S.S./Forms/C. 2118.

A.D.V.S. 50 Div

Jan

Vol VII

Instructions regarding War Diaries and Intelligence Summaries are contained in F. S. Regs., Part II. and the Staff Manual respectively. Title Pages will be prepared in manuscript.

# WAR DIARY
*or*
# INTELLIGENCE SUMMARY
*(Erase heading not required.)*

Army Form C. 2118

| Place | Date | Hour | Summary of Events and Information | Remarks and references to Appendices |
|---|---|---|---|---|
| Hooftpaaf | 1/1/16 | | Visited & Inspected Transport Lines of 151st Inf Bge & particularly the lines of the 5th Border Regt, who have had an outbreak of skin disease. Scrapings were taken from several horses & examined under the microscope, but the O.C. 50th Mobile Vety section & myself failed to find the mange Parasite. Visited & Examined H.Q's horses undergoing the Mallein test. | J.H. |
| | 2/1/16 | | Visited the 5th Border Transport Lines and issued 13 L.D. & 4 Riders. remounts, gave instructions for them to be isolated. Inspected M.M.P. & other H.Qs. staff horses under the test. Visited and examined 10 horses at Mobile Vety Section before evacuation to Base Vety Hptl. | J.H. |
| | 3/1/16 | | Visited & Examined M.M.P. horses & H.Q. Staff horses undergoing the test, no reactors. Visited Mobile Vety Section, & examined horses undergoing the test. Visited the G.O.C. horse which was retested in the opposite eye. Temp normal, & no reaction. | J.H. |

1875 Wt. W593/826 1,000,000 4/15 J.B.C. & A. A.D.S.S./Forms/C. 2118.

Instructions regarding War Diaries and Intelligence Summaries are contained in F. S. Regs., Part II. and the Staff Manual respectively. Title Pages will be prepared in manuscript.

# WAR DIARY
*or*
# INTELLIGENCE SUMMARY
*(Erase heading not required.)*

Army Form C. 2118

| Place | Date | Hour | Summary of Events and Information | Remarks and references to Appendices |
|---|---|---|---|---|
| Hoofgraaf | 4/1/16 | | Visited several units horses undergoing the test at the 24th hour. Tested 9 M. M. P. horses & 22 1/3 Fd Amb. Visited G.O.C. horse at 48th hour, temp normal, no local reaction. | J.T. |
| | 5/1/16 | | Visited & examined 1/1 & 1/3 Fd Amb horses tested previous day. Visited 1st 2nd & 3rd N. B. R. F A. Am Col horse lines. 2nd & 3rd Div Bty Horse lines. 5th D.L.I. & 5th Yorks Transport lines. Horselines are very bad, impossible to do anything with them. Visited H.Q. to confer with G.O.C. on the question of clipping draught horses trace high. I recommended the latter. Visited Mobile Vety Section & examined 8 horses before evacuation to Base Vety Hpl. | J.T. |
| | 6/1/16 | | Visited horses 1/1 & 1/3 ~~F.A.~~ Amb horses undergoing test & Div Am Col horses for same purpose, no reactors. | J.T. |

1875 Wt. W593/826 1,000,000 4/15 J.B.C. & A. A.D.S.S./Forms/C. 2118.

Instructions regarding War Diaries and Intelligence Summaries are contained in F. S. Regs., Part II. and the Staff Manual respectively. Title Pages will be prepared in manuscript.

# WAR DIARY
*or*
# INTELLIGENCE SUMMARY
*(Erase heading not required.)*

Army Form C. 2118

| Place | Date | Hour | Summary of Events and Information | Remarks and references to Appendices |
|---|---|---|---|---|
| Hoofgraaf | 7/1/16 | | Visited & examined horses in several units undergoing the test. Visited & examined 13 horses at mobile Vety Section before evacuation to Base Vety Hpl. | S.F. |
| | 8/1/16 | | Met & distributed 32 Remounts to various units. Visited & examined 16 horses at mobile Vety Section before evacuation to Base Vety Hpl. Visited & inspected transport lines & horses of 2/2 Nbn Fd Amb. | S.F. |
| | 9/1/16 | | Tested 22 horses No1 Section Div Sig Co. & 6 horses of 1/1st Nbn F. Amb & 6 1/3rd Fd Amb. Visited & inspected horses of 4th Nbn Bge Am Col undergoing test, & 4th Div Bty ditto. No reactors. Visited & inspected horses & transport lines of 5th D.L.I. | S.F. |
| | 10/1/16. | | Visited & inspected several units horses undergoing the test, no reactors. Visited the mobile Vety Section, & Divisional H.Qs. | S.F. |
| | 11/1/16. | | Inoculating animals for various units. Visited & inspected horses of units undergoing the test. Visited & examined 18 horses at mobile Vety Section before evacuation to Base Vety Hpl. | S.F. |

1875 Wt. W593/826 1,000,000 4/15 J.B.C. & A. A.D.S.S./Forms/C. 2118.

Instructions regarding War Diaries and Intelligence Summaries are contained in F. S. Regs., Part II. and the Staff Manual respectively. Title Pages will be prepared in manuscript.

# WAR DIARY
*or*
# INTELLIGENCE SUMMARY
*(Erase heading not required.)*

Army Form C. 2118

| Place | Date | Hour | Summary of Events and Information | Remarks and references to Appendices |
|---|---|---|---|---|
| Hooggraaf | 12/1/16 | | Visited & inspected horses in Units undergoing the test. | J.B. |
| | 13/1/16 | | Visited & inspected 44 Remounts at Godewaersvelde & issued them to various units, & 43 others which had arrived the previous day. Visited & examined 12 horses at Mobile Vety Section before evacuation to Base Vety Hpl. Visited H.Qs. | J.B. |
| | 14/1/16 | | Visited & examined horse at H.Qs. 5th Corps by request. Visited Mobile Vety Section to meet the G.O.C. & His Grace the Duke of Northumberland who were inspecting the Section. | J.B. |
| | 15/1/16 | | Visited & examined 14 horses at Mobile Vety Section before evacuation to Base Vety Hpl. Inoculated horses from various units. Visited & inspected horses in several Units undergoing the test. Visited & inspected 144 L.D. mules from Remounts at Godewaersvelde. | J.B. |

1875 Wt. W593/826 1,000,000 4/15 J.B.C. & A. A.D.S.S./Forms/C. 2118.

Instructions regarding War Diaries and Intelligence Summaries are contained in F. S. Regs., Part II. and the Staff Manual respectively. Title Pages will be prepared in manuscript.

# WAR DIARY
*or*
# INTELLIGENCE SUMMARY
*(Erase heading not required.)*

Army Form C. 2118

| Place | Date | Hour | Summary of Events and Information | Remarks and references to Appendices |
|---|---|---|---|---|
| Hoofpaaf | 16/1/16 | | Inoculated horses from various units. Visited & inspected units undergoing the Mallein Test. Visited Transport lines of 5th D.L.I. 5th N.F's. 6 N.F's 4th Yorks. 7th N.F. & 9th D.L.I. 5th Bords. The Transport Officer's attention was drawn to several irregularities. | J.F. |
| | 17/1/16 | | Inspected Transport Lines of 1st & 3rd Nbn F.A. | J.F. |
| | 18/1/16 | | Visited & Inspected a horse reported as suffering from Mange belonging to a Civilian Farmer, a very bad case, been affected a month, nothing had been applied, report my decision to the A.P.M. Visited H.Qrs Div Sig Co No 1 Section Transport lines, ordered one to the Mobile Vety Sect. | J.F. |
| | 19/1/16 | | Visited & examined 8 horses at Mobile Vety Section before evacuation to Base Vety Hpl. Visited & inspected horses at various units undergoing Mallein Test. Visited & inspected Transport lines 5th D.L.I. & 5th Yorks. | J.F. |

Army Form C. 2118

Instructions regarding War Diaries and Intelligence Summaries are contained in F. S. Regs., Part II. and the Staff Manual respectively. Title Pages will be prepared in manuscript.

# WAR DIARY
*or*
# INTELLIGENCE SUMMARY
*(Erase heading not required.)*

| Place | Date | Hour | Summary of Events and Information | Remarks and references to Appendices |
|---|---|---|---|---|
| Hoograaf | 20/6 | | Visited & inspected units undergoing the test | J.S. |
| | | | Visited & examined H. Le horse, lame. Visited & inspected 8 horses at Mobile Vety Section before evacuation to Base Vety Hpl. Visited & inspected 1st & 2nd & 3rd Bge Am Col R.F.A undergoing the test, no reactors. | J.S. |
| | 21/6 | | Inspected remounts before issue. Visited & inspected several units undergoing the mallein test. | J.S. |
| | 22/6 | | Visited several units undergoing the test. Inspected Transport lines 5th D.L.I. inc[illegible] | J.S. |
| | 23/6 | | Visited & examined 14 horses at Mobile Vety Section before evacuation to Base Vety Hpl. Visited & inspected Nos 1-2-&4 Cos A.S.C. | J.S. |

Instructions regarding War Diaries and Intelligence Summaries are contained in F. S. Regs., Part II. and the Staff Manual respectively. Title Pages will be prepared in manuscript.

# WAR DIARY
*or*
# INTELLIGENCE SUMMARY
*(Erase heading not required.)*

Army Form C. 2118

| Place | Date | Hour | Summary of Events and Information | Remarks and references to Appendices |
|---|---|---|---|---|
| Hooggraaf | 24/6/16 | | Visited & Inspected several Btts Transport Lines, found them deficient of Hay nets, nose bags, & grooming kits. The attention of Officers concerned was drawn to this. Sent in a report to Divisional Hd. Qrs. on the matter. | B.F. |
| | 25/6/16 | | Visited Mobile Vety Section & Units undergoing the test | B.F. |
| | 26/6/16 | | Visited & examined 17 horses at Mobile Vety Section before evacuation to Base Vety Hpl | B.F. |
| | 27/6/16 | | Met the D.D.R. at 46 Bde Amn Col who came to inspect horses for casting, other than Veterinary cases. Exchanged at same place 11 H.D. out of condition for 11 H.D. from Army H. T. Coy A.S.C. Visited Mobile Vety Section & H.Qs. | B.F. |
| | 28/6/16 | | Visiting units to examine horses undergoing Mallein Test. Visited & Inspected 3rd N Brigade R.F.A. Lines. Visited & inspected 5th D.L.I. Transport Lines. | B.F. |

Instructions regarding War Diaries and Intelligence Summaries are contained in F. S. Regs., Part II. and the Staff Manual respectively. Title Pages will be prepared in manuscript.

Army Form C. 2118

# WAR DIARY
*or*
# INTELLIGENCE SUMMARY
*(Erase heading not required.)*

| Place | Date | Hour | Summary of Events and Information | Remarks and references to Appendices |
|---|---|---|---|---|
| Hooggraaf | 29/1/16 | | Visited & examined 19 horses at Mobile Vety Section before evacuation to Base Vety Hptl. | J.J. |
| | 30/1/16 | | Visited & Inspected several units Transport Lines. | J.J. |
| | 31/1/16 | | Visited & examined 11 horses at Mobile Vety Section before evacuation to the Base Vety Hpl. | J.J. |
| | | | Summary — During the month there has not been any outbreak of a Contagious or Infectious Disease, excepting a few cases of suspected Mange, which were evacuated, and precautions taken to prevent its spreading. | |
| | | | The condition of the Heavy & Light Draught Horses has gone down owing in my opinion to the hay ration being reduced. This type suffers more than any other animal if it does not have a sufficiency of | |

1875 Wt. W593/826 1,000,000 4/15 J.B.C. & A. A.D.S.S./Forms/C. 2118.

Instructions regarding War Diaries and Intelligence Summaries are contained in F. S. Regs., Part II. and the Staff Manual respectively. Title Pages will be prepared in manuscript.

# WAR DIARY
*or*
# INTELLIGENCE SUMMARY
*(Erase heading not required.)*

Army Form C. 2118

| Place | Date | Hour | Summary of Events and Information | Remarks and references to Appendices |
|---|---|---|---|---|
| | | | bulky food. Wheat & oat straw has been issued, but very few horses will eat any quantity of either unless it is cut into chaff. Under existing conditions chaff cutting is very difficult, machines cannot be obtained readily. About 6½ tons of chaff per day would be required to give each horse in the Division a suitable quantity. I have suggested hiring a couple of windmills in the Divisional area. If this could be done the quantity could soon be cut, the difficulty would be to handle such a quantity, but with men, and large bags to hold about 5 cwt, I think even this might be overcome. I am sure if it could be, horses would assimilate their oats much better than they do, as it is, they bolt their food without chewing it, consequently the food does not get mixed with the juices of the mouth & stomach, and the oats come out in the Feces | JH |

1875 Wt. W593/826 1,000,000 4/15 J.B.C. & A. A.D.S.S./Forms/C. 2118.

Instructions regarding War Diaries and Intelligence Summaries are contained in F. S. Regs., Part II. and the Staff Manual respectively. Title Pages will be prepared in manuscript.

# WAR DIARY
*or*
# INTELLIGENCE SUMMARY
*(Erase heading not required.)*

Army Form C. 2118

| Place | Date | Hour | Summary of Events and Information | Remarks and references to Appendices |
|---|---|---|---|---|
| Hd Staff | | | whole. | |
| | | | The Horses in the Division have been mallienised by the Intra Dermal Palpebral system during the month. Only two horses showed any symptoms of reaction, one was retested in the opposite eye at the 24th course with negative results. The other is to be done. | JH. |
| | | | One of the greatest troubles out here is that horses are continually picking up nails, and unless something is done to protect their feet, the casualties from this cause will be large. I am trying a tin sole under the shoe, all over the sole, not having tried it long enough to form any opinion as to its success, I cannot express any opinion as to its usefulness, but I am afraid of the mud getting between the sole & the foot & tearing the shoe off the foot | JH. |

1875 Wt. W593/826 1,000,000 4/15 J.B.C. & A. A.D.S.S./Forms/C. 2118.

5.0

QWVS 5.0 Div

Vol VIIII

D.A.G.,

3rd Echelon.

Base

Ref your C.R. No/140/452.

Attached please find copy of February diary which was posted on to you 2.3.16.

I regret that it has gone astray in transit.

G. Franklin

Major. A.V.C.

A.D.V.S. 50th Divn.

D.HQ.

3.5.16.

Instructions regarding War Diaries and Intelligence Summaries are contained in F. S. Regs., Part II. and the Staff Manual respectively. Title Pages will be prepared in manuscript.

# WAR DIARY
*or*
# INTELLIGENCE SUMMARY
*(Erase heading not required.)*

Army Form C. 2118.

Copy

| Place | Date | Hour | Summary of Events and Information | Remarks and references to Appendices |
|---|---|---|---|---|
| Hooggraaf | 1/2/16 | | The Army Vety. Corps Sergts. (T) were warned against using Paraffin Dressings on horses' skins. All mallein syringes were returned to D.D.V.S. Second Army. | JH |
| | 2/2/16 to | | On leave .. Senior V.O. acting during my absence – Routine Work. | JH |
| | 12/2/16 | | Visited H.Qrs. & Mobile Vety. Section. | JH |
| | 13/2/16 | | Visited and examined 100 mules (Remounts) at Godewaersvelde. These animals were not in my opinion in as good condition as they ought to be. Visited and examined 8 horses at Mob. Vety. Secn. previous to their evacuation to Base Vety. Hosp. | JH |
| | 14/2/16 | | Visited Transport Lines 4th E. Yorks. to examine 2 horses with a view to reissuing them to another unit. Visited Mob. Vet. Secn. & Divl. Ammn. Coln. | JH |
| | 15/2/16 | | Visited and inspected several animals which were considered unsuitable in 2nd Bgde Amn. Coln. These horses had been issued by the Divl. Ammn. Col. & although they were not in as good condition for work as they might have been they were in my opinion fit for work. Visited H.Q. & gave them my opinion. Visited Mob. Vety Secn. | JH |
| | 16/2/16 | | Routine Work | NH |
| | 17/2/16 | | Visited Mob. Vety. Secn. & examined 12 horses before evacuation to Base Vety. Hosp. Visited York Hussars & inspected Remounts. | |
| | 18/2/16 | | Visited York Hussars & examined horses which the C.O. proposed to show the D.D.R. for casting for other than Vety. Reasons. Visited and inspected 3 horses killed & 8 injured by a bomb in the 2nd Fd. Ambce. (H'drn) & ordered the injured to be sent to Mob. Vety. Secn. Visited D.H.Q. | JH |
| | 19/2/16 | | Visited 2nd Bgde Amn. Col. to examine Remounts. Visited Mob. Vety. Secn. & examined 7 horses before evacuation to Base Vet. Hosp. Met D.D.R. at 2nd N.B.R.F.A Amn. Col. to reissue 74 H.D. | JH |

Instructions regarding War Diaries and Intelligence Summaries are contained in F. S. Regs., Part II. and the Staff Manual respectively. Title Pages will be prepared in manuscript.

# WAR DIARY
*or*
# INTELLIGENCE SUMMARY
*(Erase heading not required.)*

Army Form C. 2118.

| Place | Date | Hour | Summary of Events and Information | Remarks and references to Appendices |
|---|---|---|---|---|
| Hooggraaf | 20/2/16 | | Visited & inspected 10 horses at 7th D.L.I. transport lines which had been reported as suffering from an infectious skin disease. In my opinion they were not affected with parasitic mange. | J.H. |
| | 21/2/16 | | Visited several units in company with D.D.R. to reclassify H.D. | J.H. |
| | 22/2/16 | | Visited M.V.S. & examined 14 injured horses & 6 horses affected with skin disease before evacuation to Base Vety. Hosp. Issued 11 H.D. to 2nd N. H.Q. Ambce. to replace casualties. | J.H. |
| | 23/2/16 | | Visited & inspected horse lines of 1st Bgde. R.F.A. | J.H. |
| | | | " " " " " 5th D.L.I. & 5th Yorks Regt. | |
| | 24/2/16 | | " " " " " 1st N. H.Q. Ambce. | J.H. |
| | | | " " 14 horses at Mob. Vety. Secn. before evacuation to Base Vety. Hospital. | |
| | 25/2/16 | | " Mob. Vety. Secn to meet C.R.E. | J.H. |
| | 26/2/16 | | " & inspected horse lines of 3rd Durham Bty. R.F.A. | J.H. |
| | 27/2/16 | | " D.H.Q. & Mob. Vety. Secn & inspected of horses before evacuation to Base Vety. Hospl. | J.H. |
| | | | " GODEWAERSVELDE station to inspect remounts (75 mules & 41 other horses). | J.H. |
| | 28/2/16 | | In company with D.D.R. Second Army visited several units in the Division for the purpose of classifying H.D. horses. | J.H. |
| | | | Visited D.H.Q. & Mob. Vety. Secn. | J.H. |
| | 29/2/16 | | Visited several infantry battalions in the Div. for the purpose of obtaining the no. of H.D. horses they have. | |

Army Form C. 2118.

Instructions regarding War Diaries and Intelligence Summaries are contained in F. S. Regs., Part II. and the Staff Manual respectively. Title Pages will be prepared in manuscript.

# WAR DIARY
*or*
# INTELLIGENCE SUMMARY
*(Erase heading not required.)*

| Place | Date | Hour | Summary of Events and Information | Remarks and references to Appendices |
|---|---|---|---|---|
| Hooggraaf | 29/7/16 | | Summary:- I have pleasure in reporting that during the month there has been no serious outbreak of any disease of a contagious or infectious nature with the exception of 10 cases of suspected mange which were immediately evacuated to the Base. Neither is the number of cracked heels excessive in spite of the inclemency of the weather & the consequent state of the ground. The general condition of the horses remains satisfactory even although the condition of some of the H.D. was reduced on account of the unavoidable decrease in the hay ration, which entailed a reduction of the bulky food to which they are entitled. The quality of the forage remains good. | [illegible] |
| | | | [illegible] Major A.V.C.<br>A.D.V.S. 50th Div. | [illegible] |

2449 Wt. W14957/M90 750,000 1/16 J.B.C. & A. Forms/C.2118/12.

Instructions regarding War Diaries and Intelligence Summaries are contained in F. S. Regs., Part II. and the Staff Manual respectively. Title pages will be prepared in manuscript.

# WAR DIARY
*or*
# INTELLIGENCE SUMMARY.
*(Erase heading not required.)*

Army Form C. 2118.

| Place | Date | Hour | Summary of Events and Information | Remarks and references to Appendices |
|---|---|---|---|---|
| Hoofpraaf | 1/3/16 | | Visited H.Qs. and Mob Vety Section and examined 14 horses before evacuation to Base Vety Hpl. | J.T. |
| | 2/3/16 | | Visited & inspected the horse lines of the 1st, 2nd, 3rd, & 4th Brigade Am Cols. | J.T. |
| | 3/3/16 | | Visited the Mob Vety Section and Div H.Q. | J.T. |
| | 4/3/16 | | Visited the 2nd Brig. Am Col to inspect horses for rescue. | J.T. |
| | 5/3/16 | | Visited the 151st Inf Bge and requested the Bgde T.O. to collect 7 mules from the 149th Inf Bge. Visited the transport lines of the 5th D.L.I. | J.T. |
| | 6/3/16 | | Visited & inspected the horses of the 3rd Bty 1st Bge R.F.A. 2nd Bty 2nd Bge R.F.A. 3rd Bty 2nd Bge R.F.A. | J.T. |
| | 7/3/16 | | Visited & inspected 8 horses at Mob Vety Sect before evacuation to Base Vety Hpl. Visited Div H.Q. | J.T. |
| | 8/3/16 | | Visited Ouderdom & examined 11 horses for exchange with Army T. Co. In my opinion they had not improved greatly | J.T. |

Instructions regarding War Diaries and Intelligence Summaries are contained in F. S. Regs., Part II. and the Staff Manual respectively. Title pages will be prepared in manuscript.

# WAR DIARY
*or*
# INTELLIGENCE SUMMARY.
*(Erase heading not required.)*

Army Form C. 2118.

| Place | Date | Hour | Summary of Events and Information | Remarks and references to Appendices |
|---|---|---|---|---|
| Hoofpraaf | 8/3/16 | | with the rest for which they were originally sent. Visited Mob Vety Sect & examined 7 horses before evacuation to Base Vety Hpl. | JT |
| | 9/3/16 | | Visited Div H.Qs & Mob Vety Section | JT |
| | 10/3/16 | | Visited 1st Bde Am Col and examined 24 H.D. in exchange for 24 L.D. Visited H.Qs to report the result of examination | JT |
| | 11/3/16 | | Visited & inspected the Mob Vety Section. | JT |
| | 12/3/16 | | Visited at 4th Bde Am Col and examined 14 H.D. horses which had been drawn from Arty Bdes, in exchange for L.D. horses, all were marked X off hind quarter. Visited H.Qs to report the result of examination | JT |
| | 13/3/16 | | Visited Mob Vety Sect & examined 8 horses before evacuation to Base Vety Hpl. Visited 4th Bde Am Col & examined 8 H.D. to exchange for L.Ds. | JT |
| | 14/3/16 | | Visited 1st 2nd & 3rd Fd Amb and examined 14 H.D. horses to be exchanged for L.D. | JT |

T2134. Wt. W708—776. 500000. 4/15. Sir J. C. & S.

Instructions regarding War Diaries and Intelligence Summaries are contained in F. S. Regs., Part II. and the Staff Manual respectively. Title pages will be prepared in manuscript.

# WAR DIARY
*or*
# INTELLIGENCE SUMMARY.
*(Erase heading not required.)*

Army Form C. 2118.

| Place | Date | Hour | Summary of Events and Information | Remarks and references to Appendices |
|---|---|---|---|---|
| Hoofpaaf | 15/3/16 | | Visited Mobile Vety Section & examined 8 horses before evacuation to Base Vety Hpl. Visited Transport lines 5th D.L.I. to select & examine one H.D. in exchange for L.D. I selected the best, although it was not a good one. | [illegible] |
| | 16/3/16 | | Visited H.Qs of Mob Vety Section. | [illegible] |
| | 17/3/16. | | Visited & inspected several units, horses & Transport lines in the 150th & 151st Infantry Bdes, on the whole being good but there was still room for improvement, particularly in 5th Bord Regt. 151st M.G. Section are poor horse masters, horses are in fair condition, but the standings were very bad in places. The O.C. this Section's attention was drawn to this. | [illegible] |
| | 18/3/16. | | Attended at Rail head to meet 199 remounts coming up from the Base. A large number arrived in my opinion in poor condition; a large number of this lot were for Div Arty in exchange for heavy draughts. | [illegible] |
| | 19/3/16. | | Met 66 H.D. at 922 Central, drawn from Div Arty Bdes, reissued | [illegible] |

T2134. Wt. W708—776. 500000. 4/15. Sir J. C. & S.

Instructions regarding War Diaries and Intelligence Summaries are contained in F. S. Regs. Part II. and the Staff Manual respectively. Title pages will be prepared in manuscript.

# WAR DIARY
*or*
# INTELLIGENCE SUMMARY.
*(Erase heading not required.)*

Army Form C. 2118.

| Place | Date | Hour | Summary of Events and Information | Remarks and references to Appendices |
|---|---|---|---|---|
| Hd Quars | 19/3/16 | | some to Units in the Division the remainder were delivered to the Fd Rem Section. Visited Mob Vety Section. Visited position of 2nd Canadian Div Mob Vety Section, the probable site for the Mob Vety Sect for this Div. The situation satisfactory, but the approach is beyond description. | JH |
| | 20/3/16. | | Visited Mob Vety Section & examined 8 horses before evacuation to Base Vety Hpl. Visited & inspected Div Amm Col Lines, M.M.P. horses, & Div Sig Co. R.E. The former unit were wasting oats, by allowing them to escape from faulty sacks, the O.C's attention was drawn to this. The latter unit were wasting hay, the O.C's attention was drawn to irregularity of not using hay nets. | JH |
| | 21/3/16. | | Visited the Div Sig Co. R.E. at the request of the O.C. Found a horse injured so badly through getting impaled on a post that I ordered it to be destroyed as there was protrusion of the bowels through the rupture. | JH |

Instructions regarding War Diaries and Intelligence Summaries are contained in F. S. Regs., Part II. and the Staff Manual respectively. Title pages will be prepared in manuscript.

# WAR DIARY
*or*
# INTELLIGENCE SUMMARY.
*(Erase heading not required.)*

Army Form C. 2118.

| Place | Date | Hour | Summary of Events and Information | Remarks and references to Appendices |
|---|---|---|---|---|
| Hoofpraaf [?] | 22/3/16. | | Visited Div H.Qs. & Mob. Vet. Section | J.T. [?] |
| | 23/3/16. | | Visited the Unit Transport Lines of 9th Bde. 4th R.F.s forage poor in quality, 6th R.F.s two horses in poor condition 7th R.F. several horses in poor condition. 8th R.F. alright. The attention of the Bde. Transport Officer was drawn to these several points. | J.T. [?] |
| | 24/3/16. | | Visited Mob. Vet. Section & examined 8 horses before evacuation to Base Vet. Hpl. | J.T. [?] |
| | 25/3/16. | | Visited & inspected in company with O.C. 50th Div Mob Vet Section the position of 2nd Canadian Div Mob Vet Sect. The O.C. 50th Mob Vet Section was not at all pleased with the approach. Called on A.D.V.S. 2nd Canadian Div | J.T. [?] |
| | 26/3/16 | | Visited Div H.Qs. & Mobile Vet. Section & examined 8 horses before evacuation to Base Vet. Hpl. Visited Hd. Qs. Div Train to enquire about 2 [illegible] charges. | J.T. [?] |

Instructions regarding War Diaries and Intelligence Summaries are contained in F. S. Regs., Part II. and the Staff Manual respectively. Title pages will be prepared in manuscript.

# WAR DIARY
*or*
# INTELLIGENCE SUMMARY.
*(Erase heading not required.)*

Army Form C. 2118.

| Place | Date | Hour | Summary of Events and Information | Remarks and references to Appendices |
|---|---|---|---|---|
| Hoofpaaf | 27/3/16. | | Visited Div H.Qs & arranged with D.A.Q.M.G. about giving practical instruction in Horse & Stable management. | J.T. |
| | 28/3/16 | | Visited & examined 8 horses at Mob Vety Section before evacuation to Base Vety Hpl | J.T. |
| | 29/3/16. | | Visited & inspected 151st Inf Bde Transport lines. The 5th Borders Regt lines are still bad. The Transport Officer's attention was drawn to the want of better supervision. Visited & inspected 149th M.G. Co's lines & horses. There were two O.C. in this Co which in my opinion are not at all suitable, one very old, any age between 20 & 25, the other one blind in near eye. | J.T. J.T. |
| | 30/3/16. | | Visited the Mob Vety Section. Visited & inspected horse lines of the No 2 Co A.S.C. Found several low in condition, the O.C.'s attention was drawn to the state of these horses. Visited & inspected a Brown Mule at Div. Am. Col. Ordered it to be cast as dangerous, which has been done by D.D.R. | J.T. |

T2134. Wt. W708—776. 500000. 4/15. Sir J. C. & S.

Instructions regarding War Diaries and Intelligence Summaries are contained in F. S. Regs., Part II. and the Staff Manual respectively. Title pages will be prepared in manuscript.

# WAR DIARY
*or*
# INTELLIGENCE SUMMARY.
*(Erase heading not required.)*

Army Form C. 2118.

| Place | Date | Hour | Summary of Events and Information | Remarks and references to Appendices |
|---|---|---|---|---|
| Hoofraaf | 31/3/16. | | Visited & inspected the 7th D.L.I. horses & Transport Lines. These have improved since my last inspection, there is still room for improvement. Visited & inspected the horses & lines of the units of the 149th Inf. Bge, on the whole they were fairly good. Met several horses which had been reported as unable to work through various reasons. Visited 5th Bdrs & 9th D.L.I. & inspected remounts which had been received. | J.A. |
| | | | Summary:- The past month has been a very trying one for horses but I am pleased to say that they have withstood the strain fairly well. There has not been any outbreak of any Contagious or Infectious nature, but unfortunately there has been a number of unavoidable casualties. On the whole the horses have been made as comfortable as circumstances would permit. The forage has not attained its usual standard | J.A. J.A. |

T2134. Wt. W708–776. 500000. 4/15. Sir J. C. & S.

Instructions regarding War Diaries and Intelligence Summaries are contained in F. S. Regs., Part II. and the Staff Manual respectively. Title pages will be prepared in manuscript.

# WAR DIARY
*or*
# INTELLIGENCE SUMMARY.
*(Erase heading not required.)*

Army Form C. 2118.

| Place | Date | Hour | Summary of Events and Information | Remarks and references to Appendices |
|---|---|---|---|---|
| Hovfpraaf | | | Summary contd:- Of excellence, especially does this refer to the grain issued. During my inspections I have seen several poor samples of oats, all husk & no flour. The strictest vigilance has been preserved in examination of it to detect foreign deleterious bodies & something mixed in it by an unscrupulous foe. Several foreign bodies have been found such as nails, bits of glass. | J.A. |

T2134. Wt. W"08—776. 500000. 4/15. Sir J. C. & S.

ADVS 50 Div

Vol

Dup

Instructions regarding War Diaries and Intelligence Summaries are contained in F. S. Regs., Part II. and the Staff Manual respectively. Title pages will be prepared in manuscript.

# WAR DIARY
*or*
# INTELLIGENCE SUMMARY.
*(Erase heading not required.)*

Army Form C. 2118.

| Place | Date | Hour | Summary of Events and Information | Remarks and references to Appendices |
|---|---|---|---|---|
| Hooggraaf | 1/4/16. | | Visited the Mob Vet Section & examined 29 horses before evacuation to Base Vet Hptl. Visited Hd. Qts horses. | J.H. |
| | 2/4/16. | | Visited & inspected 5th Corps Hd Qts horses. Visited & inspected Cornwall R.E. horses, these horses were all looking fit & well. | J.H. |
| Westoutre | 3/4/16 | | 50th Div Hd. Qts removed to Westoutre, Sheet 28. M. 9. C. 3.5 | J.H. |
| | 4/4/16 | | Visited & inspected Div Signal Co R.E. horses & lines fairly good. Visited & inspected lines & horses of following units. 4th Yorks. 4th E. Yorks. 5th Yorks. 5th D.L.I. & 150th M.G. Section. These units lines were fairly good & the horses are improving. Examined the Div Chaplains horse very lame near fore leg, in my opinion due to a defective [illegible]. also examined Capt Clegg horse lame off fore foot from [illegible]. | J.H. |
| | 5/4/16. | | Met the D.D.R. at M.17 d.4.4 Sheet 28 who came to inspect H.D. in exchange for L.D. The Div Field Co R.E. turned out 20 H.D. all good ones. The Field Amb 12 useful ones. Visited Mob Vet Section in the old area to obtain information about | J.H. |

T2134. Wt. W708—776. 500000. 4/15. Sir J. C. & S.

Instructions regarding War Diaries and Intelligence Summaries are contained in F. S. Regs., Part II. and the Staff Manual respectively. Title pages will be prepared in manuscript.

# WAR DIARY
*or*
# INTELLIGENCE SUMMARY.
*(Erase heading not required.)*

Army Form C. 2118.

| Place | Date | Hour | Summary of Events and Information | Remarks and references to Appendices |
|---|---|---|---|---|
| Westoutre | 5/4/16 | | (contd) suitable men in the Section for promotion to Sgts A.V.C. for attachment to R.F.A. units | J.T. |
| | 6/4/16 | | Visited & examined A.S.C. 3 horse at Divisional Hd Qrs lines, lame near fore leg from Splint. Visited 1st Northumbrian Bde & examined a horse with several Shrapnel wounds, particularly about head & neck, ordered it into the Section. Mobile Vet Section moved into new area. | J.T. |
| | 7/4/16 | | Visited the Mob Vet Section & inspected the lines & camp. Visited & inspected Nos 2nd 3rd & 4th Div Train A.S.C. The O.C. 4th Co had reported some about the water supply being contaminated, which had caused several of his horses ~~to~~ slight colicky pains. Another supply was found with beneficial results to the horses. | J.T. |
| | 8/4/16. | | ~~Inspected~~ Visited & inspected the lines, horses & forage, at the following units. Hd Qrs. 4th 5th 6th & 7th Nbn Fusiliers, & 149 Machine Gun Section. Found all the horses improving in condition. | J.T. |

T2134. Wt. W708—776. 500000. 4/15. Sir J. C. & S.

Instructions regarding War Diaries and Intelligence Summaries are contained in F. S. Regs., Part II. and the Staff Manual respectively. Title pages will be prepared in manuscript.

# WAR DIARY
*or*
# INTELLIGENCE SUMMARY.
*(Erase heading not required.)*

Army Form C. 2118.

| Place | Date | Hour | Summary of Events and Information | Remarks and references to Appendices |
|---|---|---|---|---|
| Westoutre | 8/4/16 | | contd. The horse lines left by the Division which this Division succeeded were left in a very dirty & insanitary condition. | [initials] |
| | 9/4/16 | | Visited Mob Vety Section & examined 8 horses before evacuation to Base Vety Hpl. Visited the Fd. Remount Section & inspected a number of L.Ds. in exchange for H.Ds. I was only able to select 8. | [initials] |
| | 10/4/16 | | Visited Mob. Vety. Section & examined 11 horses before evacuation to Base Vety Hpl. Visited & inspected Yorks Hussars Squadron. Found two lame which in my opinion will soon be sound & fit for work. Visited & inspected 1/1st Fd Amb. | [initials] |
| | 11/4/16 | | Visited & inspected 151st Bde. Hd Qts horses, and the following units 6th, 8th, 9th D.L.I. 5th Border Regt, 151st Machine Gun Section. The same remarks apply to this Bde Horse lines, they were left by the last Division in a very insanitary condition, the only good feature about this position is that there is a good water supply. The horses were all looking fairly well. | [initials] |

Instructions regarding War Diaries and Intelligence Summaries are contained in F. S. Regs., Part II. and the Staff Manual respectively. Title pages will be prepared in manuscript.

# WAR DIARY
*or*
# INTELLIGENCE SUMMARY.
*(Erase heading not required.)*

Army Form C. 2118.

| Place | Date | Hour | Summary of Events and Information | Remarks and references to Appendices |
|---|---|---|---|---|
| Westoutre | 12/4/16 | | Visited & inspected horses & lines 7th D.L.I. Pioneer Btt. Reposition was good, no covering in bad weather. Ordered a very lame horse to be floated into Section as it was unfit to travel. Visited Mob Vety Section & examined 13 horses before evacuation to Base Vety Hptl. | J.F. |
| | 13/4/16. | | Visited & inspected horses & lines at Hd Qrs, Div Amn Col. & Nos 1-2 & 3 Sections Div Amn Col. Horse standings fairly good, surroundings very bad. Visited & inspected 2nd & 3rd Cos A.S.C. Horse standings good. Met & distributed 128 Remounts at Railhead. 66 mules for Div Amn Col were a good draft. 62 remounts were good excepting two, one a very old & broken-winded one, & lame near hind lock from sprain, the other unsuitable to carry an officer 6 ft. weighing 14 St. | J.F. J.F. |
| | 14/4/16. | | Distributing Remounts at Yorks Hussars lines to various units. Visited & inspected horses & lines 2/2nd Fd Amb. | J.F. |

Instructions regarding War Diaries and Intelligence Summaries are contained in F. S. Regs., Part II. and the Staff Manual respectively. Title pages will be prepared in manuscript.

# WAR DIARY
*or*
# INTELLIGENCE SUMMARY.
*(Erase heading not required.)*

Army Form C. 2118.

| Place | Date | Hour | Summary of Events and Information | Remarks and references to Appendices |
|---|---|---|---|---|
| Westoutre | 14/4/16 | | contd] Horses were all in good working condition. Visited Mob Vet Section. | J.T. |
| | 15/4/16. | | I was asked by the O.C. Div Train ASC to call & examine a Brown mare, in my opinion she was suffering from either a blood clot on the brain, or some growth there. a very peculiar & interesting case. This mare had had Facial Paralysis on the off side for a long time, the Brain symptoms were probably secondary. Visited & inspected the horse lines of 2nd Bty, 1st Bge, R.F.A. very bad & in a filthy condition. In my opinion there are dozens of tons of manure left close to the lines. | J.T. / J.T. |
| | 16/4/16. | | Visited & inspected horses & lines 1/3 (N.M.) Fd Amb. 2nd Bty 2nd Bge R.F.A. Lines very bad, too much manure had been left by the late unit occupying these lines. consequently it is next to impossible to do anything with it. 1st Bty, 1st Bge R.F.A the same remarks apply to these lines. | J.T. |

T2134. Wt. W708—776. 500000. 4/15. Sir J. C. & S.

Instructions regarding War Diaries and Intelligence Summaries are contained in F. S. Regs., Part II. and the Staff Manual respectively. Title pages will be prepared in manuscript.

# WAR DIARY
*or*
# INTELLIGENCE SUMMARY.
*(Erase heading not required.)*

Army Form C. 2118.

| Place | Date | Hour | Summary of Events and Information | Remarks and references to Appendices |
|---|---|---|---|---|
| Lestrem (?) | 16/4/16 | contd. | Visited & inspected the horses & lines of 2nd Fd Co. R.E. Found an improvement in this unit. Visited & inspected Hd Qrs lines & horses of 150th Inf Bge. Very good. Visited & inspected 8 horses at Mob. Vet. Section before evacuation to Base Vet. Hpl. | J.H. |
| | 17/4/16. | | Attended at 149th Bge Hd Qrs & met the Transport officers, & Sergts & gave them a few practical hints on Horse management in its relation to health & disease, particularly watering & feeding & the consequent dangers which arise from any irregularities in this branch. Visited & inspected lines & horses of S.P. Cable section, horses well cared for, but the lines in places were poor & wanted repairing. | J.H. |
| | 18/4/16. | | Visited 3rd Bge Am Col, lines very bad. Visited & inspected lines & horses of 5th Bty, 4th (How) Bge, & ordered a very old horse broken winded & debilitated to the Mob. Vet. Section. Visited Mob. Vet. section & examined a horse with a very large Ventral Hernia in the off flank, | J.H. |

T2134. Wt. W708—776. 500000. 4/15. Sir J. C. & S.

Instructions regarding War Diaries and Intelligence Summaries are contained in F. S. Regs., Part II. and the Staff Manual respectively. Title pages will be prepared in manuscript.

# WAR DIARY
*or*
# INTELLIGENCE SUMMARY.
*(Erase heading not required.)*

Army Form C. 2118.

| Place | Date | Hour | Summary of Events and Information | Remarks and references to Appendices |
|---|---|---|---|---|
| Westoutre | 18/4/16 (cont) | | the largest I have ever seen, as it was a very old horse & kept on having slight attacks of Colic. I ordered it to be destroyed. | |
| | 19/4/16. | | Visited & inspected 4 Durham (How) Bty, these horses are not looking at all well, their lines are in a very exposed position, & I think unsuitable. Visited & inspected 1st Bde Am Col, found the horses in this Col looking bad, starved, tucked up, in fact showing signs of debility, ordered one into Mob Vet Section. Visited & inspected horses & Vet Equipment of Yorks Hussars, found them all well & fit to go into training. Visited & examined horses at Mob Vet Sec before evacuating to B.V.H. | |
| | 20/4/16. | | Visited & inspected horses & lines of 7th Fd Co R.E. very good, considering that a large number of horses in this Co are aged they have come through the winter very well. Visited 151st Inf Bde Hd Qrs horses & lines, found all correct. | |
| | 21/4/16. | | Visited & inspected transport horses & lines of 4th Yorks | |

T2134. Wt. W708—776. 500000. 4/15. Sir J. C. & S.

Instructions regarding War Diaries and Intelligence Summaries are contained in F. S. Regs., Part II. and the Staff Manual respectively. Title pages will be prepared in manuscript.

# WAR DIARY
*or*
# INTELLIGENCE SUMMARY.
(*Erase heading not required.*)

Army Form C. 2118.

| Place | Date | Hour | Summary of Events and Information | Remarks and references to Appendices |
|---|---|---|---|---|
| Westoutre | 21/4/16 | | ...da. Regt. & 4th Yorks Regt. Pleased to say I found both these units improved. Visited & examined 15 horses at Mob Vety Section before evacuation to Base Vety Hpl | JA |
| | 22/4/16. | | Met D.D.V.S. II Army who visited & inspected the Section & afterwards examined several men in Veterinary Science with a view to their being promoted Army Vety Corps Sgts. & then becoming attached to artillery units | JA |
| | 23/4/16 | | Met 38 remounts at Bailleul Station and distributed them to the units concerned. One animal very lame, & in my opinion ought never to have been sent. Visited the Section. | JA |
| | 24/4/16 | | The A.A. & Q.M.G. 50th Div visited & inspected the Mob Vety Section. | JA |
| | 25/4/16. | | 50th Divisional Head Qrs removed to new area. Visited & examined 15 horses at Mob Vety Section before evacuation to Base Vety Hpl | JA |
| Flêtre | 26/4/16 | | Visited the position of 11th Mob Vety Section III Div and | |

Instructions regarding War Diaries and Intelligence Summaries are contained in F. S. Regs., Part II. and the Staff Manual respectively. Title pages will be prepared in manuscript.

# WAR DIARY
*or*
# INTELLIGENCE SUMMARY.
*(Erase heading not required.)*

Army Form C. 2118.

| Place | Date | Hour | Summary of Events and Information | Remarks and references to Appendices |
|---|---|---|---|---|
| Flêtre | 26/4/16 | | interviewed the O.C. | J.H. |
| | 27/4/16 | | Visited & inspected 151st Inf Bde Head Qrs lines & horses, one lot of stabling was very bad, no ventilation. Visited & inspected transport lines & horses of 151st Machine Gun Co. 8th D.L.I. & 6th O.L.I. horses improving, & lines all good. Visited & inspected Horses & lines of 43rd Bg R.F.A. Found several horses backward in condition. Brick standings very good, but surroundings are very bad & foul. I doubt the water supply of this unit, as there has been several cases of Colic in a week. I ordered the O.C. to find a fresh supply. | J.H. |
| | 28/4/16 | | Visited 149th Bde Hd Qrs Horses & 5th Btt N.Hum Fus found them improving in condition. Visited Mob Vety Section & detailed 5 A.V.C. Sgts to various Arty Units. Visited Hd Qrs Co A.S.C. & examined a horse which had been injured. Examined 16 horses at the Mob Vety Section before evacuation to the Base Vety Hpl. | J.H. |

Instructions regarding War Diaries and Intelligence Summaries are contained in F. S. Regs., Part II. and the Staff Manual respectively. Title pages will be prepared in manuscript.

# WAR DIARY
*or*
# INTELLIGENCE SUMMARY.
*(Erase heading not required.)*

Army Form C. 2118.

| Place | Date | Hour | Summary of Events and Information | Remarks and references to Appendices |
|---|---|---|---|---|
| Flêtre | 29/4/16 | | Visited & examined 13 horses at Mob Vet Section before evacuation to Base Vet Hpl. Attended at conference of A.D.V.S. Division at Bailleul, we were addressed by the D.D.V.S. II Army, very instructive particularly that portion relating to the Sanitation of Camps. | S.T. |
| | 30/4/16 | | 1/1 North. Mob. Vet Section arrived in new area, I met them they had stood the march well. | S.T. |
| | | | Summary. I have pleasure in reporting that the horses in the 50th Division are in good health, and continuing in condition. There has not been any attack of a Contagious or Infectious nature during the month. The forage on the whole has been good, the oats have not been quite so good as in previous months, they have been poor in weight, & not quite so clean as they ought to be. The remounts issued to the Division were satisfactory, especially the Light Draughts, the riders were not at all good. I am endeavouring to obtain | S.T. S.T. |

Instructions regarding War Diaries and Intelligence Summaries are contained in F. S. Regs., Part II. and the Staff Manual respectively. Title Pages will be prepared in manuscript.

# WAR DIARY
*or*
# INTELLIGENCE SUMMARY
*(Erase heading not required.)*

Army Form C. 2118

| Place | Date | Hour | Summary of Events and Information | Remarks and references to Appendices |
|---|---|---|---|---|
| Flete. | 30/4/16. | | a small issue of Rock Salt for the horses in the Division, cognisant of its efficacy in aiding horses to improve & retain their condition. | |
| | | | E. Franklin<br>Major AVC<br>ADVS. 50th Division | |

1875 Wt. W593/826 1,000,000 4/15 J.B.C. & A. A.D.S.S./Forms/C. 2118.

Instructions regarding War Diaries and Intelligence Summaries are contained in F. S. Regs., Part II. and the Staff Manual respectively. Title pages will be prepared in manuscript.

# WAR DIARY
*or*
# INTELLIGENCE SUMMARY.
*(Erase heading not required.)*

ADVS 50 Div
Vol XI

Army Form C. 2118.

| Place | Date | Hour | Summary of Events and Information | Remarks and references to Appendices |
|---|---|---|---|---|
| Flêtre | 1/5/16. | | Visited D.D.V.S. II Army Hd Qts, & discussed the question of the malleability of the iron from which shoes for the Army are issued. | JH. |
| | 2/5/16. | | Visited Hd Qts, C.R.A. Visited & inspected 150th Bge Machine Gun Section, Visited & inspected Hd Qts horses, 1st (Nbn) Bge R.F.A. Visited & inspected 1st Bty, 1st Bge R.F.A. horses improving in condition. Visited & inspected 2nd Bty R.F.A. Found them out grazing. Visited & inspected 3rd Bty R.F.A. not improving at all. Visited 1st Bge Am Col, improving. | JH. |
| | 3/5/16. | | Visited & inspected Hd Qts, 2nd (Nbn) Bge R.F.A. improving. Visited & inspected 1st Bty, 2nd Bge, these horses were all in fair working condition, the shoeing was not good. the O.C. attention was drawn to this. Visited 2nd Bty, 2nd Bge, room for a great deal of improvement in this Bty. The same applies to the 3rd Bty of this Brigade. Visited the 2nd Bge Am Col. Horses were looking better. Returned the | JH. |

Instructions regarding War Diaries and Intelligence Summaries are contained in F. S. Regs., Part II. and the Staff Manual respectively. Title pages will be prepared in manuscript.

# WAR DIARY
*or*
# INTELLIGENCE SUMMARY.
*(Erase heading not required.)*

Army Form C. 2118.

| Place | Date | Hour | Summary of Events and Information | Remarks and references to Appendices |
|---|---|---|---|---|
| Fletre | 3/5/16. | | Army Vety Corps Sgts in the afternoon on Horse management. | J.H. |
| | 4/5/16. | | Visited & inspected Hd Qts horses 3rd Bge R.F.A. room for improvement. Visited & inspected the 3rd Bge Am. Col. Horses improving. Visited & inspected 1st, 2nd, & 3rd Btys of this Brigade. Horses are beginning to improve. Gave instructions to all O.C. Btys to take advantage of all the grass they could find along the Country lanes by letting the horses have as much as they could. | J.H. |
| | 5/5/16. | | Visited & inspected a horse at the 2/3rd (Nln) Fd Co. R.E. found it to be suffering from a very nasty Quittor, as it was very old, I ordered it to be destroyed. Visited & inspected 61st Bty atta 4th (Nln) Bge R.F.A. This unit has a number of old horses which in my opinion are past the age for working. I saw three which were very old, anything between 25 & 30 years of age. | J.H. |
| | 6/5/16. | | Visited the Hd Qts 150th Inf Bge & lectured the Transport Officers on Horse management. Visited Fd Remount Section to select chargers for Staff Officers. Visited & attended a foal | |

Army Form C. 2118.

Instructions regarding War Diaries and Intelligence Summaries are contained in F. S. Regs., Part II. and the Staff Manual respectively. Title pages will be prepared in manuscript.

# WAR DIARY
*or*
# INTELLIGENCE SUMMARY.
*(Erase heading not required.)*

| Place | Date | Hour | Summary of Events and Information | Remarks and references to Appendices |
|---|---|---|---|---|
| Flêtre | 6/5/16 contd | | in this town belonging to a Farmer, found it very ill suffering from Colic. | J.T. |
| | 7/5/16 | | Visited & inspected the Divisional Sig Co. R.E. lines & horses. Ordered a roan mare to the Section suffering from a large serous abscess on the chest. Visited & examined Div Hd Qts horses particularly the Q.M.G. mare, found it much improved. Visited & examined the Farmers foal twice, very poorly. | J.T. |
| | 8/5/16. | | Visited & inspected 107th Bty. R.F.A. All excepting two were well & in good condition. Visited & examined charger belonging Brigade Commander, 150th Inf Bde. Found it lame in my opinion from Splints, gave instructions for treatment. Visited & examined 16 horses before evacuation to Base Vety Hospital. | J.T. |
| | 9/5/16 | | Visited & examined C.R.E.'s mare, wound in shoulder. Visited & inspected 4th Yorks Inf Btn Transport lines & horses | J.T. |

Instructions regarding War Diaries and Intelligence Summaries are contained in F. S. Regs., Part II. and the Staff Manual respectively. Title pages will be prepared in manuscript.

# WAR DIARY
*or*
# INTELLIGENCE SUMMARY.
*(Erase heading not required.)*

Army Form C. 2118.

| Place | Date | Hour | Summary of Events and Information | Remarks and references to Appendices |
|---|---|---|---|---|
| Flêtre | 9/5/16 cont | | Found them improving, also the same applies to the 5th D.L.I. Visited & inspected 1/3 (Nbn) Fd Amb, saw one horse suffering from bad septic broken knees, all the others well. Visited & inspected 4th Yorks, lines & horses, excepting two which will improve all were looking well. As I was passing the 150th Bde Hd Qrs I examined the Brigade Commanders Ch mare & ordered it to Mob Vet section for treatment. | J.A. |
| | 10/5/16 | | Visited the Mob Vet Section. Visited & inspected the 5th Border Regt Transport lines & horses, a slight improvement on my last inspection, but there is still room for more improvement. The forage issued to this unit was not good. Visited & inspected the 9th D.L.I. Regt transport lines & horses, lines were good, horses in good working condition. | J.A. |
| | 11/5/16 | | Was asked to examine a Civilian farmers horse suffering from an excoriated mouth, prescribed | J.A. |

Instructions regarding War Diaries and Intelligence Summaries are contained in F. S. Regs., Part II. and the Staff Manual respectively. Title pages will be prepared in manuscript.

# WAR DIARY
*or*
# INTELLIGENCE SUMMARY.
*(Erase heading not required.)*

Army Form C. 2118.

| Place | Date | Hour | Summary of Events and Information | Remarks and references to Appendices |
|---|---|---|---|---|
| Ilette | 11/5/16 cont. | | Visited & inspected Transport lines of 149th Machine Gun Co not at all good, wants better supervision. 4th N.F. Btt, horses & lines not good. 5th N.F. Btt no attempt to clean up lines, ordered 2 animals to Mob Vet Section. Visited & inspected 1/1st Fd Amb transport lines & horses horses in good condition. | [illegible] |
| | 12/5/16. | | Visited & examined 15 horses at Mob Vet Section before evacuation to Base Vet Hpl. Visited & inspected 1/2nd Fd Amb, very good. Visited 2nd & 3rd Sections Div Amn Col. Mules ought to begin to improve in condition, but they do not as much as I should like. I assisted the V.O. i/c of this unit to make a P.M. on a mule which had died very quickly. It had ruptured a blood vessel in the mesentery it had also a very large spleen. I examined a large number of horses which had been detailed to No 4 Section, some of them were | [illegible] |

Instructions regarding War Diaries and Intelligence Summaries are contained in F. S. Regs., Part II. and the Staff Manual respectively. Title pages will be prepared in manuscript.

# WAR DIARY
*or*
# INTELLIGENCE SUMMARY.
*(Erase heading not required.)*

Army Form C. 2118.

| Place | Date | Hour | Summary of Events and Information | Remarks and references to Appendices |
|---|---|---|---|---|
| Steke | 12/5/16 ctd. | | in poor condition, but they will improve as they are a suitable age. | S.A. |
| | 13/5/16. | | Attended a conference of A.D's V.S Divisions presided over by the D.D.V.S. 2nd Army, very instructive & enjoyable. The discussion on Cutting & Fired bone diseases good. | S.A. |
| | 14/5/16. | | Visited the Mob Vet Section, Inspected lines & horses of 7th D.L.I. these horses will improve as the officer in charge is a practical horseman. Visited 1/1st Fd Co R.E. not as good as usual. Visited No 2 Co Div Train A.S.C. horses in good condition. Visited & examined a Bn mare at 6th N.F. Btt Hd Qts suffering from intestinal trouble. The D.A.A. & Q.M.G mare still lame | S.A. |
| | 15/5/16. | | Visited C.R.A Hd Qts, & Div Am Col. Inspected 30 horses collected by No 2 Section Div Am Col, a very poor lot, 3 were issued lame, 1 suspicious skin eruption. Visited Mob Vet Section | S.A. |

T2134. Wt. W708—776. 500000. 4/15. Sir J. C. & S.

Instructions regarding War Diaries and Intelligence Summaries are contained in F. S. Regs., Part II. and the Staff Manual respectively. Title pages will be prepared in manuscript.

# WAR DIARY
*or*
# INTELLIGENCE SUMMARY.
*(Erase heading not required.)*

Army Form C. 2118.

| Place | Date | Hour | Summary of Events and Information | Remarks and references to Appendices |
|---|---|---|---|---|
| Ilette | 16/8/16 | | Visited Lothians & Border Horse (Sqd) & examined a H.D. Br mare obtained from 198th Co A.S.C. 25th Div. It had symptoms of skin eruption, ordered it into Mobile Vet Section. Visited & inspected 30 remounts at No 1 Section Div Am Col, two or three in poor condition but they will soon improve. Visited & inspected No 3 Sect Div Am Col, especting 8 a few old ones the same remarks applies to these Remounts. Visited the Mob Vet Section. | J.T. |
| | 17/8/16 | | Visited Mob Vet Section to examine patients. Had a conference with A.V.C. Sergts in the afternoon & gave them instructions on their duties. | J.T. |
| | 18/8/16 | | Visited the Fd Remount Section to select remounts for the Division. The mules were good but rides were a very poor lot. 34 were collected & distributed. | J.T. |
| | 19/8/16 | | Visited the Mob Vet Section & examined 8 horses before evacuation to the Base Vet Hpl. Conference with | J.T. |

T2134. Wt. W708—776. 500000. 4/15. Sir J. C. & S.

Instructions regarding War Diaries and Intelligence Summaries are contained in F. S. Regs., Part II. and the Staff Manual respectively. Title pages will be prepared in manuscript.

# WAR DIARY
*or*
# INTELLIGENCE SUMMARY.
(*Erase heading not required.*)

Army Form C. 2118.

| Place | Date | Hour | Summary of Events and Information | Remarks and references to Appendices |
|---|---|---|---|---|
| Fletre | 19/5/16 | | V.O.'s in my office. | J.T. |
| | 20/5/16 | | Visited & inspected the horses & lines of the 443rd Bty R.F.A. horses have improved in condition since my last visit. Visited & inspected transport lines & horses of 8th D.L.I. & 6th D.L.I. and 151st Machine Gun Section. | J.T. |
| | 21/5/16. | | Visited & inspected transport lines & horses of 5th Border Regt. pleased to say this units horses have improved. Visited & inspected transport lines & horses of 9th D.L.I. these are improving, which I hope will continue. Visited the Mob. Vety Section. | J.T. |
| | 22/5/16 | | Visited & inspected 10 horses of the Divisional Artillery for casting. Visited Mob Vety Section. Visited 150th Bge Hd Qrs & examined a Ch Ride G. 6 years old, fit for reissue. | J.T. |
| | 23/5/16 – 1/6/16 | | On leave. | J.T. |

T2134. Wt. W708—776. 500000. 4/15. Sir J. C. & S.

Instructions regarding War Diaries and Intelligence Summaries are contained in F. S. Regs., Part II. and the Staff Manual respectively. Title pages will be prepared in manuscript.

# WAR DIARY
*or*
# INTELLIGENCE SUMMARY.
*(Erase heading not required.)*

Army Form C. 2118.

| Place | Date | Hour | Summary of Events and Information | Remarks and references to Appendices |
|---|---|---|---|---|
| | | | Summary. I have pleasure in reporting that during the past month, ~~that~~ there has not been any outbreak of a contagious or infectious nature among the horses of the 50th Division. | J.A. |
| | | | F. Franklin<br>Major A.V.C.<br>A.D.V.S. 50th (Nbn) Division. | |

Instructions regarding War Diaries and Intelligence Summaries are contained in F. S. Regs., Part II. and the Staff Manual respectively. Title pages will be prepared in manuscript.

# WAR DIARY
*or*
# INTELLIGENCE SUMMARY.
*(Erase heading not required.)*

Army Form C. 2118.

ADVS 50 DW

Vol 12

| Place | Date | Hour | Summary of Events and Information | Remarks and references to Appendices |
|---|---|---|---|---|
| Westoutre | 1/6/16 | | Returned to the Division from leave | S.F. |
| | 2/6/16 | | Visited D.D.V.S. 2nd Army on the subject of reinforcements from England. Visited Mob Vet Section. | S.F. |
| | 3/6/16 | | Attended fortnightly conference at Bailleul of A.D.V.S. of 2nd Army, a very interesting subject "Quittor" was discussed, causes & treatment. Samples of oats were also discussed which had become contaminated by a larva named Canealis "Dancoides". They are not poisonous, & have not any feeding properties, being largely composed of woody matter. | S.F. |
| | 4/6/16. | | Visited & inspected the transport lines of 7th N. F. & found a horse suffering from Opthalmia, not serious enough for evacuation. 149th Machine Gun Sect, all moving. Visited & inspected the 1/1st Nhm Fd Amb, saw a Chest mare with all the symptoms of a simple fracture of the Tibia, a very peculiar & interesting case, decided to give her a chance as she was a very useful young L.D. mare. Visited & inspected | S.F. |

Army Form C. 2118.

Instructions regarding War Diaries and Intelligence Summaries are contained in F. S. Regs., Part II. and the Staff Manual respectively. Title pages will be prepared in manuscript.

# WAR DIARY
*or*
# INTELLIGENCE SUMMARY.
*(Erase heading not required.)*

| Place | Date | Hour | Summary of Events and Information | Remarks and references to Appendices |
|---|---|---|---|---|
| Nestoutre | 4/6/16 | | Ch. transport lines of 4th, 5th & 6th R. W. F. found these units were being looked after, excepting one or two minor cases had not anything to show me. | |
| | 5/6/16 | | Visited & examined 23 horses at Mob Vet Section before evacuation to Base Vety Hpl. | S.T. |
| | 6/6/16 | | Visited & inspected 2/2nd (Wln) Fd Amb, found horses all looking well. Visited & inspected Div Hd Qts horses all looking well. Visited 1/3rd (Wln) Fd Amb found a bay H. D. mare had been kicked during the night, not serious. Visited C. R. A. Hd Qts horses no fault to find. | S.T. |
| | 7/6/16. | | Visited & inspected 2/2nd (Wln) Fd Amb (mobile section) ~~and~~ being well looked after. Visited & inspected 3rd Sec Div Am Col. found too many in the sick lines. Visited & inspected Div Sig Co R. E. too many kicks in this unit, the O. C. of this Co attention was drawn to this. Visited & inspected No 1 Sect Div Am Col in company with D. D. V. S. 2nd Army | S.T. |

T2134. Wt. W708—776. 500000. 4/15. Sir J. C. & S.

Instructions regarding War Diaries and Intelligence Summaries are contained in F. S. Regs., Part II. and the Staff Manual respectively. Title pages will be prepared in manuscript.

# WAR DIARY
*or*
# INTELLIGENCE SUMMARY.
*(Erase heading not required.)*

Army Form C. 2118.

| Place | Date | Hour | Summary of Events and Information | Remarks and references to Appendices |
|---|---|---|---|---|
| Westoutre | 7/6/16 (contd) | | Found too many sick horses in the lines, ordered them into Mob Vet Sect, & the V.O. i/c was warned about this irregularity | |
| | 8/6/16 | | Met the D.D.R. 2nd Army at M.17.C. & inspected a number of old, worn out, vicious horses for other than veterinary reasons, he cast 16 from various units. Visited & inspected the 151st Inf Bgde. transport lines & horses. & machine gun Section. not anything to report. | E.F. |
| | 9/6/16 | | Visited & examined 24 sick animals at Mob Vet Section before evacuation to Base Vet Hpl. Visited & inspected transport lines & horses of 7th D.L.I. Found them improved very much since my last visit. | E.F. |
| | 10/6/16 | | Visited & inspected Mob Vet Sect. & in company with O.C. of the section went to look at a place where it is proposed to move the Section, situation good. close to the road consequently easy to get at. | E.F. |

Instructions regarding War Diaries and Intelligence Summaries are contained in F. S. Regs., Part II. and the Staff Manual respectively. Title pages will be prepared in manuscript.

# WAR DIARY
*or*
# INTELLIGENCE SUMMARY.
*(Erase heading not required.)*

Army Form C. 2118.

| Place | Date | Hour | Summary of Events and Information | Remarks and references to Appendices |
|---|---|---|---|---|
| Wesloutre | 11/6/16. | | D.D.V.S. 2nd Army visited & inspected the 1/1st (Wln) Mob Vet Section. He also inspected a new draft which had arrived, & detailed the men of the section to the various R.F.A. Batteries. | S.F. |
| | 12/6/16. | | Visited Hd Qtrs Div Am Col. Saw O.C. about several irregularities which the DDVS spoke about | S.F. |
| | 13/6/16. | | Visited & examined 24 horses before evacuation to Base Vety Hpl, also 6 horses suffering from Skin Disease, & 16 horses were sent with this draft which had been cast by the DDVS. Visited & inspected B. Bty 251st Bde. found them in good health. Visited & inspected No 3 Co ASC & No 2 Co ASC. Very bad horse lines, but animals in good health. Visited & inspected D Bty 251st Bde, horses & lines, very bad lines. C Bty 251st Bde, found this unit not taking care of its forage, left out in the rain. | S.F. |

Instructions regarding War Diaries and Intelligence Summaries are contained in F. S. Regs., Part II. and the Staff Manual respectively. Title pages will be prepared in manuscript.

# WAR DIARY
*or*
# INTELLIGENCE SUMMARY.
*(Erase heading not required.)*

Army Form C. 2118.

| Place | Date | Hour | Summary of Events and Information | Remarks and references to Appendices |
|---|---|---|---|---|
| Westoutre | 14/6/16 | | Visited & inspected A Bty, 251st Bde. Very bad horse lines, animals in poor condition, watering arrangements bad, the latter being contaminated by wastage from ablution bench, ordered this unit to find fresh lines. Visited & inspected C Bty, 250th Bde & examined a horse which had fallen into a trench, ordered it to be destroyed as its off hind tibia was fractured. Interviewed A.V.C. Sgts on their routine work. | R.F. |
| | 15/6/16 | | Visited 150 Inf Bde Hd Qrs to examine a bay mare, found it blind in both eyes (cataract). Visited & inspected 5th Btl D.L.I. found an aged bay g. doing with colic as it had been affected several times I ordered it to M.V.S. Visited & inspected horses & lines of the following units & found them doing better 4th Btl E. Yorks, 4th Btl Yorks, 5th Btl Yorks. Visited & inspected the 150th Bde Machine Gun Co. Very dirty | R.F. |

Instructions regarding War Diaries and Intelligence Summaries are contained in F. S. Regs., Part II. and the Staff Manual respectively. Title pages will be prepared in manuscript.

# WAR DIARY
*or*
# INTELLIGENCE SUMMARY.
*(Erase heading not required.)*

Army Form C. 2118.

| Place | Date | Hour | Summary of Events and Information | Remarks and references to Appendices |
|---|---|---|---|---|
| Westoutre | 15/6/16 | | (A) lines, no hay nets, consequently hay is wasted. The O.C. of this Co attention was drawn to these irregularities | J.T. |
| | 16/6/16. | | Went with D.A. & I.M.G. to pick out L.D. from Inf Bges in exchange for mules. Afterwards visited & inspected horses & lines of D.Bty/250th Bge R.F.A. Examined a bay mare which had become affected across the loins. She walked with difficulty, ordered it into Section, I do not think she will do any good. | J.T. |
| | 17/6/16 | | Visited the units of the 149th Inf Bge. & 150th Inf Bge to pick out if possible more L.D. I managed to pick out a few more. | J.T. |
| | 18/6/16. | | Visited Inf Bges to ascertain if they had their establishment of H.D. 73rd Inf Bge Mel. Gun Co horses are well done. Visited & inspected 1/1st (Nor) Fd Co R.E. this unit is doing well | J.T. |

Instructions regarding War Diaries and Intelligence Summaries are contained in F. S. Regs., Part II. and the Staff Manual respectively. Title pages will be prepared in manuscript.

# WAR DIARY
*or*
# INTELLIGENCE SUMMARY.
*(Erase heading not required.)*

Army Form C. 2118.

| Place | Date | Hour | Summary of Events and Information | Remarks and references to Appendices |
|---|---|---|---|---|
| Westoutre | 18/6/16 | | (A) Visited & inspected A Bty 250th Bde R.F.A. A want of better stable supervision is required in this Bty. Forage being wasted, too many sick horses in the lines, not using horse bags, consequently horses are not looking as they should. | [illegible] |
| | 19/6/16. | | Visited Div Am Col. Hd Qrs to ascertain their number of H.D. horses, found they had 2 surplus, one was issued to the Div Train A.S.C. the second being in poor condition was sent into Mob Vet Section. Visited the Div Train A.S.C. for a similar purpose, found 2 surplus Rides issued them to the 150th M.G. Co. Visited No 4 Sec. Div Am Col, found the animals of this Section were being looked after well. | [illegible] |
| | 20/6/16 | | Visited Mobile Vety Section & examined 14 horses before proceeding to Base Vet Hpl. Visited & inspected horses & lines C/250th Bde R.F.A. & B/250th | [illegible] |

Army Form C. 2118.

# WAR DIARY
*or*
# INTELLIGENCE SUMMARY.
*(Erase heading not required.)*

Instructions regarding War Diaries and Intelligence Summaries are contained in F. S. Regs., Part II. and the Staff Manual respectively. Title pages will be prepared in manuscript.

| Place | Date | Hour | Summary of Events and Information | Remarks and references to Appendices |
|---|---|---|---|---|
| Westoutre | 20/6/16 | | Bge R.F.A. wagon lines. Visited & inspected horses & lines D.V. Cable section, good. Visited & inspected 7th Fd Co. R.E. excepting they were not dealing with Excreta properly, this unit was good. | SL |
| | 21/6/16 | | Visited at Bailleul Station & examined H.Q. Remounts several were lame, one showed symptoms of skin disease. Visited No 3 Sec. Div Am Col, not at all good. Visited Mob Vet Section. | SL |
| | 22/6/16 | | Visited & examined A/252 Bge, R.F.A. horses which were undergoing the mallein test. Visited & inspected B/252 Bge R.F.A. This Bty have a number of very old horses in poor condition. Visited C/252 Bge RFA found horses & lines clean & well cared for. Visited & inspected D/252 Bge R.F.A. excepting two aged & worn out horses this bty is good. Visited Mob Vet Section & examined 8 horses | SL |

Instructions regarding War Diaries and Intelligence Summaries are contained in F. S. Regs., Part II. and the Staff Manual respectively. Title pages will be prepared in manuscript.

# WAR DIARY
*or*
# INTELLIGENCE SUMMARY.
*(Erase heading not required.)*

Army Form C. 2118.

| Place | Date | Hour | Summary of Events and Information | Remarks and references to Appendices |
|---|---|---|---|---|
| Westoutre | 22/6/16. | | Before proceeding to Base Vety Hpl. | E.A. |
| | 23/6/16 | | Visited & inspected A/252 Bge R.F.A. no reactors. Visited & inspected B/251 Bge R.F.A. horses & lines good. Visited & inspected No 2 Sec. Div Am Col. This section was not as good as usual, a want of better & keener stable supervision is needed. | E.A. |
| | 24/6/16. | | Visited & inspected A/250 Bge, R.F.A. No reactors. Visited Mob Vety Section to make arrangements for the evacuation of sick horses by road. | E.A. |
| | 25/6/16. | | Visited Bailleul Station to inspect 42 Remounts for 5th Corps Cavalry & 35 for this Division, this draft was not at all good. Several arrived with dirty itchy skins. | E.A. |
| | 26/6/16. | | Visited Mobile Vety Section and examined 5 horses before proceeding by road to St Omer, they were all in my opinion fit to march. Visited No 1 Co Div | E.A. |

Instructions regarding War Diaries and Intelligence Summaries are contained in F. S. Regs., Part II. and the Staff Manual respectively. Title pages will be prepared in manuscript.

# WAR DIARY
*or*
# INTELLIGENCE SUMMARY.
*(Erase heading not required.)*

Army Form C. 2118.

| Place | Date | Hour | Summary of Events and Information | Remarks and references to Appendices |
|---|---|---|---|---|
| Lestouche | 26/6/16 | | Am Col and examined the horses in this unit affected with Skin Disease, ordered 4 to Mob Vet Section, gave instructions about treating the rest. Visited Hd Qrs C.R.A. Div Signal Co R/s 3rd (Wln) Fd Amb, & 2nd (Wln) Fd Amb. | S.F. |
| | 27/6/16 | | Visited & inspected 20th Labour Btt (Notts & Derby Regt) horse lines & arranged for Vet attendance, very poor lot. Visited with the D.A. & Q.M.G. to select L.D. from Engineering units, we selected 42 from these units & gave them mules. | S.F. |
| | 28/6/16 | | Visited & inspected A Squad Royal Wilts Yeo (attached) very bad lines, forage wasted, altogether an improvement in stable management is required. B Squad Royal Wilts Yeo. this unit have had Mange & I can understand why they have it, & will always if they have not better stable supervision. Visited & inspected C Squad Hants | S.F. |

Instructions regarding War Diaries and Intelligence Summaries are contained in F. S. Regs., Part II. and the Staff Manual respectively. Title pages will be prepared in manuscript.

# WAR DIARY
*or*
# INTELLIGENCE SUMMARY.
*(Erase heading not required.)*

Army Form C. 2118.

| Place | Date | Hour | Summary of Events and Information | Remarks and references to Appendices |
|---|---|---|---|---|
| Westoutre | 28/6/16 | | Yeomanry. Very good, quite a contrast to the 2 Squadrons of Wilts Yeo. | |
| | 29/6/16. | | Attended a conference of A.D.V.S.s Divisions at Bailleul presided over by the D.D.V.S. II Army. A new scheme of evacuation of sick horses was described, and in my opinion when it has got into working order ought to develop into a good scheme. Visited & inspected the 1/2nd Mou[nted] Fd Amb—a section is away from its Base. Very good. | J.T. |
| | 30/6/16 | | Visited & inspected several Chronic Skin diseases in 7th D.T.[?] I lines, ordered four to the section, the rest in this unit are improving. | J.T. |
| | | | Visited & inspected A Bty 253 Bde R.F.A. which arrived on the 28th inst. I found many poor horses, ~~[illegible]~~ one wonders why they look as well as they do considering the amount of forage which | J.T. |

Instructions regarding War Diaries and Intelligence Summaries are contained in F. S. Regs., Part II. and the Staff Manual respectively. Title pages will be prepared in manuscript.

# WAR DIARY
*or*
# INTELLIGENCE SUMMARY.
*(Erase heading not required.)*

Army Form C. 2118.

| Place | Date | Hour | Summary of Events and Information | Remarks and references to Appendices |
|---|---|---|---|---|
| Westoutre | 30/6/16 | | is wasted. Visited B/Bty 253 Bde R.F.A. slight improvement on the last Bty. Visited C/Bty 253 Bde R.F.A. The horses in this Bty are very poor & thin, but from information received & considering they had been marching 5 days, & a large number had had sand colic I can quite understand their poor condition, but with good feeding, proper stable management, they will soon recover, most of them are a good age to do so. | J.F. |
| | | | Summary:- I regret during the last month there has been a recrudescence of Skin Disease in this Division, a number of horses having broken out again. A section Div Am Col were unfortunate in having a number of poor horses issued to them, susceptible animals for this disease. They have been isolated, and the worst cases | J.F. |

Instructions regarding War Diaries and Intelligence Summaries are contained in F. S. Regs., Part II. and the Staff Manual respectively. Title pages will be prepared in manuscript.

# WAR DIARY
*or*
# INTELLIGENCE SUMMARY.
*(Erase heading not required.)*

Army Form C. 2118.

| Place | Date | Hour | Summary of Events and Information | Remarks and references to Appendices |
|---|---|---|---|---|
| Westoutre. | | | have been evacuated to the Base Vety Hpl. A horse in A/Bty 252 Bde R.F.A. which had been evacuated sick to Base Vety Hpl reacted to the Mallein Test, all the horses in the Bty were tested with negative results. This horse was a remount issued to this Division last September, it was tested Jan 1916 with negative results. The forage has been good. In other respects the health & condition of the horses is good. | |
| | | | E. Franklin. Major AVC | |
| | | | ADVS 50th (North) Division | |

T2134. Wt. W708–776. 500000. 4/15. Sir J. C. & S.

50

Vol 13

Confidential

War Diary

A.D.V.S. 50th Division

From 1st July 1916

To 31st July 1916

Volume XI

Instructions regarding War Diaries and Intelligence Summaries are contained in F. S. Regs., Part II. and the Staff Manual respectively. Title Pages will be prepared in manuscript.

# WAR DIARY
*or*
# INTELLIGENCE SUMMARY
*(Erase heading not required.)*

Army Form C. 2118.

| Place | Date | Hour | Summary of Events and Information | Remarks and references to Appendices |
|---|---|---|---|---|
| Westoutre | 1/7/16 | | Visited the horses & lines 12th Labour Btt. Horses & lines in good & clean condition. Visited Signal Co. att.d 149 Inf Bde, to examine mare with a fractured leg, & ordered it to be destroyed. Visited & inspected Hd Qts 150th Inf Bde horses. Found a horse suffering from Strangles & ordered it to the Mob Vety Section. Saw several trusses of hay in this unit which were very bad, & in my opinion quite unfit for horses, reported this to the Staff Captain. Visited & inspected Transport horses & lines of the 4th Yorks, 5th Yorks, 4th E. Yorks, 5th D.L.I. found the horses & lines in these units good & clean. Visited 1st Entrenching Btt, horses & lines good & clean. I impressed on all units the necessity of keeping all picketing ropes, brushes, harness, & everything very clean. | J.T. |

2449 Wt. W14957/M90 750,000 1/16 J.B.C. & A. Forms/C.2118/12.

Army Form C. 2118.

Instructions regarding War Diaries and Intelligence Summaries are contained in F. S. Regs., Part II. and the Staff Manual respectively. Title Pages will be prepared in manuscript.

# WAR DIARY
*or*
# INTELLIGENCE SUMMARY
*(Erase heading not required.)*

| Place | Date | Hour | Summary of Events and Information | Remarks and references to Appendices |
|---|---|---|---|---|
| Westoutre | 1/7/16 | | ct. and that everything must be thoroughly washed in antiseptic solution. | [illegible] |
| | 2/7/16. | | Met the C.R.A. at C/Bty 253 horse lines & examined the horses with the V.O. This unit had just returned to the Division, and had marched 95 miles in six days. I found a large number of very thin animals. I advised a liberal diet of Linseed mashes, with as much green food as could be got. Visited & inspected the 150th Bge M. Gun Co good. | [illegible] |
| | 3/7/16. | | Visited & examined several horses to parade for the D.D.R. II Army with a view to their being cast. 150th Bge HdQrs. 2 Fd Co R.E. A Squad hills Jeo. ~~19th Cheshire Labour Btl~~ Visited & inspected horses in the 19th Cheshire Labour Btl. found nine suffering from Ringworm. as this Btl had only just arrived in this Area they brought this | [illegible] |

Instructions regarding War Diaries and Intelligence Summaries are contained in F. S. Regs., Part II. and the Staff Manual respectively. Title Pages will be prepared in manuscript.

# WAR DIARY
*or*
# INTELLIGENCE SUMMARY
*(Erase heading not required.)*

Army Form C. 2118.

| Place | Date | Hour | Summary of Events and Information | Remarks and references to Appendices |
|---|---|---|---|---|
| Westoutre | 3/7/16 | | disease with them. The O.C. was given instructions to deal with it. Visited & inspected 2/2nd (N) Fd Co R.E. horses & lines were in a good & clean condition. Visited & inspected transport horses & lines of the 6th D.L.I. & 8th D.L.I. both the horses & lines in these units were good. The 9th D.L.I. & 5th Borders were not either horses or lines in as good condition. Visited Mob. Vet Sec & examined 32 sick horses before evacuation to Base [illegible] Rd. | [illegible] |
| | 4/7/16 | | Visited & inspected B. Squad Hussars Yeo horses & lines, this unit has several horses suffering from mange gave instructions to the Fr Sgt about a better supervision being given to stamp it out. Visited C Squad Hants. Yeo. found them erecting a new [illegible] & floor | [illegible] |

Army Form C. 2118.

# WAR DIARY
*or*
# INTELLIGENCE SUMMARY
*(Erase heading not required.)*

Instructions regarding War Diaries and Intelligence Summaries are contained in F. S. Regs., Part II. and the Staff Manual respectively. Title Pages will be prepared in manuscript.

| Place | Date | Hour | Summary of Events and Information | Remarks and references to Appendices |
|---|---|---|---|---|
| [illegible] | 4/7/16. | | horses in good condition. Visited & inspected horses & lines of Div Sig Co. R.E. I examined a horse which had been injured & found it had fractured the off hind Tibia, ordered it to be destroyed, there is a great improvement in the horses of this unit, but the lines were not as clean as they ought to be, the O.C's attention was called to this. | |
| | 5/7/16. | | Visited & examined several more horses in various units for Casting. Visited the horse lines of the 149 Inf Bde M. Gun Co. Horses were in good condition & well looked after, but the lines were not too clean. The O.C's attention was drawn to this, likewise the necessity of moving the dung. Visited & inspected the 2/3rd Fd Amb, also the R.A.M.C. park, these units horses | JH |

2449 Wt. W14957/M90 750,000 1/16 J.B.C. & A. Forms/C.2118/12.

# WAR DIARY
*or*
# INTELLIGENCE SUMMARY
*(Erase heading not required.)*

Instructions regarding War Diaries and Intelligence Summaries are contained in F. S. Regs., Part II. and the Staff Manual respectively. Title Pages will be prepared in manuscript.

| Place | Date | Hour | Summary of Events and Information | Remarks and references to Appendices |
|---|---|---|---|---|
| Westoutre | 5/7/16. | | are very good in every way. Visited the Mob. Vet. Section. | R.T. |
| | 6/7/16. | | Met the D.D.V.S. II Army. He cast eleven as worn out and aged. | R.T. |
| | 7/7/16. | | Visited & inspected horses & lines H.Q. the 149 Inf Bde, & the following units 4th, 5th, 6th, & 7th (North) Fusiliers. The 4th 6th & 7th are very good. The 5th are not so. There is a want of better supervision in this unit. Conference with the V.O.s of the Division. | R.T. |
| | 8/7/16. | | Attended at Railway station to meet 77 Remounts. Of this number 37 mules were for the Div Am Col. Several of them showed symptoms of mange, [illegible] for them to be isolated. Otherwise they were a useful lot of animals. | R.T. |

Army Form C. 2118.

Instructions regarding War Diaries and Intelligence Summaries are contained in F. S. Regs., Part II. and the Staff Manual respectively. Title Pages will be prepared in manuscript.

# WAR DIARY
*or*
# INTELLIGENCE SUMMARY
*(Erase heading not required.)*

| Place | Date | Hour | Summary of Events and Information | Remarks and references to Appendices |
|---|---|---|---|---|
| Westoutre | 9/7/16. | | Attended at Hd Qts II Army to interview the D.D.V.S. on evacuation of sick horses by road by a new route & a new method of leading horses. | [illegible] |
| | 10/7/16 | | Visited & inspected C/250 Bty R.F.A. B/250 Bty R.F.A. – These 2 units having a number of poor old horses do not improve in condition, [illegible] Visited the A/253 Bty R.F.A. this unit lines are not well situated, Visited D/251 Bty R.F.A. & C/200 Bty R.F.A. These two units are too close together. Visited & examined 62 horses before being evacuated to Base Vety Hosp by road. | [illegible] |
| | 11/7/16. | | Visited the A/250 Bty R.F.A. Dirty lines wasting forage and altogether a better supervision is required in this unit. Found 2 cases of Ringworm. | [illegible] |

2449 Wt. W14957/M90 750,000 1/16 J.B.C. & A. Forms/C.2118/12.

Army Form C. 2118.

Instructions regarding War Diaries and Intelligence Summaries are contained in F. S. Regs., Part II. and the Staff Manual respectively. Title Pages will be prepared in manuscript.

# WAR DIARY
*or*
# INTELLIGENCE SUMMARY
*(Erase heading not required.)*

| Place | Date | Hour | Summary of Events and Information | Remarks and references to Appendices |
|---|---|---|---|---|
| Westoutre | 11/7 | 12 noon | Visited C/257 Bty R.F.A. good all round, clean horses & harness. The last 2 or 3 days I have seen several cases of Ophthalmia, in my opinion it is not the Contagious form. | [initials] |
| | 12/7/16. | | Visited D.D.V.S. II Army reported to him peculiar symptoms which one of the V.Os. in this Division had had in some mules, the latter had sent me some peculiar seeds which he had obtained from the oats ration the day before, no fatal results from eating the corn, but the animals had symptoms of having eaten something which did not agree with them. | [initials] |
| | 13/7/16. | | Attended in company with D.D.V.S. II Army and examined some mules which had arrived from Remounts, several of these were suffering from mange. He ordered them into Mob Vet Section for evacuation. Visited Mob Vet Sec & examined 8 horses for evacuation to the Base Vet Hpl. | [initials] |

2449 Wt. W14957/M90 750,000 1/16 J.B.C. & A. Forms/C.2118/12.

Army Form C. 2118.

# WAR DIARY
*or*
# INTELLIGENCE SUMMARY
*(Erase heading not required.)*

Instructions regarding War Diaries and Intelligence Summaries are contained in F. S. Regs., Part II. and the Staff Manual respectively. Title Pages will be prepared in manuscript.

| Place | Date | Hour | Summary of Events and Information | Remarks and references to Appendices |
|---|---|---|---|---|
| Westoutre | 13/7/16 | | Visited & inspected in company with the V.O. of the Section a new siding for the entrainment of sick horses. With slight alterations & accommodation it will be alright. | BT |
| | 14/7/16 | | Visited & inspected 3rd Sec Div Am Col & inspected horses & lines. The horses are improving in condition, the lines were clean, but there is far too much forage scattered about. Visited & inspected No 1 Sec Div Am Col, the horses in this unit are improving. Visited & inspected B/Bty 252 R.F.A. on the whole good but there are several thin horses. C/Bty 252 Bde R.F.A. not so good, better line supervision & method is required in this unit. D/Bty 252 Bde on the whole satisfactory. A/Bty 252 Bde R.F.A. very good. Examined A.P.M.'s charger. | BT |
| | 15/7/16 | | Visited & inspected Hd Qts horses & lines Div Train A.S.C. very good. Visited & inspected Hd Qts No 1 Co A.S.C. Too many thin horses in this Co. The O.C. | BT |

Army Form C. 2118.

# WAR DIARY
*or*
# INTELLIGENCE SUMMARY
*(Erase heading not required.)*

Instructions regarding War Diaries and Intelligence Summaries are contained in F. S. Regs., Part II. and the Staff Manual respectively. Title Pages will be prepared in manuscript.

| Place | Date | Hour | Summary of Events and Information | Remarks and references to Appendices |
|---|---|---|---|---|
| [illegible] | 15/7 | [illegible] | attention was drawn to their condition. No 2. 3. & 4 Co. All were in a better condition but there is room for improvement in these Cos. Visited Hd Qrs 253 Bge R.F.A. Several old & thin horses. Visited No 4 Sec D.A.C. too many Girth galls in this unit as well as shoulder galls. The mules in this unit are working very hard. Visited & inspected C/Bty 253 Bge R.F.A. these horses have improved considerably. The standings are in a very dilapidated condition & want repairing, but unfortunately there are no bricks to be got. | [illegible] |
| | 16/7/16 | | Visited & inspected 7th D.L.I. Since this unit has had a new Transport Officer they have considerably improved. Visited A/Bty 252 Bge R.F.A. to examine a mare which had been injured, ordered its destruction. Visited B/Bty 251 Bge R.F.A. This unit are generally very good, but on this inspection I had to complain of the waste of forage. | [illegible] |

2449 Wt W14957/M90 750,000 1/16 J.B.C. & A. Forms/C.2118/12.

Army Form C. 2118.

# WAR DIARY
*or*
# INTELLIGENCE SUMMARY

*(Erase heading not required.)*

Instructions regarding War Diaries and Intelligence Summaries are contained in F. S. Regs., Part II. and the Staff Manual respectively. Title Pages will be prepared in manuscript.

| Place | Date | Hour | Summary of Events and Information | Remarks and references to Appendices |
| --- | --- | --- | --- | --- |
| Westoutre | 16/7/16 | | Visited A/Bty 257 Bde R.F.A. Bad, lack of method & stricter supervision is what is required in this unit. Visited 2nd Sec Div Am Col, although there are a number of thin horses in this unit, they are fit, the muscle they have on them is firm & in good condition, in my opinion they are fit to do any amount of work. Visited D/Bty 253 Bde R.F.A very good. one skin disease. The D.V.S. visited the Divisional Mobile Vety Section | J.T. |
| | 17/7/16. | | Visited & inspected 43 sick horses before marching to receiving Vety Hpl, St Omer. Visited & inspected 150th Inf Bde. 4th Yorks 4th E. Yorks. 5th D.L.I. & 5th Yorks. all good. Visited 50th Div Sig Co horses are in good & clean condition but the lines are bad, want repairing. | G.T. |

Army Form C. 2118.

# WAR DIARY
*or*
# INTELLIGENCE SUMMARY
*(Erase heading not required.)*

Instructions regarding War Diaries and Intelligence Summaries are contained in F. S. Regs., Part II. and the Staff Manual respectively. Title Pages will be prepared in manuscript.

| Place | Date | Hour | Summary of Events and Information | Remarks and references to Appendices |
|---|---|---|---|---|
| Westoutre | 18/7/16. | | Visited & inspected 2/2nd Fd Amb, & 1/3 Fd Amb, & R.A.M.C. horse park, found them all in a clean & good condition. Visited & inspected 151 Machine Gun Co. horses & mules looking well. | S.B. |
| | 19/7/16. | | Visited & inspected 1st Fd Co R.E. Horses clean & in good condition, no sick. Visited 1st Entrenching Battn. horses clean & in good condition. 2nd Fd Co R.E. on the whole good two sick cases. Visited 84th Fd Co R.E. good. Visited 149th Inf Bde Hd Qrs, horses alright but standings very bad, & smelly, the floor is laid with wooden sleepers, in my opinion these are a failure, because dung & urine gets between the joints & this decomposes & smells very bad. Visited the 4th N.F. very good. 5th N.F. not good, wants better line & horse supervision. 6th N.F. good. 7th N.F. moderate, room for improvement. | S.B. |

2449 Wt. W14957/M90 750,000 1/16 J.B.C. & A. Forms/C.2118/12.

Instructions regarding War Diaries and Intelligence Summaries are contained in F. S. Regs., Part II. and the Staff Manual respectively. Title Pages will be prepared in manuscript.

# WAR DIARY
*or*
# INTELLIGENCE SUMMARY
*(Erase heading not required.)*

Army Form C. 2118.

| Place | Date | Hour | Summary of Events and Information | Remarks and references to Appendices |
|---|---|---|---|---|
| Westoutre | 19/7/16. | | Visited 7th Fd Co R.E. good. Examined a mule for exchange, as it was too small. Visited 11th Lancashire Batt, good. | S.F. |
| | 20/7/16. | | attended on the D.D.V.S. II Army who came to inspect horses for casting, 7 were put on the role. Visited Mobile Vet Section. | S.F. |
| | 21/7/16. | | Visited D.D.V.S. II Army, & obtained Calcium Sulphide. Met 56 Remounts at L17 d 4.6. one arrived showing symptoms of mange, one ditto Strangles. | S.F. |
| | 22/7/16. | | Visited & inspected 7th D.L.I. horses & lines. Improving. Visited 5th Bord. Regt. The dung in these lines is too near, asked Transport Officer to move it, although he has two incinerators going it cannot be got rid of fast enough. | S.F. |
| | 23/7/16. | | In company with V.O. i/c Div Am Col I visited the | |

2449 Wt. W14957/M90 750,000 1/16 J.B.C. & A. Forms/C.2118/12.

Instructions regarding War Diaries and Intelligence Summaries are contained in F. S. Regs., Part II. and the Staff Manual respectively. Title Pages will be prepared in manuscript.

# WAR DIARY
*or*
# INTELLIGENCE SUMMARY
*(Erase heading not required.)*

Army Form C. 2118.

| Place | Date | Hour | Summary of Events and Information | Remarks and references to Appendices |
|---|---|---|---|---|
| Westoutre | 23/7 | Contd. | Sec of the Column which had had the 53 Remounts distributed amongst them on their arrival on the 21st inst. In my opinion there are several more showing symptoms of mange. 1 with Poll Evil. I think this lot of remounts were sent away from the Vety Hpl too soon, otherwise they are a very useful lot. Visited & inspected 35 horses at Mob Vet Section before going down to Receiving Vety Hpl. | [illegible] |
| | 24/7/16 | | Visited & inspected Hd Qrs 151 Inf Brigade horses. Visited & inspected Transport lines & horses 6th D.L.I. good, one lame horse. Visited & inspected 8th D.L.I. good. Visited & inspected 9th D.L.I. not so good, found one with suspicious mange. Visited & inspected Transport lines & horses 7th Fd Co. R.E. found them alright, no sick. | [illegible] [illegible] |

2449 Wt. W14957/M90 750,000 1/16 J.B.C. & A. Forms/C.2118/12.

Army Form C. 2118.

# WAR DIARY
*or*
# INTELLIGENCE SUMMARY
*(Erase heading not required.)*

Instructions regarding War Diaries and Intelligence Summaries are contained in F. S. Regs., Part II. and the Staff Manual respectively. Title Pages will be prepared in manuscript.

| Place | Date | Hour | Summary of Events and Information | Remarks and references to Appendices |
|---|---|---|---|---|
| Westoutre | 25/7/16 | | Visited & inspected horses B/Bg 250 Bge R.F.A. good, one sick. Visited & inspected horses A Bg 253 Bge R.F.A. Bad lines want repairing, pleased this unit had found a new water supply. Visited & examined C/Bg 250 Bge R.F.A. Found 3 suspicious skin diseases which the V.O. informed had been contracted whilst up at the gun position. Reported to O.C. Bge that this unit wastes too much forage, consequently they have a number of thin horses. Visited D/Bg 250 Bge R.F.A. Bad lines but unfortunately cannot be moved, horses looking fit. Visited D/Bg 251 Bge R.F.A. Several animals were looking very tired & poor, working hard. Visited Hd Qts 250 Bge R.F.A. alright | SA<br>SA. |

2449 Wt. W14957/M90 750,000 1/16 J.B.C. & A. Forms/C.2118/12.

Army Form C. 2118.

Instructions regarding War Diaries and Intelligence Summaries are contained in F. S. Regs., Part II. and the Staff Manual respectively. Title Pages will be prepared in manuscript.

# WAR DIARY
*or*
# INTELLIGENCE SUMMARY
*(Erase heading not required.)*

| Place | Date | Hour | Summary of Events and Information | Remarks and references to Appendices |
|---|---|---|---|---|
| Westoutre | 26/7/16. | | Visited & inspected 4th Sect D.A.C. although these mules are on the Rd from 10 to 12 hours every day they are in my opinion in good condition, but they appear to be getting foot sore. Visited & inspected B/Bde 253 Bde R.F.A. found this unit alright. Conference in the afternoon with A.V.C. Sgts attached to units. Spoke to them on the importance of dealing with the principal sources of mange. | J.F. |
| | 27/7/16. | | Met & distributed 79 Remounts, poor condition, & very dirty. Attended in the afternoon at 4th Sec D.A.C. lines & met the D.D.R. II Army who came to reclassify H.D. Inspected & examined 23 H.D. at Div Train A.S.C. 18 of these were sent to Fd Rem Section. | J.F. |

2449 Wt. W14957/M90 750,000 1/16 J.B.C. & A. Forms/C.2118/12.

Instructions regarding War Diaries and Intelligence Summaries are contained in F. S. Regs., Part II. and the Staff Manual respectively. Title Pages will be prepared in manuscript.

# WAR DIARY
*or*
# INTELLIGENCE SUMMARY
*(Erase heading not required.)*

Army Form C. 2118.

| Place | Date | Hour | Summary of Events and Information | Remarks and references to Appendices |
|---|---|---|---|---|
| Westoutre | 28/7/16. | | Met the D.A. & Q.M.G. 50th Div. at Canada Corner to inspect surplus horses from the Div Arty. He issued a certain number to units in the Division, 4 sick ones to M.V.S. & 12 to Fd Remount Section, one of this last number went lame & only 11 were sent. Visited & inspected 252 Bge R.F.A. A/Bty very good. B/Bty fair, C/Bty moderate lot of room for improvement D/Bty. very good. | J.A. |
| | 29/7/16. | | Visited & inspected A/Bty 250 Bge R.F.A. Supervision improved, but the lines are very bad, & unfortunately owing to the small space there is not room to move them. Visited & inspected C/Bty 250 Bge R.F.A. gone off slightly, not as good as on my last inspection, too many Kicks. Met the D.D.V.S. II Army, he inspected | J.A. |

Army Form C. 2118.

# WAR DIARY
*or*
# INTELLIGENCE SUMMARY
*(Erase heading not required.)*

Instructions regarding War Diaries and Intelligence Summaries are contained in F. S. Regs., Part II. and the Staff Manual respectively. Title Pages will be prepared in manuscript.

| Place | Date | Hour | Summary of Events and Information | Remarks and references to Appendices |
|---|---|---|---|---|
| Westoutre | 29/7/16 | ct. | several remounts which arrived on the 21/7/16. These horses had been diagnosed as suffering from mange. He confirmed it, & ordered them to be dressed on the lines. Visited the Mob. Vet Sect in the evening & examined scrapings from the above with negative results. | J.T. |
| | 30/7/16. | | Visited No 6 Sick Horse Halt to collect lime & sulphur to make the Liq Calcis Sulph, so that it can be applied in the fresh state, with all due deference to everyone's opinion, I submit it is not any use for Sarcoptic mange, the mites thrive on it. Visited & inspected A/BG. 257 Bde R.F.A. one case of suspicious mange this horse has been dressed 3 times in 15 days with Liq Calcis, & still not cured. | J.T. |

Instructions regarding War Diaries and Intelligence Summaries are contained in F. S. Regs., Part II. and the Staff Manual respectively. Title Pages will be prepared in manuscript.

Army Form C. 2118.

# WAR DIARY
*or*
# INTELLIGENCE SUMMARY

*(Erase heading not required.)*

| Place | Date | Hour | Summary of Events and Information | Remarks and references to Appendices |
|---|---|---|---|---|
| Westoutre | 30/7/16 | Ct. | Visited & inspected A/Bty 251 Bde R.F.A. this units horses doing well. | JH |
| | 31/7/16. | | Visited 2nd Sect D.A.C. Visited A/Bty 251 Bde & called on Capt Atkinson & gave him & the Sgts All instruction how to prepare Lig Calcis Sulph as laid down in Cir Memo No 77 d 5/7/16. Visited Mobile Vety Section & examined 41 cases prior to their evacuation by road to 23, R.V.H. Inspected Hd Qts C.R.A. horses & M.M.P. Found them alright. | JH |
| | | | Summary. I regret to say that during the past month the number of mange cases in the 50th Division has slightly increased, this in my opinion is owing to a number of | JH |

2449 Wt. W14957/M90 750,000 1/16 J.B.C. & A. Forms/C.2118/12.

Instructions regarding War Diaries and Intelligence Summaries are contained in F. S. Regs., Part II. and the Staff Manual respectively. Title Pages will be prepared in manuscript.

# WAR DIARY
*or*
# INTELLIGENCE SUMMARY
*(Erase heading not required.)*

Army Form C. 2118.

| Place | Date | Hour | Summary of Events and Information | Remarks and references to Appendices |
|---|---|---|---|---|
| | | | Remounts being sent to the Division affected with symptoms of mange, the worst case has been evacuated to the Base, the others have been isolated, dressed, & are being worked. Every other precaution has been taken to prevent the spread of the infection. The forage during the past month has not been up to the usual standard. The system of evacuating sick horses which are able to march by road to the Receiving Hospital at St Omer, has up to the present work satisfactorily. | |
| | | | E. Franklin. Major A.V.C. A.D.V.S. 50th (Nbn) Division | |

2449 Wt. W14957/M90 750,000 1/16 J.B.C. & A. Forms/C.2118/12.

Vol 14

WAR DIARY

- of -

A. D. V. S. 50th DIVISION .

AUGUST 1916.

Vol. XI.

Army Form C. 2118.

# WAR DIARY
*or*
# INTELLIGENCE SUMMARY
*(Erase heading not required.)*

Instructions regarding War Diaries and Intelligence Summaries are contained in F. S. Regs., Part II. and the Staff Manual respectively. Title Pages will be prepared in manuscript.

| Place | Date | Hour | Summary of Events and Information | Remarks and references to Appendices |
| --- | --- | --- | --- | --- |
| Lestouke | 1/8/16. | | Visited & inspected mallened horses of 28th Army Troops. R.E. at the 24th hour, no reactions. Visited & inspected 7th D.L.I. horses & lines. Visited & inspected horses & lines of 5th Border Regt. Visited & inspected 7th Fd Co R.E., & 2nd Fd Co R.E. no sick horses to report in either of these units. Visited & inspected 1/1st Nbn Fd Amb, 11th Labour Btl & 12th Labour (Devon) Btl. All these units were good. | J.F. |
| | 2/8/16. | | Visited & inspected R.A.M.C. (horse park) all the horses right, not anything to report. Visited the 1/3rd Fd Amb, one poor H.D. horse sent to Mob Vet Sect. Visited & inspected Mob. Vet Section. Conference with A.V.C. Sgts. attached to units, & explained the procedure when leaving sick horses with inhabitants | J.F. |
| | 3/8/16. | | Visited & inspected No 32 Co. A.S.C. (Reserve Park), as this unit had just become attached to the 50th Div. I found several | J.F. |

Army Form C. 2118.

# WAR DIARY
*or*
# INTELLIGENCE SUMMARY
*(Erase heading not required.)*

Instructions regarding War Diaries and Intelligence Summaries are contained in F. S. Regs., Part II. and the Staff Manual respectively. Title Pages will be prepared in manuscript.

| Place | Date | Hour | Summary of Events and Information | Remarks and references to Appendices |
|---|---|---|---|---|
| Westoutre | 3/8/16 | | 4 poor horses in the unit, these ~~one~~ were from 5th Corps Cavalry & attached for supplies. Four horses in this unit are affected with mange, - ordered one to the Section. Visited & inspected No 2 Co. A.S.C. several poor horses in this Co. No 3 Co A.S.C. found a horse in this Co. suffering from acute Dermatitis. No 4 Co. A.S.C. very good. No 1 Co. A.S.C. not so good several poor horses, altogether the A.S.C. of this the 50th Division are not bad. | J.T. |
| | 4/8/16. | | Visited & inspected No. 3 Sec. Div Am. Col. slight improvement on my last visit. No. 1 Sec. Div. Amn Col. have six cases of mange. No 2 Sec. Div. Amn Col found 2 or 3 horses getting gradually poorer, ordered V.O. to have their teeth well examined. Visited Mob. Vet Section. | J.T. |
| | 5/8/16. | | Visited & inspected the 149 Inf Bde Machine Gun Co. | J.T. |

2449 Wt. W14957/M90 750,000 1/16 J.B.C. & A. Forms/C.2118/12.

Instructions regarding War Diaries and Intelligence Summaries are contained in F. S. Regs., Part II. and the Staff Manual respectively. Title Pages will be prepared in manuscript.

# WAR DIARY
*or*
# INTELLIGENCE SUMMARY
*(Erase heading not required.)*

Army Form C. 2118.

| Place | Date | Hour | Summary of Events and Information | Remarks and references to Appendices |
|---|---|---|---|---|
| Westoutre | 5/8/16. | | I am pleased to report favourably on this Brigade. Visited & inspected 150 Inf Bge, Machine Gun Co everything alright except that the lines were dirty - reported this to O.C. Visited & inspected Hd Qrs, Div Am Col, very good. | |
| | 6/8/16. | | Visited Mob. Vet. Section & inspected 44 horses before evacuation to Base Vety Hpl, good. A stray horse was sent into section suffering from mange this horse had strayed into 5th Border Transport lines in the night. | J.H. |
| | 7/8/16. | | Visited & inspected a civilian's horse suffering from mange in Westoutre, still suffering in my opinion, ordered it to be redressed. Visited & inspected 4th Sec. Div Am Col. good. Visited & inspected 4th Yorks & 5th D.L.I. horses & lines, good. Visited Mob Vet Section to examine horse with wound in the chest. | J.H. |

2449 Wt. W14957/M90 750,000 1/16 J.B.C. & A. Forms/C.2118/12.

Instructions regarding War Diaries and Intelligence Summaries are contained in F. S. Regs., Part II. and the Staff Manual respectively. Title Pages will be prepared in manuscript.

# WAR DIARY
*or*
# INTELLIGENCE SUMMARY
*(Erase heading not required.)*

Army Form C. 2118.

| Place | Date | Hour | Summary of Events and Information | Remarks and references to Appendices |
|---|---|---|---|---|
| Westoutre | 8/8/16. | | 50th (Nly) Div moved to Flêtre, I handed over maps & contents of Office to A.D.V.S. 19th Division. The Section fittings were also handed over by O/C. Visited Mob. Vet. Section & inspected 3 Riders & 1 pack horse collected from Fd Rem Section. | J.H. |
| Flêtre | 9/8/16 | | Met & distributed 38 Remounts at Caestre. Delivered 30 head Collars & ropes to Fd Rem Section. Visited & examined two H.D. at 5th Nlu Fs by 4th Nlu Fs found them in my opinion fit for work. Visited Mob Vet Section. | J.H. |
| | 10/8/16. | | Visited & inspected Div Sig Co R.E. & examined a horse which had been kicked during the night. It was fit to move with the Co to their new area. | J.H. |
| | 11/8/16. | | 50th Div moved into 9th Corps, 3rd Army area | J.H. |

Army Form C. 2118.

# WAR DIARY
*or*
# INTELLIGENCE SUMMARY
*(Erase heading not required.)*

Instructions regarding War Diaries and Intelligence Summaries are contained in F. S. Regs., Part II. and the Staff Manual respectively. Title Pages will be prepared in manuscript.

| Place | Date | Hour | Summary of Events and Information | Remarks and references to Appendices |
|---|---|---|---|---|
| Bernaville | 11/8/16 | | Met the Mob Vet Section on the march, alright, gave O.C. instructions where to go. | J.T. |
| | 12/8/16 | | Visited & inspected 1/1 Nrn Fd Co R.E. This Co had 3 miles to go to water. Visited 5th Nrn Fs. 5th Yorks & 4th Yorks, these units were alright. Visited & examined the C.R.E. charger, found it suffering from Ophthalmia, ordered it to the section. | J.T. |
| | 13/8/16 | | Visited Mob Vet Section, & routine work. | J.T. |
| | 14/8/16 | | Visited Mob Vet Section & gave instructions to OC about moving from Bernaville. He must get away before 3-30 am the following morning. | J.T. |
| | 15/8/16 | | Mob Vet Section left at 3-20 am. to march to Vignacourt, arrived latter place 8-15 am. - picketed horses in stubble field men bivouacked. arrived safely. I marched with them. | J.T. |

2449 Wt. W14957/M90 750,000 1/16 J.B.C. & A. Forms/C.2118/12.

Army Form C. 2118.

# WAR DIARY
*or*
# INTELLIGENCE SUMMARY
*(Erase heading not required.)*

Instructions regarding War Diaries and Intelligence Summaries are contained in F. S. Regs., Part II. and the Staff Manual respectively. Title Pages will be prepared in manuscript.

| Place | Date | Hour | Summary of Events and Information | Remarks and references to Appendices |
|---|---|---|---|---|
| Vignacourt | 16/8/16 | | Mob Vet Sect left at 6 am en route for Montigny arrived about 12 noon, found a good place for men & horses. came through very well. | S.H. |
| Montigny | 17/8/16 | | Mob-Vet Sect left Montigny at 9-30 for Baizeux. arrived at noon. Men were billeted in barns. & horses picketed in orchard. not at all a suitable place. Visited A & C/Btys 253 Bge R.F.A. marched through without any serious casualty. Visited C & D/Btys 251 Bge R.F.A. allright came through without any casualty. A very trying day both for horses & men. very hot. | S.H. |
| " | 18/8/16. | | Visited Div. Amn. Col, Hd Qts to ascertain what number of sick horses had been left behind during the march. Visited 250 Bge R.F.A. this Bge excepting a few galls had no casualties. | S.H. |

2449 Wt. W14957/M90 750,000 1/16 J.B.C. & A. Forms/C.2118/12.

Army Form C. 2118.

Instructions regarding War Diaries and Intelligence Summaries are contained in F. S. Regs., Part II. and the Staff Manual respectively. Title Pages will be prepared in manuscript.

# WAR DIARY
*or*
# INTELLIGENCE SUMMARY
*(Erase heading not required.)*

| Place | Date | Hour | Summary of Events and Information | Remarks and references to Appendices |
|---|---|---|---|---|
| Mortigny | 19/8/16 | | Visited & inspected Div. Hd. Qts horses, M. M. P. horses & Div Sig Co. R.E. excepting the latter unit the others had not anything to report. Visited D.D.V.S. IV Army | J.T. |
| | 20/8/16. | | Attended at Railhead 6 a.m. to meet Remounts. Did not arrive until 3 p.m., a long weary wait. A very useful lot of Remounts. | |
| | 21/8/16. | | Visited Div. Am. Col. & distributed remounts. Visited Mob. Vet. Section. 7th R.P.L.I. & 149 Inf Bge. all good. | J.T. |
| | 22/8/16. | | Visited Mob Vet Section & examined 16 horses before evacuation to Base Vety Hpl. | J.T. |
| | 23/8/16. | | Visited & inspected 1/1st Fd Co. R.E. Visited & inspected 150 Inf Bge, all horses in my opinion are in good hard working condition. Called at Mob Vet Section | J.T. |

Instructions regarding War Diaries and Intelligence Summaries are contained in F. S. Regs., Part II. and the Staff Manual respectively. Title Pages will be prepared in manuscript.

# WAR DIARY
*or*
# INTELLIGENCE SUMMARY
*(Erase heading not required.)*

Army Form C. 2118.

| Place | Date | Hour | Summary of Events and Information | Remarks and references to Appendices |
|---|---|---|---|---|
| Montigny | 24/8/16. | | Visited & inspected 3 Btys 253 Bde R.F.A. in company with V.O. gave instructions about keeping horse lines very clean according to III Corps orders. Visited & inspected 7th Fd Co R.E. very smelly & dirty lines, & a better line supervision must be exercised. The O/C's attention was drawn to this. Visited & inspected 2/2nd Fd Co R.E. & 1/1st Fd Amb. found these units alright. | J.T. J.T. |
| | 25/8/16. | | Visited & inspected Hd Qts, A.S.C. Hd Qts Co, No 1-2-&3 Co A.S.C. of this Division. Excepting that several were in poor condition, the others were in good health. no sick. | J.T. |
| | 26/8/16 | | Visited & inspected C/Bty 253 Bde, R.F.A. horses which were reported as in poor condition. In my | J.T. |

Army Form C. 2118.

Instructions regarding War Diaries and Intelligence Summaries are contained in F. S. Regs., Part II. and the Staff Manual respectively. Title Pages will be prepared in manuscript.

# WAR DIARY
*or*
# INTELLIGENCE SUMMARY
*(Erase heading not required.)*

| Place | Date | Hour | Summary of Events and Information | Remarks and references to Appendices |
|---|---|---|---|---|
| Montigny | 20/8/16 | | A. opinion These horses are improving in condition. The O.C. Bge wanted an extra ration of forage for about 30. Divisional Hd. Qrs. could not sanction it. Visited 1/3 Fd Amb alright. Visited & inspected A/252, B/252. C/252. In good health & condition excepting three in the C/115 which were thin, D/252 were in good health. Visited Hd Qrs 251 Bge R.F.A. not anything to report. | J.F. |
| | 27/8/16. | | Visited & inspected 151 Inf Bge, & Machine Gun Co. found the horses & mules with about 3 exceptions clean & in good condition & health. Visited the Mob Vet Section. | J.F. |
| | 28/8/16. | | Visited & attended C.R.E. charger which was affected with Colic (twice) Visited the Mob Vet Section. | J.F. |

Army Form C. 2118.

# WAR DIARY
*or*
# INTELLIGENCE SUMMARY
*(Erase heading not required.)*

Instructions regarding War Diaries and Intelligence Summaries are contained in F. S. Regs., Part II. and the Staff Manual respectively. Title Pages will be prepared in manuscript.

| Place | Date | Hour | Summary of Events and Information | Remarks and references to Appendices |
|---|---|---|---|---|
| Montigny | 29/8/16. | | Visited & examined C/B[y] 253 Bde R.F.A. in company with the D.A. & Q.M.G. There are about fifteen really in poor condition, but with care, attention & proper supervision several of these ought to improve. They belong to the number of horses in this B[y] which were affected with Sand Colic whilst training at [illegible] & although they have improved very much since they returned to the Division they do not improve so quickly as the O.C. the Bde would like. Representations have been made to the Division for extra rations but it has not been granted. Visited & examined C.R.E. horse twice — improving, but not fit to take away from Sick Lines. | JJ [?] |
| | 30/8/16 | | Visited Div HdQrs & examined G.S.O. II horses which he reported as coughing. Also the C.R.E. Horse, improvement maintained. Visited 252 Bde R.F.A. Visited No 3 Sec. D.A.C. ordered a lame & debilitated horse into Sec. | JJ [?] |

2449 Wt. W14957/M90 750,000 1/16 J.B.C. & A. Forms/C.2118/12.

Instructions regarding War Diaries and Intelligence Summaries are contained in F. S. Regs., Part II. and the Staff Manual respectively. Title Pages will be prepared in manuscript.

# WAR DIARY
*or*
# INTELLIGENCE SUMMARY
*(Erase heading not required.)*

Army Form C. 2118.

| Place | Date | Hour | Summary of Events and Information | Remarks and references to Appendices |
|---|---|---|---|---|
| Montigny | 30/8/16. | | Visited No 2 Sec D.A.C. horses were alright considering the bad weather which they had to undergo, in fact the lines had to be moved the previous night on a/c of the sudden downpour of rain. | JT |
| | 31/8/16. | | Visited Mob Vet Section in company with the O.C. & visited the 15th Div Mob Vet Section, and called on the A.D.V.S. 15th Division. | JT |
| | | | <u>Summary</u>. Considering the 50th Division has been on the move during <u>the month</u> there have been very few sick horses. Unfortunately a number have been killed by Shell Fire since we arrived in this area. I am pleased to say there has not been any outbreak amongst the horses in the Division of any Infectious or Contagious | JT |

Instructions regarding War Diaries and Intelligence Summaries are contained in F. S. Regs., Part II. and the Staff Manual respectively. Title Pages will be prepared in manuscript.

# WAR DIARY
*or*
# INTELLIGENCE SUMMARY
*(Erase heading not required.)*

Army Form C. 2118.

| Place | Date | Hour | Summary of Events and Information | Remarks and references to Appendices |
|---|---|---|---|---|
| Montigny | | " | nature. The health & condition of the horses on the whole is satisfactory. | G.J. |
| | | | G. [illegible], Major A.V.C. A.D.V.S. 50th (Nbn) Division | |

2449 Wt. W14957/M90 750,000 1/16 J.B.C. & A. Forms/C.2118/12.

Instructions regarding War Diaries and Intelligence Summaries are contained in F. S. Regs., Part II. and the Staff Manual respectively. Title Pages will be prepared in manuscript.

# WAR DIARY
*or*
# INTELLIGENCE SUMMARY
*(Erase heading not required.)*

Army Form C. 2118.

ADVS 50 D
Vol 15

| Place | Date | Hour | Summary of Events and Information | Remarks and references to Appendices |
|---|---|---|---|---|
| Montigny | 1/9/16. | | Visited & inspected No. 4 Sec. D.A.C. 1/2 Sec. No 2. & 1/2 Sec. No 3 (the two latter had moved back). Not anything to report. Visited & examined at Mob Vet Sec. 8 horses before evacuation to Base Vety Hpl. | J.F. |
| | 2/9/16. | | Met the D.D.R. IV Army who came to inspect horses for Casting for other than Veterinary Reasons, several were redistributed to other units in the Division on his authority. | J.F. |
| | 3/9/16. | | Visited & examined at Mob. Vet. Sect. 16 horses before evacuation to Base Vety Hpl. Visited the Railhead to see these horses entrained. | J.F. |
| | 4/9/16. | | In company with the O.C. Divisional Train I visited the advanced Field Remount Section & examined H.D.s. Visited & inspected Div Hd. Qrs. & Div Sig Co. horses not anything to report. | J.F. |
| | 5/9/16. | | Visited & examined 16 horses at Mob. Vet. | J.F. |

2449 Wt. W14957/M90 750,000 1/16 J.B.C. & A. Forms/C.2118/12.

Army Form C. 2118.

Instructions regarding War Diaries and Intelligence Summaries are contained in F. S. Regs., Part II. and the Staff Manual respectively. Title Pages will be prepared in manuscript.

# WAR DIARY
*or*
# INTELLIGENCE SUMMARY
*(Erase heading not required.)*

| Place | Date | Hour | Summary of Events and Information | Remarks and references to Appendices |
|---|---|---|---|---|
| Montigny | 5/9/16. | | Ct. Section before evacuation to Base Vety. Hpl. With the O/C Mob. Vet. Section I visited several places in the Divl. Area to choose a fresh position for the Section. | SA |
| | 6/9/16. | | Visited & inspected 150th Inf Bge. & M. Gun Co. Found them alright. I was shown a horse from Amx. Horse Tram Co. attached for water duty to this Bge. This animal should never have been sent as it was lame, very poor in condition. Met & distributed 69 Remounts at Railhead. Excepting one a good lot. | SA |
| | 7/9/16. | | Visited Mob. Vet. Sect. to make enquiries about return of Head Collars & Ropes. Called at 253 Bge. R.F.A. Hd. Qts. about 9 Remounts which they had received in Error. Visited & inspected 9th D.L.I. several affected with Ringworm. Visited 5th Bordr. lines for a similar reason. Visited | SA |

Instructions regarding War Diaries and Intelligence Summaries are contained in F. S. Regs., Part II. and the Staff Manual respectively. Title pages will be prepared in manuscript.

# WAR DIARY
*or*
# INTELLIGENCE SUMMARY.
*(Erase heading not required.)*

Army Form C. 2118.

| Place | Date | Hour | Summary of Events and Information | Remarks and references to Appendices |
|---|---|---|---|---|
| Montigny | 7/9/16 | | Ct & Inspected the 149th Inf. Bde. Mach. Gun Co. Nothing to report only that they had received a poor, thin Remount. I examined this horse, & although it was poor, it was quite fit to work. Picked up on the line of march two | J.H. |
| | ~~4/..~~ | | lame horses 167th Bde R.F.A. 33 Div. too lame to travel, & had them evacuated through Mob. Vet. Section next day | |
| | 8/9/16 | | Visited B. Echelon to enquire if they had received the 9 Remounts from Hd Qts 253 Bde R.F.A. Visited Hd Qts. 251 Bde R.F.A. Found a horse suffering very badly from Lymphangitis & Debility. Ordered it to be destroyed. Visited Mob. Vet. Section & examined 8 horses before evacuation to Base Vet. Hpl. | J.G. |
| | 9/9/16 | | Div. Hd. Qts. & Mob. Vet. Sect. moved into new area. Examined G.O.C. horse, had a nasty cut on its Poll. dressed & made it as comfortable as possible. Visited 9th D.L.I. & 5th Bdr. animals suffering from Ringworm | J.H. |

Instructions regarding War Diaries and Intelligence Summaries are contained in F. S. Regs., Part II. and the Staff Manual respectively. Title Pages will be prepared in manuscript.

# WAR DIARY
*or*
# INTELLIGENCE SUMMARY
*(Erase heading not required.)*

Army Form C. 2118.

| Place | Date | Hour | Summary of Events and Information | Remarks and references to Appendices |
|---|---|---|---|---|
| Millencourt | 9/9/16 contd. | | Found an improvement in them. | S.A. |
| | 10/9/16. | | Visited, examined, & dressed G.O.C. horses head twice, no worse. Visited Mob. Vet. Section. Visited & examined a mule at R.E. Hd Qts. | |
| | 11/9/16. | | Visited Div. Train. Hd. Qts. to obtain position of their refilling points, & make some arrangements to try & reduce the number of cases of P.U.K. Visited Mob. Vet. Sect. & found 14 mules fit for walking work. | S.A. |
| | 12/9/16. | | Visited & inspected 1/3 Wlns. Fd. Amb. This unit was not up to its usual standard, attention was drawn to these defects. Visited & interviewed R.T.O. & R.S.O. at Edgehill Siding to make arrangements about evacuating sick horses. Visited & inspected 3rd Sec. D.A.C. Dirty lines & wasting forage consequently through Nelatte horses are not looking well | S.A. |

2449 Wt. W14957/M90 750,000 1/16 J.B.C. & A. Forms/C.2118/12.

Instructions regarding War Diaries and Intelligence Summaries are contained in F. S. Regs., Part II. and the Staff Manual respectively. Title Pages will be prepared in manuscript.

# WAR DIARY
*or*
# INTELLIGENCE SUMMARY
*(Erase heading not required.)*

Army Form C. 2118.

| Place | Date | Hour | Summary of Events and Information | Remarks and references to Appendices |
|---|---|---|---|---|
| Millencourt | 9/9/16 | | found an improvement in them. | |
| | 10/9/16 | | Visited, examined, & dressed G.O.C. horses head twice, no worse. Visited Mob. Vet. Section. Visited & examined a mule at R.E. Hd Qrs. | S.A. |
| | 11/9/16 | | Visited Div. Train Hd. Qrs. to obtain position of their refilling points, & make some arrangements to try & reduce the number of cases of P.U.K. Visited Mob. Vet. Sect. & found 4 mules fit for walking work. | S.A. |
| | 12/9/16 | | Visited & inspected 1/3 Nhns. Fd. Amb. This unit was not up to its usual standard, attention was drawn to these defects. Visited & interviewed R.T.O. & R.S.O. at Edgehill Siding to make arrangements about evacuating sick horses. Visited & inspected 3rd Sec. D.A.C. Dirty lines & wasting forage consequently through the latter horses are not looking well. | S.A. |

2449 Wt. W14957/M90 750,000 1/16 J.B.C. & A. Forms/C.2118/12.

Instructions regarding War Diaries and Intelligence Summaries are contained in F. S. Regs., Part II. and the Staff Manual respectively. Title Pages will be prepared in manuscript.

# WAR DIARY
*or*
# INTELLIGENCE SUMMARY
*(Erase heading not required.)*

Army Form C. 2118.

| Place | Date | Hour | Summary of Events and Information | Remarks and references to Appendices |
|---|---|---|---|---|
| Millencourt | 10/9/16 | | Visited & inspected 2nd Sect. Div. Am. Col. Several poor horses. Visited 1/2 of No. 4 Sec. Div. Am. Col. Good. | [initials] |
| | 13/9/16 | | Visited & inspected A/Bg. B/Bg. C/Bg. & D/Bg. 250th Bde R.F.A. I found a large number of thin horses in my opinion, their from overwork, as they were doing about 36 miles per day. Inspected horses of A/Bg. B/Bg. C/Bg. & D/Bg. 252 Bde. R.F.A. excepting A/Bg. which are & have always been good. The same remarks apply as above to the remaining 3 Batteries. Visited & examined sick horses at Mob. Vet. Section. | [initials] |
| | 14/9/16 | | Attended a conference of A.D.V.S. at D.D.V.S. Office on conducting parties for sick horses. | [initials] |
| | 15/9/16 | | Visited & inspected 9th D.L.I. mules affected with Ringworm, improving, not quite safe to discharge. Placed an advanced collecting post for sick horses | [initials] |

2449 Wt. W14957/M90 750,000 1/16 J.B.C. & A. Forms/C.2118/12.

Army Form C. 2118.

Instructions regarding War Diaries and Intelligence Summaries are contained in F. S. Regs., Part II. and the Staff Manual respectively. Title Pages will be prepared in manuscript.

# WAR DIARY
*or*
# INTELLIGENCE SUMMARY

*(Erase heading not required.)*

| Place | Date | Hour | Summary of Events and Information | Remarks and references to Appendices |
|---|---|---|---|---|
| Millencourt | 16/9/16 | | Met the V.O's of the Division at Advanced Collecting Post and spoke to them about the large number of debilitated horses I had found in the Divisional Arty. & Div Am Col. Visited & examined 16 horses before evacuation to Base Vet. Hpl. | [illegible] |
| | 17/9/16 | | Visited & inspected B/B.y 251. good. A/B.y 251. not using hay nets. D/251 Bty R.F.A. not using hay nets. Visited & inspected 7th. R.L.I. lines & horses, found them alright, no sick. 7th Fd. Co. R.E. alright no sick 2nd Fd. Co. R.E. one suspicious skin case. 1st Fd. Co. R.E. alright. All these units complained to me of not being able to obtain hay nets. Issued 14 [illegible] to units concerned. | [illegible] |
| | 18/9/16 | | Met the D.D.V.S. 4th Army at the Guards Division Mob. Vet. Section to make final arrangements for evacuation of sick horses. | [illegible] |

2449 Wt. W14957/M90 750,000 1/16 J.B.C. & A. Forms/C.2118/12.

Army Form C. 2118.

Instructions regarding War Diaries and Intelligence Summaries are contained in F. S. Regs., Part II. and the Staff Manual respectively. Title Pages will be prepared in manuscript.

# WAR DIARY
*or*
# INTELLIGENCE SUMMARY
*(Erase heading not required.)*

| Place | Date | Hour | Summary of Events and Information | Remarks and references to Appendices |
|---|---|---|---|---|
| Millencourt | 18/9/16 | | Visited & examined 16 horses at Mob. Vet. Section before evacuation to Base Vet. Hpl. Requested the V.Os of the Division to exercise more care in the diagnosis of lame animals sent into Section. Those that can do walking work must not be sent. | J.F. |
| | 19/9/16. | | Visited & inspected Hd. Qrs. 251 Bde, R.F.A. found several very poor horses, gave the V.O. the instructions to send them into the Section. | J.F. |
| | 20/9/16 | | Visited Mob. Vet. Section & examined several very bad float cases. | J.F. |
| | 21/9/16. | | Met 70 Remounts at Albert Station at 6 am. Many of them not in as good condition as they ought to have been. Visited & inspected 8 horses at Mob. Vet. Section before evacuation to Base Vet. Hpl. Visited & inspected B/A/C/D 252 Bde R.F.A. A/C/B/252. | J.F. |

2449 Wt. W14957/M90 750,000 1/16 J.B.C. & A. Forms/C.2118/12.

Instructions regarding War Diaries and Intelligence Summaries are contained in F. S. Regs., Part II. and the Staff Manual respectively. Title Pages will be prepared in manuscript.

# WAR DIARY
*or*
# INTELLIGENCE SUMMARY
*(Erase heading not required.)*

Army Form C. 2118.

| Place | Date | Hour | Summary of Events and Information | Remarks and references to Appendices |
|---|---|---|---|---|
| Millencourt | 21/9/16 | | At A/Bg & D/Bg 251 Bge R.F.A. Considering the amount of work these Batys are doing they were all in fair condition excepting A/Bg 252 Bge which had several poor horses. | [illegible] |
| | 22/9/16. | | Visited & examined 8 horses in Mob. Vet. Section before evacuation to Base Vet. Hpl. In company with O/C Mob. Vet. Section I went to choose a place to move the Section to. | [illegible] |
| | 23/9/16. | | Visited & inspected advanced collecting sick horse post & examined an animal sent in by D/Bg 250. In my opinion it was suffering from debility. Visited & inspected 150th Inf Bge. Not anything sick, but the shortage of hay nets in this Bge is bad. I informed Ordnance of this. If they have not hay nets, hay must be soiled, & animals particularly horses will not eat soiled hay. | [illegible] |
| | 24/9/16. | | Visited & examined the A.P.M. mare lame in fore from bruised sole. ordered the usual | [illegible] |

2449 Wt. W14957/M90 750,000 1/16 J.B.C. & A. Forms/C.2118/12.

Instructions regarding War Diaries and Intelligence Summaries are contained in F. S. Regs., Part II. and the Staff Manual respectively. Title Pages will be prepared in manuscript.

# WAR DIARY
*or*
# INTELLIGENCE SUMMARY
*(Erase heading not required.)*

Army Form C. 2118.

| Place | Date | Hour | Summary of Events and Information | Remarks and references to Appendices |
|---|---|---|---|---|
| Millencourt | 24th cont. | | treatment viz:- Cot poultices. Visited & examined 8 horses at Mob. Vet. Section before evacuation to Base Vet. Hpl. Marched with Mob. Vet. Section to their new position. | [illegible] |
| | 25/9/16. | | Visited & inspected 149th Inf. Bde. Hd. Qrs, & 4th 5th 6th & 7th N.F.s transport lines & animals found them doing well, only short of hay nets. Visited & examined 8 horses before evacuation to the Base Vet. Hpl. Visited & inspected 1st Sec. Div. Am. Col. Not using hay nets, consequently forage is wasted. I spoke to the O/C section about this wastage. Visited & examined 8 horses at Mob. Vet. Section before evacuation to receiving lines. | [illegible] |
| | 26/9/16 | | Visited & examined 1st Nth. Fd. Amb. Found the sick horses were improving excepting a Bde mare with bad food. Visited & inspected | [illegible] |

2449 Wt. W14957/M90 750,000 1/16 J.B.C. & A. Forms/C.2118/12.

Army Form C. 2118.

# WAR DIARY
*or*
# INTELLIGENCE SUMMARY
*(Erase heading not required.)*

Instructions regarding War Diaries and Intelligence Summaries are contained in F. S. Regs., Part II. and the Staff Manual respectively. Title Pages will be prepared in manuscript.

| Place | Date | Hour | Summary of Events and Information | Remarks and references to Appendices |
|---|---|---|---|---|
| Millencourt | 26/9/16 | | (?) C.R.A. Hd Qrs horses & lines, one sick H.D. mare with a pinched wither, not anything serious, tried to fit a saddle to the C.R.A. mare. Visited Hd. Qrs. & examined A.D.V.S. mare, lame in foot, advised shoe to be removed & foot poulticed. Visited & examined 3 sick horses before evacuation to sick horse receiving lines. | J.F. |
| | 27/9/16 | | Visited & examined 8 horses at Mob. Vet. Section before evacuation to sick horse receiving lines. Visited & inspected 9th D.A.C. not anything sick to report. Called on the C.R.A. Several other units. | J.F. |
| | 28/9/16 | | Met 31 Remounts at Albert Station & distributed them to Artillery & Div. Amm. Col. units. Visited & inspected ~~H~~ Div Hd. Qrs. & Div. Sig. Co. horse lines, found many nasty cuts in Signal Co. from barbed wire. | |

2449 Wt. W14957/M90 750,000 1/16 J.B.C. & A. Forms/C.2118/12.

Instructions regarding War Diaries and Intelligence Summaries are contained in F. S. Regs., Part II. and the Staff Manual respectively. Title Pages will be prepared in manuscript.

# WAR DIARY
*or*
# INTELLIGENCE SUMMARY
*(Erase heading not required.)*

Army Form C. 2118.

| Place | Date | Hour | Summary of Events and Information | Remarks and references to Appendices |
|---|---|---|---|---|
| Millencourt | 28/9/16 | | Visited & inspected 8 sick horses at Mob. Vety. Section before evacuation to Receiving sick horse lines. | JA |
| " | 29/9/16 | | Visited 150 Inf. Bde. Hd. Qrs. re the [illegible] of a L.D. Visited 151 Inf. Bde. Hd. Qrs. & ordered two stray animals into the Mob. Vet. Section. Visited Mob. Vet. Section & examined Ammunit. Col. Column. Visited & examined Div. Hd. Qrs. & Div. Sig. Co. sick horses. | JA |
| | 30/9/16 | | Visited & examined sick horses at 1/1st (N) Fd Amb, found them considerably improved. Visited & examined sick horses at Div. Sig. Co. These were also improving. | JA |
| | | | Summary:– I regret to say that the 50th (Nbn) Divisional Artillery & Ammunition Column horses have gone down in condition during the past month. They have had an increased amount of work | JA |

2449 Wt. W14957/M90 750,000 1/16 J.B.C. & A. Forms/C.2118/12.

Army Form C. 2118.

Instructions regarding War Diaries and Intelligence Summaries are contained in F. S. Regs., Part II. and the Staff Manual respectively. Title Pages will be prepared in manuscript.

# WAR DIARY
*or*
# INTELLIGENCE SUMMARY
*(Erase heading not required.)*

| Place | Date | Hour | Summary of Events and Information | Remarks and references to Appendices |
|---|---|---|---|---|
| Millencourt. | | | on a decreased forage ration; the latter falling as low as 8½lbs of oats, & 10 lbs of hay per issue, and no equivalents to make up the deficiency. 8½ lbs of oats, & 10 lbs of hay is not sufficient for horses doing long hard days work over very heavy ground. Two horses have died from exhaustion, & 46 have been evacuated for debility from this cause alone. Shortage of hay nets will account for a certain wastage of Hay. From enquiries made, this is not the fault of units not indenting for them, but because they are not being sent up from the Base.<br>J. Franklin<br>Major A.V.C.<br>A.D.V.S. 50th (Nbn) Division | JH |

2449 Wt. W14957/M90 750,000 1/16 J.B.C. & A. Forms/C.2118/12.

Vol 16

Confidential

War Diary

of

A. D. of V. S. 50th Division

from 1st Oct. to 31st Oct. 1916.

Volume XIII

Instructions regarding War Diaries and Intelligence Summaries are contained in F. S. Regs., Part II. and the Staff Manual respectively. Title Pages will be prepared in manuscript.

# WAR DIARY
*or*
# INTELLIGENCE SUMMARY
*(Erase heading not required.)*

War Diary of A.D. of V.S. 50th Division

Army Form C. 2118.

| Place | Date | Hour | Summary of Events and Information | Remarks and references to Appendices |
|---|---|---|---|---|
| Millencourt | 1/10/16 | | Visited & inspected 1/3rd (Nbn) Fd Amb, R.A.M.C. Found several lame horses, this was explained to me, that they had been doing too much work on very uneven & bad Roads. Visited & inspected A/Bty 253 Bge R.F.A. A want of better line supervision is ~~wanted~~ noticed in this Bge. B/Bty 253 Bge R.F.A. This battery is good, although they have a few horses thin. C/Bty 253 Bge R.F.A. Good, the best battery in the Bge. Visited & examined 9 horses at Mob. Vet. Section before evacuation to Base Vet. Hpl. Visited C.R.A. Hd. Qts. & examined the horse with bruised heel, improving. | H |
| | 2/10/16 | | Visited & examined sick horses at Div. Hd. Qts. Div. Sig. Co. R.E., & C.R.A. Hd Qts. I discharged several fit for duty. Visited Mob. Vet. Section on its arrival. | H |

2449 Wt. W14957/M90 750,000 1/16 J.B.C. & A. Forms/C.2118/12.

Instructions regarding War Diaries and Intelligence Summaries are contained in F. S. Regs., Part II. and the Staff Manual respectively. Title Pages will be prepared in manuscript.

# WAR DIARY
*or*
# INTELLIGENCE SUMMARY
*(Erase heading not required.)*

Army Form C. 2118.

| Place | Date | Hour | Summary of Events and Information | Remarks and references to Appendices |
|---|---|---|---|---|
| Millencourt | 3 | 10/16. | Visited & examined sick horses at 1/1st Fd. Amb R.A.M.C. since my last visit to this unit the sick have improved & discharged two fit for duty. Visited Mob. Vet. Section. Visited & examined lame H.D. in Div. Hd. Qr. lines, found it lame from having been pricked in shoeing. Reported shoeing smith to Camp Commandant as this was the 3rd he had lamed in a week. | J.F. |
| | 4 | 10/16 | Visited & examined sick horses at Div. Hd. Qr. lines & Hd. Qrs. C.R.A. found them improving. | J.F. |
| | 5 | 10/16. | Visited & inspected A/Bg. B/Bg. C/Bg. & D/Bg. 257 Bde, R.F.A. I moved several poor & unthrifty animals into Section for evacuation. In my opinion considering the work these horses are doing they are not getting sufficient food to keep them up, otherwise considering all things I thought them good. | J.F. |

2449 Wt. W14957/M90 750,000 1/16 J.B.C. & A. Forms/C.2118/12.

Instructions regarding War Diaries and Intelligence Summaries are contained in F. S. Regs., Part II. and the Staff Manual respectively. Title Pages will be prepared in manuscript.

# WAR DIARY
*or*
# INTELLIGENCE SUMMARY
*(Erase heading not required.)*

Army Form C. 2118.

| Place | Date | Hour | Summary of Events and Information | Remarks and references to Appendices |
|---|---|---|---|---|
| Millencourt | 5 10/16 | | A. Visited & inspected A. B. C. D/Btys. 252 Bde. The same remarks as overleaf apply to this Bde. | S.T. |
| | 6 10/16. | | Visited & inspected 4th, 5th, 6th, & 7th Nbn. Fs. Transport lines & Hd. Qrs. found them alright, no serious case to show me. Visited & examined sick horses at 1/1st Nbn. Fd. Amb. found them improving, Capt. Shields mare walking well. | S.T. |
| | 7 10/16 | | Visited Mob. Vet. Section & examined 16 horses before evacuation to Base Vet. Hpl. Met & distributed 69 Remounts at Frechencourt Station. A very useful draft. | S.T. |
| | 8 10/16. | | Visited & inspected Hd. Qrs. Div. Am. Col. Very good. Visited & inspected No. 1 Sec. D.A.C. animals are all in as good condition as they might be. No 2. 3. & 4 Sec. D.A.C. are standing the rough conditions & hard work very well. Visited & inspected 7 D.L.I. alright, one old horse which is in my opinion will not stand the work. Visited & examined sick animals at 1/1st Nbn. Fd. Amb. R.A.M.C. Sent one in Mob. Vet. Sect. with debility. | S.T. |

2449 Wt. W14957/M90 750,000 1/16 J.B.C. & A. Forms/C.2118/12.

Instructions regarding War Diaries and Intelligence Summaries are contained in F. S. Regs., Part II. and the Staff Manual respectively. Title Pages will be prepared in manuscript.

# WAR DIARY
*or*
# INTELLIGENCE SUMMARY
*(Erase heading not required.)*

Army Form C. 2118.

| Place | Date | Hour | Summary of Events and Information | Remarks and references to Appendices |
|---|---|---|---|---|
| Millencourt | 9 10/16. | | Visited & inspected A/Bty. 250 Bge. R.F.A. Found several poor horses ordered one into Mob. Vet. Sect. the rest were in good hard working condition. Visited & inspected B/Bty. 250 Bge. R.F.A. Several poor horses in this Bty, but fit for work. C/Bty 250 Bge. very poor indeed, no proper supervision in this Bty. I found several lacerated heels caused by getting their feet fast in the bundles of fascines at the watering troughs, reported this matter to Div. Hd. Qrs. Visited Mob. Vet. Section & examined 16 horses before evacuation to the Base Vet. Hpl. | JY |
| | 10 10/16. | | Visited Mob. Vet. Section & examined 24 horses before evacuation to Base Vety. Hpl. Visited & inspected 150th Inf. Bge. Hd. Qrs. lines good. also 4th Yorks. & 4th E. Yorks. 5th D.L.I. & 5th Yorks. Transport lines all well excepting C.O. rider in 5th D.L.I. which was suffering from a bad attack of Laryngitis. | JY |

Army Form C. 2118.

Instructions regarding War Diaries and Intelligence Summaries are contained in F. S. Regs., Part II. and the Staff Manual respectively. Title Pages will be prepared in manuscript.

# WAR DIARY
*or*
# INTELLIGENCE SUMMARY
*(Erase heading not required.)*

| Place | Date | Hour | Summary of Events and Information | Remarks and references to Appendices |
|---|---|---|---|---|
| Millencourt | 10 | 10/16 | Ct. 150 Machine Gun Section good. This Infantry Bge is good altogether, the Officers take a great interest in their animals. | J.A. |
| | 11 | 10/16 | Visited D.D.V.S. IV Army Hd. Qts. to consult him on certain affairs. Visited Mob. Vet. Section and examined 48 horses before evacuation to Base Vet. Hpl. | J.A. |
| | 12 | 10/16. | Visited & inspected 151 Inf. Bge, 5th Borders, excepting 2 or 3 which might be in better condition are alright. 151 Machine Gun Co have no haynets, no shackles, or heel pegs, but the horses & mules were in good condition. Bge. Hd. Qts. & 9th D.L.I. together were good. 8th D.L.I. 6th D.L.I. good. altogether a good Brigade. | J.A. |
| | 13 | 10/16. | Visited & inspected 7th Fd Co R.E. This Co have erected a very good shed for the horses for the winter. Their horses were in good working condition. They had ~~been~~ had issued this morning 6 bundles of badly weathered oat straw, worn, & | J.A. |

2449 Wt. W14957/M90 750,000 1/16 J.B.C. & A. Forms/C.2118/12.

Army Form C. 2118.

# WAR DIARY
*or*
# INTELLIGENCE SUMMARY
*(Erase heading not required.)*

Instructions regarding War Diaries and Intelligence Summaries are contained in F. S. Regs., Part II. and the Staff Manual respectively. Title Pages will be prepared in manuscript.

| Place | Date | Hour | Summary of Events and Information | Remarks and references to Appendices |
|---|---|---|---|---|
| Millencourt | 13 | 10/16 | very nasty & this in lieu of hay, how can horses be kept fit for hard work on such muck, what I saw was not fit to put in bullock yards, naturally the horses wouldn't eat it, whatever price it cost if only one penny per bundle it was dear. | SH |
| | | | Visited 1/1st Fd. Co. R.E. & 1/2nd Fd. Co. R.E. same remark applies to these Cos. Called at No 4. Sec D.A.C. & examined 9 mules which had been injured by shell fire the previous day ordered all of them to the Sec. Visited & inspected Hd. Qrs. Co. Div. Train. A.S.C. not at all good several horses with galled shoulders, & several in sick lines through kicks. I pointed this out to the O.C. & told him he wanted better line supervision. | |
| | | | Visited Mob. Vet. Section & examined 37 sick horses before evacuation to the Base. | SH. |
| | 14 | 10/16 | Visited & inspected Nos 2. 3. & 4 Cos Div. Train. A.S.C. not as good as they ought to be, the horses have fallen | |

Army Form C. 2118.

# WAR DIARY
*or*
# INTELLIGENCE SUMMARY
*(Erase heading not required.)*

Instructions regarding War Diaries and Intelligence Summaries are contained in F. S. Regs., Part II. and the Staff Manual respectively. Title Pages will be prepared in manuscript.

| Place | Date | Hour | Summary of Events and Information | Remarks and references to Appendices |
|---|---|---|---|---|
| Millencourt | 14 | 10/16 (cont.) | away in condition since my last inspection. Visited & inspected 2/3rd Fd. Amb. R.A.M.C., ordered two lame riders into Mob. Vet. Section. | RA |
| | 15 | 10/16. | Visited & inspected C/251 Bde R.F.A. ordered 1 to Mob. Vet. Section. Visited & inspected B/251 Bde R.F.A. one sick horse others doing well. Visited & inspected A/251, ordered 5 horses to be sent to Mob. Vet. Section, two for debility. Visited & inspected a mule at Hd. Qrs. 149 Inf. Bde. with a superficial cut wound, not amounting to much. As the A.V.C. Sgt had been reported to me sick I ordered a man to go to this Bde. to look after the sick. | RA |
| | 16 | 10/16. | Visited & examined two horses for casting at A/250 Bde R.F.A. one lame sent into Section the other was a D.D.R. case. Visited & inspected A/253 Bde R.F.A. a large number of horses in this Bde are thin & poor, but are not debilitated in my opinion. | RA |

2449 Wt. W14957/M90 750,000 1/16 J.B.C. & A. Forms/C.2118/12.

Army Form C. 2118.

Instructions regarding War Diaries and Intelligence Summaries are contained in F. S. Regs., Part II. and the Staff Manual respectively. Title Pages will be prepared in manuscript.

# WAR DIARY
*or*
# INTELLIGENCE SUMMARY

*(Erase heading not required.)*

| Place | Date | Hour | Summary of Events and Information | Remarks and references to Appendices |
|---|---|---|---|---|
| Millencourt. | 16 10/16 | | Visited & inspected B/253. Bge R.F.A. On the whole the horses in this Brigade are in fair condition. Visited & inspected C/253 Bge. R.F.A. Examined a Remount which this Bty had had about a month, 25 to 30 years old, & it was in very poor condition. Excepting two or three ~~old~~ old ones this Bty horses are good, all can work. D/251. Bge R.F.A. a few poor horses in this Bty, otherwise alright. Examined Hd. Qrs. 250 Bge, R.F.A. good. Visited advanced Veterinary Collecting post. alright. | J.J. |
| | 17 10/16 | | Visited 4th Army Hd. Qrs. & attended a conference of A.D.V.S.s Divisions. Visited Mob. Vet. Section & examined 16 sick horses before evacuation to Base Vety. Hpl. | J.J. |
| | 18 10/16 | | Visited Mob. Vet. Section & examined 53 sick horses before evacuation to Base Vety. Hpl. Visited & inspected 4th Bt. S. Yorks. found them alright. Called at Hd. Qs. Div. Train A.S.C. & ordered Capt | J.J. |

2449 Wt. W14957/M90 750,000 1/16 J.B.C. & A. Forms/C.2118/12.

Instructions regarding War Diaries and Intelligence Summaries are contained in F. S. Regs., Part II. and the Staff Manual respectively. Title Pages will be prepared in manuscript.

# WAR DIARY
*or*
# INTELLIGENCE SUMMARY
*(Erase heading not required.)*

Army Form C. 2118.

| Place | Date | Hour | Summary of Events and Information | Remarks and references to Appendices |
|---|---|---|---|---|
| Millencourt | 18 | 10/16 | Portenis to attend 252 Bde R.F.A. who were ordered back to rest. | J.F. |
| | 19 | 10/16 | Visited & inspected Hd Qts C.R.A. 1 Ride still lame & not fit for duty. Visited & inspected Div Hd Qts. 1 sick horse which was not fit for duty. Quar Mrs charger had a suspicious bearing out in its loins. Visited & inspected Div Sig Co R.E. four sick animals not fit for duty. Visited Mob Vet section & examined 16 sick horses before evacuation to Base Vety Hpl. | J.F. |
| | 20 | 10/16 | Visited & inspected Hd Qts 252 Bde R.F.A. very good. Visited A/252 Bde R.F.A. 8 poor & thin horses, ordered them into Mob Vet Sect. Visited B/252. Several poor horses, the rest were in working condition. Visited C/252, about 6 poor & thin animals ordered them into Mob Vet Sect. Visited C/251, the same remarks applies to this Bty. | J.F. |
| | 21 | 10/16 | Visited Mob Vet Sect & examined 16 horses before evacuation to Base Vety Hpl. Visited & inspected | J.F. |

2449 Wt. W14957/M90 750,000 1/16 J.B.C. & A. Forms/C.2118/12.

Instructions regarding War Diaries and Intelligence Summaries are contained in F. S. Regs., Part II. and the Staff Manual respectively. Title Pages will be prepared in manuscript.

# WAR DIARY
*or*
# INTELLIGENCE SUMMARY
*(Erase heading not required.)*

Army Form C. 2118.

| Place | Date | Hour | Summary of Events and Information | Remarks and references to Appendices |
|---|---|---|---|---|
| Millencourt | 21 | 10/16 | A Dplg 251 Bgde R.F.A. not at all good. Visited & inspected 4 Secs & Hd Qts Div. Am. Col. several poor horses, otherwise considering their work & conditions the rest were in good hard condition. | J.H. |
| | 22 | 10/16 | Visited Mob. Vet. Section & examined 16 sick horses before evacuation to Base Vety Hpl. Visited the Div. Hd. Qts new position to find ground for Mob. Vet. Section. Called upon A.D.V.S. 9th Division. Visited Capt. Atkinson A.V.C. at Div. Am. Col. lines & gave him instructions about debilitated animals. | J.H. |
| | 23 | 10/16 | Visited & inspected 2/2nd (Wm) Fd. Amb. at Ramullies. Found their animals in good condition. | J.H. |
| | 24 | 10/16 | Visited Mob. Vet. Section & examined 16 sick horses before evacuation to Base Vety Hpl. | J.H. |
| | 25 | 10/16 | Div. Hd. Qts. moved to new area. Attended at Edge Hill received & distributed 96 Remounts | J.H. |

2449 Wt. W14957/M90 750,000 1/16 J.B.C. & A. Forms/C.2118/12.

Instructions regarding War Diaries and Intelligence Summaries are contained in F. S. Regs., Part II. and the Staff Manual respectively. Title Pages will be prepared in manuscript.

# WAR DIARY
*or*
# INTELLIGENCE SUMMARY
*(Erase heading not required.)*

Army Form C. 2118.

| Place | Date | Hour | Summary of Events and Information | Remarks and references to Appendices |
|---|---|---|---|---|
| Fricourt Farm. | 26 | 10/16. | Visited Mob. Vet. Section which had moved into new position. Attended at Edgehill, met & distributed 41 Remounts, all for the Div. Arty. & Div. Am. Col. | J.F. |
| | 27 | 10/16 | Visited & inspected Hd. Qts. Div. Am. Col, very good. No 1 Sec. Div. Am. Col, on the whole the horses were in good working condition. No 2 Sec. Div. Am. Col were troubled with several animals affected with Colic, this in my opinion was due to the horses being kept too long without water & food, gave instructions how to remedy it. No 3 Sec. Div. Am. Col, this unit [animals] are troubled with 13 cases of septic ulcers on the legs, these have been caused by wounds contracted at the watering troughs. No 4 Sec. Div. Am. Col, good. Visited Mob. Vet. Section & examined 24 sick horses before evacuation to Base Vet. Hpl. | J.F. |

2449 Wt. W14957/M90 750,000 1/16 J.B.C. & A. Forms/C.2118/12.

Army Form C. 2118.

Instructions regarding War Diaries and Intelligence Summaries are contained in F. S. Regs., Part II. and the Staff Manual respectively. Title Pages will be prepared in manuscript.

# WAR DIARY
*or*
# INTELLIGENCE SUMMARY
*(Erase heading not required.)*

| Place | Date | Hour | Summary of Events and Information | Remarks and references to Appendices |
|---|---|---|---|---|
| Fricourt Farm | 28 | 10/16. | Visited 151 Inf. Bde. H.Qts. alright. Visited & inspected 5th D.L.I. 5th Border, 8th D.L.I. & 9th D.L.I. Found the horses in this Bde alright & in good condition, but they will not be the latter long if they are not able to receive hay nets, for as the Transport lines are in such a bleak spot unless they can be issued the Hay will all be blown away. Visited & inspected 149 Inf Bde Hd Qts & the 4th, 5th, 6th, & 7th N.F.s found this Bde horses alright excepting one with a peculiar skin, & lame. The same remarks as above apply to this Bde, no hay nets, blowing all over the place. Visited & inspected 150 Inf Bde, alright. The same complaint, cannot get hay nets. Called at C/250 Bde R.F.A & examined an animal suffering from open hock joint, & it would not do any good for further service ordered its destruction. Called at Hd. Qts 250 Bde R.F.A & examined the C.O. ride, had to order its destruction from similar symptoms & causes. | W.F. |

2449 Wt. W14957/M90 750,000 1/16 J.B.C. & A. Forms/C.2118/12.

# WAR DIARY
*or*
# INTELLIGENCE SUMMARY
*(Erase heading not required.)*

Army Form C. 2118.

Instructions regarding War Diaries and Intelligence Summaries are contained in F. S. Regs., Part II. and the Staff Manual respectively. Title Pages will be prepared in manuscript.

| Place | Date | Hour | Summary of Events and Information | Remarks and references to Appendices |
|---|---|---|---|---|
| Fricourt Farm | 29 | 10/16 | Visited & inspected C/Bg. 250 Bge R.F.A. Vet Sergt reported one horse had had to be destroyed through floundering into a shell hole & breaking its leg. A/Bg 250 Bge. R.F.A. very bad no proper methodical line supervision, & although they had haynets were not ~~using~~ using them. B/Bg. 250 Bge. R.F.A. on the whole fairly good, take the Bge as a whole it is not good there appears to be no proper supervision. Visited & inspected D/251 Bge R.F.A a slight improvement, still there is plenty of room for it. Visited Mob. Vet. Section & examined 16 sick animals before being evacuated to the Base Vet. Hpl. | [illegible] |
| | 30 | 10/16 | Sick with Rheumatism but able to perform routine work | |
| | 31 | 10/16 | Same remarks as above | [illegible] |

2449 Wt. W14957/M90 750,000 1/16 J.B.C. & A. Forms/C.2118/12.

Army Form C. 2118.

Instructions regarding War Diaries and Intelligence Summaries are contained in F. S. Regs., Part II. and the Staff Manual respectively. Title Pages will be prepared in manuscript.

# WAR DIARY
*or*
# INTELLIGENCE SUMMARY
*(Erase heading not required.)*

| Place | Date | Hour | Summary of Events and Information | Remarks and references to Appendices |
|---|---|---|---|---|
| Fremicourt Farm | 31/10/16 | | During past month the artillery horses in the Divn. have lost condition rapidly, consequently there has been a large number of debility cases evacuated. This is owing partly to the heavy condition of the ground through which they have to go, I have seen it myself up to the knees & hocks, the extra 2lbs of oats has helped them along a lot, but it is not only oats they want, but a bit more hay. I have been troubled with several cases of tender feet in animals caused by the shoe being cast in the heavy ground, I am trying experiments in the Mob. Vet. Section with a crêpe sole, but I fear it will beat us, at any rate I shall in my next Diary say how it has progressed. There is no Contagious or Infectious Disease in the Division. | GF |
| | | | G. Franklin<br>Major AVC.<br>A.D.V.S. 50 (Nbn) Division<br>B.E. Force<br>France | |

2449 Wt. W14957/M90 750,000 1/16 J.B.C. & A. Forms/C.2118/12.

Confidential

War Diary

of

A. D. of V. S.

50th Division

from

Nov. 1st 1916 to Nov: 30th 1916

Vol. XIV

Army Form C.

Instructions regarding War Diaries and Intelligence Summaries are contained in F. S. Regs., Part II. and the Staff Manual respectively. Title pages will be prepared in manuscript.

# WAR DIARY
or
# INTELLIGENCE SUMMARY.
(Erase heading not required.)

War Diary of A.D.V.S., 50th Division

| Place | Date | Hour | Summary of Events and Information | Remarks and references to Appendices |
|---|---|---|---|---|
| Fricourt Farm | 1/11/16 | 10 AM | (1). A.D.V.S. confined to bed - muscular rheumatism<br>(11). Informed D.D.V.S. that no more M.V.S. men wished to go to Farriers School | J.R.C. |
| " | 2/11/16 | | (1). Had several art. horses inspected with a view to having them cast by D.D.R. Several proved Debility cases and were ordered to M.V.S. One was for casting & one for pack.<br>(11). Inspected 16 animals prior to evacuation to Base Vet. Hospital. | J.R.C. |
| " | 3/11/16 | | (1). Wire D.D.R. 4th Army for 2 H.D. for S Staff. Labour Batt.<br>(11). Drew attention of V.O. i/c 3rd Fld. Coy (48th Div) to sending animals to M.V.S. with labels. | J.R.C. |
| " | 4/11/16 | | (1). A.D.V.S. to Corps Rest Station Beaucourt. Capt J. R. Crone appointed acting A.D.V.S.<br>(11). Inspected 33 animals prior to evacuation to the Base Hospital<br>(111). Requested D.A.C. to return Capt Taylors riders to M.V.S. for re-issue. | J.R.C. |
| " | 5/11/16 | | (1). Issued Capt. Taylors Riders to (1) Capt Newton A.V.C. (2) Lt. Brown A.V.C.<br>(11). Wrote D.D.V.S. on Major Franklin's removal to Rest Station<br>(111). Inspected the horses of the 253rd Bde R.F.A. | J.R.C. |
| " | 6/11/16 | | (1). Wired units to concerned to meet remounts Edgehill 9 a.m. Met and distributed the above 74 remounts. | J.R.C. |

A5834 Wt. W4973/M687 750,000 8/16 D. D. & L. Ltd. Forms/C.2118/13.

Instructions regarding War Diaries and Intelligence Summaries are contained in F. S. Regs., Part II. and the Staff Manual respectively. Title pages will be prepared in manuscript.

# WAR DIARY
*or*
# INTELLIGENCE SUMMARY.
*(Erase heading not required.)*

Army Form C. 2118.

| Place | Date | Hour | Summary of Events and Information | Remarks and references to Appendices |
|---|---|---|---|---|
| Fricourt Farm. | 6/11/16 | | (II) Wrote C.R.A. & 151st Inf Bde to return remount head-collars to M.V.S. | |
| | | | (III) Inspected animals of the 7th D.L.I. pioneer Batt. | J.R.C. |
| " | 7/11/16 | | (I) Wired Capt Porteus to remain at Montigny and take over Veterinary charge of Art. Bdes arriving there. | |
| | | | (II) Wired asking Staff Captains 149th & 150th I Bgds if they would take 6 HDs for water carts and exchange 6 mules for them at M.V.S | |
| | | | (III) Inspected 32 animals prior to evacuation to the Base. Hospital | J.R.C. |
| | | | (IV) Wrote to V.O.s to submit confidential report on all A.V.C. sergeants | J.R.C. |
| " | 8/11/16 | | (I) Informed D.D.V.S. of Sgt Stewart 25 A.D. A.V.C. being evacuated sick to England | |
| | | | (II) Inspected animals of 50th Div. D.A.C. | |
| | | | (III) Requested Capt Newton to attend 149th I Bde whilst I was engaged as A.D.V.S at Headquarters | J.R.C. |
| " | 9/11/16 | | (I) Gave Q a tabulated list of diseases from which horses had suffered when evacuated to B.V.H. during the previous week. | |
| | | | (II) 48 animals were to day evacuated to Base Vet. Hospital | J.R.C. |
| " | 10/11/16 | | (I) Inspected horses of D/267 R.F.A. and found several very poor and debilitated and reported state of affairs to C.R.A. | |
| | | | (II) Inspected 32 animals prior to evacuation to B.V.H. | J.R.C. |

A5834 Wt. W4973/M687 750,000 8/16 D. D. & L. Ltd. Forms/C.2118/13.

Instructions regarding War Diaries and Intelligence Summaries are contained in F. S. Regs., Part II. and the Staff Manual respectively. Title pages will be prepared in manuscript.

# WAR DIARY
*or*
# INTELLIGENCE SUMMARY.
*(Erase heading not required.)*

Army Form C. 2118.

| Place | Date | Hour | Summary of Events and Information | Remarks and references to Appendices |
|---|---|---|---|---|
| Fricourt Farm | 11/11/16 | | (i) Submitted a confidential Report to D.D.V.S, 4th Army on all A V C serjeants att. to units of this Division, other than M.V.S | |
| | | | (ii) Applied to D A C. for assistance (6 men) for M.V.S who had had such a large number of sick to cope with - Granted. | |
| | | | (iii) Inspected 16 animals prior to being evacuated to B.V.H | J.R.C. |
| " | 12/11/16 | | (i) Forwarded copy of Corps wire to all V.O.s on evacuation of too many debility cases. (ii) Issued Rider to D.A.C. | |
| | | | (iii) Applied again to D.A.C. for assistance for M.V.S. - granted. | |
| | | | (iv) Instructed Capts Atkinson & Pattens on their work when Art moved back. | |
| | | | V Inspected 40 animals prior to evacuation to B.V.H | J.R.C. |
| " | 13/11/16 | | (i) Requested Capt H Newton to report on condition of Cavalry Pack horses lent to this Division | |
| | | | (ii) Instructed Capt Newton to attend 2 HD's requiring attention at Shelter wood. | |
| | | | (iii) Issued to V.Os. D D V S letter on applying a strip of tin over the frog as a protection to soles. Asked them to try the system & be ready to report on it. | J.R.C. |
| | | | (IV) 32 animals were evacuated to B.V.H. mostly suffering from Debility | |
| " | 14/11/16 | | (i) Visited Cavalry Pack myself & forwarded report to Q. Inspected all the animals of the 149th Inf Bde and found them in very good condition | J.R.C. |

A5834 Wt. W4973/M687 750,000 8/16 D. D. & L. Ltd. Forms/C.2118/13.

Instructions regarding War Diaries and Intelligence Summaries are contained in F. S. Regs., Part II. and the Staff Manual respectively. Title pages will be prepared in manuscript.

# WAR DIARY
*or*
# INTELLIGENCE SUMMARY.
*(Erase heading not required.)*

Army Form C. 2118.

| Place | Date | Hour | Summary of Events and Information | Remarks and references to Appendices |
|---|---|---|---|---|
| Fricourt Farm | 15/11/16 | | (i) Submitted to Q for Corps a detailed list of all cases of debility evacuated for the week ending 10.11.16. | |
| | | | (ii) Wired A D V S 1st Division to see if he was taking over our M V S position (NO) | |
| | | | (iii) Wired to 5th Division A D V S to ask if they expected a SS as one had arrived to 50th Division in error. | |
| | | | IV. Visited and inspected 23 animals being evacuated to B V H | |
| | | | V Visited 1st & 2nd North'd Fld Amb animals in good condition | JRC |
| " | 16/11/16 | | (i) Applied to Camp Commandant for Mc Envelly's return to M V S during the A D V S's absence sick | |
| | | | (ii) Wrote to O.C. M V S instructing him to be prepared to move on Saturday (18th) to BAIZIEUX chose his own sight, leave an advanced collecting post for units still in the line and personally attend units at rest in LAVIEVILLE. | |
| | | | (iii) Wired C.R.A. giving them new position of M V S. after 18th inst. | |
| | | | IV) Wired 5th Division informing them of SS Chambers dispatch to BETHUNE. | |
| | | | V) Inspected animals belonging to 157th Inf Bde. | |
| | | | VI) of the 253rd Bde R F A found a good many of them very thin and showing signs of hard work. | JRC |

A5834 Wt. W4973/M687 750,000 8/16 D. D. & L. Ltd. Forms/C.2118/13.

Instructions regarding War Diaries and Intelligence Summaries are contained in F. S. Regs., Part II. and the Staff Manual respectively. Title pages will be prepared in manuscript.

# WAR DIARY
*or*
# INTELLIGENCE SUMMARY.
*(Erase heading not required.)*

Army Form C. 2118.

| Place | Date | Hour | Summary of Events and Information | Remarks and references to Appendices |
|---|---|---|---|---|
| Fricourt Farm. | 17/11/16 | | (I) Wrote to D.D.V.S. informing him of 3 Sgts AVC surplus to estabs. caused through changes in composition of Artillery. | |
| | | | (II) Forwarded to Q. S.S. Watson's fathers application for his sons release from service on domestic grounds. | |
| | | | (III) Requested O.C. B/257 to alter Sgt Smiths &d pay book on account of his being promoted to rank of Paid Acting Sgt. | |
| | | | IV) Inspected 16 animals prior to being evacuated to B.V.H. | |
| | | | (V) Consulted with OC M.V.S. & Adjt C.R.E. on construction of a shed to accommodate Debility cases for treatment not poor enough to be sent to B.V.H | |
| | | | VI) Wired to C.R.A. to return surplus Sgt A.V.C. to M.V.S | |
| | | | VII Wired OC 141st Fld Amb to retain horse of 2/3 N.F.A. until our float could collect. | |
| | | | VIII Visited & inspected horses of the 250th Bde RFA. (many poor) | J.R.C. |
| " | 18/11/16 | | (I) Wired D.D.V.S. weekly casualty list for 16.11.16 | |
| | | | (II) " Capt Portens to discontinue evacuating to No 35 M.V.S. | |
| | | | (III) " " Newton & Brown position of advanced collecting Post. | |
| | | | IV " Q position of M.V.S. & advanced collecting post. | |
| | | | V Visited A & B Batteries of 253rd Bde R.F.A. | J.R.C. |

Instructions regarding War Diaries and Intelligence Summaries are contained in F. S. Regs., Part II. and the Staff Manual respectively. Title pages will be prepared in manuscript.

# WAR DIARY
*or*
# INTELLIGENCE SUMMARY.
*(Erase heading not required.)*

Army Form C. 2118.

| Place | Date | Hour | Summary of Events and Information | Remarks and references to Appendices |
|---|---|---|---|---|
| Albert | 19/11/16 | | (i) D.H.Q moved to Albert. | |
| | | | (ii) Informed O.C. 9 M.V.S. that I was sending 3 Sgt A.V.C. to the section and wrote to Base and requesting him to dispatch them to Edgehill station. Informed O.C. No 2 Base Veterinary Hospital to expect their arrival. Also informed O.C. A.V.C. records of their return. | |
| | | | (iii) Wired D.D.V.S. of move of H.Q. & M.V.S. giving present position | JRC |
| | | | IV. Visited 149th Inf Bde & A.P.M.'s Lines (Picked up mail.) | |
| " | 20/11/16 | | (i) Returned Sgt Richardsons application for special leave as he gets it from the O.C. of unit to which he is attached. | |
| | | | II Wrote A.D.V.S. 1st Division handing over to him at Fricourt units that had been attached to this Division for administration | |
| | | | III Visited and inspected 16 animals prior to being dispatched to the B.V.H. | |
| | | | IV Informed Capt Newton of having withdrawn these units from his charge. | |
| | | | V Instructed Capt Porteus to accompany 251 & 252nd Bde R.F.A. when they return to action on 22/23. | |
| | | | VI Instructed 9th Div V.O.'s to render their returns to A.D.V.S. 1st Division. | JRC |

A5834 Wt. W4973/M687 750,000 8/16 D. D. & L. Ltd. Forms/C.2118/13.

Instructions regarding War Diaries and Intelligence Summaries are contained in F. S. Regs., Part II. and the Staff Manual respectively. Title pages will be prepared in manuscript.

# WAR DIARY
*or*
# INTELLIGENCE SUMMARY.
*(Erase heading not required.)*

Army Form C. 2118.

| Place | Date | Hour | Summary of Events and Information | Remarks and references to Appendices |
|---|---|---|---|---|
| Albert | 21/11/16 | | (i) Replied to A D V S 1st Division on leaving 5 men behind attached to a M V S. | |
| | | | (ii) Wrote asking Capt Newton to visit 3rd NFA Bottom Wood. | |
| | | | (iii) " " " Patens to send his returns to this office | |
| | | | (iv) Wired Capt Patens to return surplus Sgt A V C to the M V S | |
| | | | V Enquired from D A Q M G if advanced collecting post was to admit 9th Div animals in the line (no) | |
| | | | VI. 16 animals sent to B.V.H today | |
| | | | VII. Visited M M P horses & those of Signals Coy R E. found them all in very good condition | JRC |
| " | 22/11/16 | | (i) Visited and examined 149th Inf Bde animals all were looking very well, in spite of having no standings or over-head cover | |
| | | | (ii) Inspected 21 animals prior to going to B.V.H | JRC |
| " | 23/11/16 | | (i) Suggested to Q to attach one infantry man to each Battery of R.F.A for instruction in cold-shoeing | |
| | | | (iii) Instructed 4th Yks & 150 B H Q to collect a mule & a rider from M V S. Instructed 5th Yks to collect H D from 150 I Bde | |
| | | | Visited Signals R E & M M P. horses 3 lame (pricked) | JRC |

A5834 Wt. W4973/M687 750,000 8/16 D. D. & L. Ltd. Forms/C.2118/13.

Army Form C. 2118.

Instructions regarding War Diaries and Intelligence Summaries are contained in F. S. Regs., Part II and the Staff Manual respectively. Title pages will be prepared in manuscript.

# WAR DIARY
*or*
# INTELLIGENCE SUMMARY.
*(Erase heading not required.)*

| Place | Date | Hour | Summary of Events and Information | Remarks and references to Appendices |
|---|---|---|---|---|
| Albert. | 24/11/16 | | (i) Informed D.D.V.S. of another Sgt A.V.C. surplus to establishment | |
| | | | (ii) Visited D.A.C. & R.E.'s some of the former mules very thin | |
| | | | (iii) 26 animals were sent to Base Veterinary Hospital | JRG |
| " | 25/11/16 | | (i) Instructed Capt. Portens to attend C/50th Bde 9th Division | |
| | | | (ii) " Lt Brown to attend D.A.C. in lieu of 151st Bde &c | |
| | | | (iii) " Capt Wright to attend 151st Bde H.Q. at Millencourt – | |
| | | | IV Visited Divisional H.Q. horses all very good – | |
| | | | V Issued circular memo to all V.O's of this Division to keep a sharp look out for Mange at this time of the year and to instruct Sgts A.V.C. attached likewise – | JRG |
| " | 26/11/16 | | (i) Met and distributed 99 Remounts from Edgehill – | |
| | | | (ii) Informed D.D.V.S. of having handed over all 9th Division remainders to A.D.V.S. 1st Division in accordance with his 1843.1 | |
| | | | (iii) Wired to 250th, 251st & 252nd Bdes R.F.A. to collect 56 remounts from D.A.C. | |
| | | | IV Visited 149th Inf Bde transport lines – | |
| | | | V Inspected 16 animals prior to being sent to B.V.H. | JRG |

A5834 Wt. W4973/M687 750,000 8/16 D. D. & L. Ltd. Forms/C.2118/13.

Army Form C. 2118.

Instructions regarding War Diaries and Intelligence Summaries are contained in F. S. Regs., Part II. and the Staff Manual respectively. Title pages will be prepared in manuscript.

# WAR DIARY
*or*
# INTELLIGENCE SUMMARY.
*(Erase heading not required.)*

| Place | Date | Hour | Summary of Events and Information | Remarks and references to Appendices |
|---|---|---|---|---|
| Albert | 27/11/16 | | (i) Informed G.O.C. 151st Inf Bde rules relating to clipping horses trace high. (no objection to it). | |
| | | | (ii) Requested O.C., M.V.S. to return Sgt Scott A.V.C. to the No 2 Veterinary Hospital Havre. | |
| | | | (iii) Informed O.C. i/c Records of above transfer. | |
| | | | IV Submitted to D.D.V.S. a preliminary report on the results accruing from shoeing using a tin-plate protection (for frog & pedal joint) against P.V. Nails. | |
| | | | V Wired to V.O's to report on this system at the conclusion of the tests. | J.R.B. |
| " | 28/11/16 | | (i) Visited Signals R.E. & M.M. Police horses also the | |
| | | | (ii) 149th Inf Bde Amiens Road. some improvement. | |
| | | | (iii) Inspected 23 animals prior to going to B.V.H. | J.R.B. |
| " | 29/11/16 | | (i) Visited M.V.S. at BAZZIEUX. | |
| | | | (ii) Met DDVS and consulted with him about tin plates for horses feet to prevent P.V. Nails | |
| | | | (iii) Wrote to Capt Newton to attend the animals of the D.A.C. | |
| | | | IV Sent Pack pony from Hd Qrs to the 5th N.F. | |
| | | | V Visited the A.P.M's horse. | J.R.B. |

A5834 Wt. W4973/M687 750,000 8/16 D. D. & L. Ltd. Forms/C.2118/13.

Instructions regarding War Diaries and Intelligence Summaries are contained in F. S. Regs., Part II. and the Staff Manual respectively. Title pages will be prepared in manuscript.

# WAR DIARY
*or*
# INTELLIGENCE SUMMARY.
*(Erase heading not required.)*

Army Form C. 2118.

| Place | Date | Hour | Summary of Events and Information | Remarks and references to Appendices |
|---|---|---|---|---|
| Albert | 30/11/16 | | (i) Visited and inspected horses at 251st Bde R.F.A. Contalmaison which they wished to be cast for other than Veterinary Reasons<br>(ii) Visited and inspected D.A.C. animals proposed for Casting other than Veterinary Reasons —<br>(iii) Wrote Capt Newton to attend the D.A.C | JRC |
| | | | **Summary** | |
| " | 30/11/16 | | The animals of this Division during the month have had a very strenuous time and as a result many had to be evacuated for Debility. There was a shortage of hay for about three weeks which told its tale amongst the animals. Hay nets were unobtainable and as a result a good deal of hay was trampled under foot and destroyed. Remounts were of good quality and a fair supply. Roads up to Gun positions during the month were much improved.<br>Joseph R Crone Capt. R.V.C.<br>a/a D.V.S 50th Division | JRC |

A5834 Wt. W4973/M687 750,000 8/16 D. D. & L. Ltd. Forms/C.2118/13.

Confidential

# WAR DIARY

OF

# A.D.V.S., 50th DIVISION.

FROM DECEMBER 1st to DECEMBER 31st 1916.

VOLUME XV.

8129

Instructions regarding War Diaries and Intelligence Summaries are contained in F. S. Regs., Part II. and the Staff Manual respectively. Title pages will be prepared in manuscript.

# WAR DIARY
*or*
# INTELLIGENCE SUMMARY.
*(Erase heading not required.)*

Army Form C. 2118.

of A.D.V.S. 50th Division
for Dec 1916
Vol. XV

| Place | Date | Hour | Summary of Events and Information | Remarks and references to Appendices |
|---|---|---|---|---|
| BAIZIEUX | 1/12/16 | | (I) Made a fresh distribution of Veterinary Officers for the work of Division | |
| | | | (II) Wired ADVS 48th Division to send Lt Jackson to Baizieux & report. | |
| | | | (III) D.H.Q. moved to Baizieux (rest area) Wired DDVS my position. | J.R.C. |
| " | 2/12/16 | | (I) Informed Records A.V.C base of Pte Martins return to Base surplus. | |
| | | | (II) Instructed Capt Atkinson to attend Unit of 150th Inf Bde Contry. | |
| | | | (III) " Lt Brown to attend 149th Inf Bde & 1/1st NFA at Laviaville | |
| | | | (IV) Wired H.Q. 250 Bde RFA a second time to report if Sgt Manton AVC had yet reported there for duty. | |
| | | | (V) Wired Advanced Vety Stores re 25 lbs chest having gone astray in transit & still lost. | |
| | | | (VI) Inspected 16 animals prior to evacuation to the B.V.H. | J.R.C. |
| " | 3/12/16 | | (I) Visited and inspected animals of the 151st Inf Bde at Warloy. | |
| | | | (II) " " " " Divisional Signals R.E. | J.R.C. |
| " | 4/12/16 | | Informed DDVS of Serjeant Mantons AVC arrival for duty with 250th Bde RFA | |
| | | | (II) Inspected 16 animals prior to evacuation to the B.V. Hospital | |
| | | | (III) Notified all V.Os to order the burial of all dead horses in their vicinity irrespective of whose unit or Division | |
| | | | (IV) Called for an explanation as to why Lt Brown AVC had not seen 149th Inf Bde when instructed to do so by letter on the 2nd inst. | J.R.C. |

A5834 Wt. W4973/M687 750,000 8/16 D. D. & L. Ltd. Forms/C.2118/13.

Instructions regarding War Diaries and Intelligence Summaries are contained in F. S. Regs., Part II. and the Staff Manual respectively. Title pages will be prepared in manuscript.

# WAR DIARY
*or*
# INTELLIGENCE SUMMARY.
*(Erase heading not required.)*

Army Form C. 2118.

| Place | Date | Hour | Summary of Events and Information | Remarks and references to Appendices |
|---|---|---|---|---|
| BAIZIEUX | 4/12/16 | | (v) Wired Capt Porteus to attend 3rd N.F.A. Bottom Wood and enquire for location of C/50 Bde (9th Div) from C.R.A. as the D.D.V.S. wished this Battery to be administered by this Division | |
| | | | (vi) Wired Capt Atkinson to attend 2nd F.A. 48th Division at Warloy (D.D.V.S. orders to A.D.V.S. 15th Div) latter could not arrange. | |
| | | | (vii) Inspected 16 animals prior to evacuation to the B.V.H. | |
| | | | (viii) Wired all units (except Artillery) collecting remounts on 26th inst to return all head collars to the M.V.S. at once. | JRC |
| " | 5/12/16 | | (i) Wired Capt Newton to attend 3rd N.F.A. | |
| | | | (ii) Informed Q that 15th Division M.V.S. did not hand over to Nth'd M.V.S. and that no stores were handed over. | |
| | | | (iii) Visited and inspected 250th Bde R.F.A. horses | JRC |
| " | 6/12/16 | | (i) Inspected 14 animals prior to evacuation to the B.V. Hospital | |
| | | | (ii) Received a note from O.C. D.A.C. to make an examination of a dead animal in old position which had died under suspicious circumstances | |
| | | | (iii) Wired Capt Newton to meet me there. | |
| | | | (iv) Visited and examined animals of the 5th Yks & 5th D.L.I. also examined the horses of the M.M.P. at Headquarters. | JRC |

Army Form C. 2118.

Instructions regarding War Diaries and Intelligence Summaries are contained in F. S. Regs., Part II. and the Staff Manual respectively. Title pages will be prepared in manuscript.

# WAR DIARY
*or*
# INTELLIGENCE SUMMARY.
*(Erase heading not required.)*

| Place | Date | Hour | Summary of Events and Information | Remarks and references to Appendices |
|---|---|---|---|---|
| BAIZIEUX | 7/12/16 | (i) | Visited and made a PM on dead horse at old lines of the DAC and reported to DAC that death was due to internal haemorrhage. | |
| | | (ii) | Wrote to OC DAC stating that horse-line supervision in DAC was slack & requesting him to issue instruction to ameliorate | |
| | | (iii) | Explained to OC MVS that animals sent into MVS without tickets from DAC were not sent in on my authority. | |
| | | (iv) | Wrote to Capt Newton on two cases of suspected mange having been admitted into MVS from DAC and drew his attention to my circular letter on Mange of the 25th inst. | |
| | | V | Informed DDVS that there were no shoeing-smiths in the MVS capable or suitable for appointment of instructors at the Base. | |
| | | VI | Informed DDVS that in my opinion I considered a water-cart necessary for a MVS in an area such as this, being often so situated as to be unable to draw water from neighbouring units, water often having to be carried a distance in petrol tins. | |
| | | VII | Wired Capt Newton to attend serious case at 3rd NFA B'de [illegible] | |
| | | VIII | Acknowledged DO from CRA. | |
| | | IX | Wired Capt Newton to meet me at the DAC lines | |
| | | X | Visited and inspected animals & horse lines of the 149th Inf Bde. | JRC |

Army Form C. 2118.

Instructions regarding War Diaries and Intelligence Summaries are contained in F. S. Regs., Part II. and the Staff Manual respectively. Title pages will be prepared in manuscript.

# WAR DIARY
*or*
# INTELLIGENCE SUMMARY.
*(Erase heading not required.)*

| Place | Date | Hour | Summary of Events and Information | Remarks and references to Appendices |
|---|---|---|---|---|
| BAIZIEUX | 8/12/16 | I | Wrote to A D V S 48th Division informing him of the non-arrival of Lt H Jackson A.V.C. for duty with this Division. | |
| | | II | Visited & inspected animals of the D.A.C. found the standing bad and many animals with no shelter. Impressed upon Capt Newton to lay off work at once any animals that were beginning to show signs of Debility. | |
| | | III | Asked Town Major for permission to erect a hut as an office for A.D.V.S. – granted. | |
| | | IV | Visited and inspected the advance collecting Post. | |
| | | V | 12 animals sent down to the B V H today. | |
| " | 9/12/16 | (I) | Informed D A Q M G that of the 6 pack animals to be disposed of by Signals Co. – 2 were being retained, one lost, 1 each to 6th & 9th D.L.I. & 5th N.F. | JRC |
| | | II | Informed D D V S. that Lt Jackson AVC had reported for duty and had attached him to the D.A.C. as V.O. i/c. | |
| " | 10/12/16 | (I) | Applied to D D V S for Capt Newton's leave. | JRC |
| | | (II) | Instructed 6th & 9th D.L.I. & 6th N.F. to each collect a pack animal from Div. Signals Co. | |
| | | III | Visited and inspected the animals lines of the 5th Yks & 5th D L I no standings nor shelter and much mud. | |
| | | IV | Inspected 12 animals prior to being evacuated to the B.V.H. | JRC |

A5834 Wt. W4973/M687 750,000 8/16 D. D. & L. Ltd. Forms/C.2118/13.

Army Form C. 2118.

Instructions regarding War Diaries and Intelligence Summaries are contained in F. S. Regs., Part II. and the Staff Manual respectively. Title pages will be prepared in manuscript.

# WAR DIARY
*or*
# INTELLIGENCE SUMMARY.
*(Erase heading not required.)*

| Place | Date | Hour | Summary of Events and Information | Remarks and references to Appendices |
|---|---|---|---|---|
| BAIZIEUX | 10/12/16 | V | Explained to DDVS why a duplicate note had been sent re a horse collected by MVS from an inhabitant. | |
| | | VI | Instructed Capt Newton to hand over DAC to Lt W.M. Jackson AVC | JRb |
| " | 11/12/16 | II | Wrote to Lt Jackson stating that drugs for the DAC were already on indent (by late V.O. i/c), and that I would visit his worst cases of Debility & suspected skin disease. | |
| | | III | Visited & inspected animals of the 149th Inf Bde. | JRb |
| " | 12/12/16 | I | Inspected 14 animals prior to evacuation to the B.V. Hospital. | |
| | | II | Wrote to O.C. D/251 to collect from MVS an animal under treatment cured. | |
| | | III | Wired V.Os. for report on Anti-tetanic serum as a basis for treatment in cases of Tetanus. | |
| | | IV | Visited and inspected animals in the DAC as arranged. Found several suffering from Debility and a few with skin disease which was not surprising seeing that this unit had been in action for four months with practically no rest. | |
| " | 13/12/16 | I | Wrote to Lt Jackson that it was essential to use labels when sending sick & lame animals into the M.V.S. | JRb |
| | | II | Notified DDVS of intention to move M.V.S. to Millencourt. | |
| | | III | Inspected 13 animals prior to being sent to the B.V.H. | |
| | | IV | Wrote DDVS for authority to entrain sick animals at Albert. | |
| | | V | Requested Capt Newton to arrange to hand over to Lt Jackson this units while he was away on leave. | JRb |

A5834 Wt. W4973/M687 750,000 8/16 D. D. & L. Ltd. Forms/C.2118/13.

Instructions regarding War Diaries and Intelligence Summaries are contained in F. S. Regs., Part II. and the Staff Manual respectively. Title pages will be prepared in manuscript.

# WAR DIARY
*or*
# INTELLIGENCE SUMMARY.
*(Erase heading not required.)*

Army Form C. 2118.

| Place | Date | Hour | Summary of Events and Information | Remarks and references to Appendices |
|---|---|---|---|---|
| BAIZIEUX | 14/12/16 | I | Applied to D.D.V.S. 4th Army for a reinforcement for M.V.S. to replace 1 O.R. evacuated sick to England. | |
| | | II | Informed Capt Porteus that 3rd N.F.A. were attended by Capt Newton and that the latter unit would be attended by Lt Jackson during his absence on leave. | |
| | | III | Wired D.D.V.S. that "lost charger" widely advertised had not been traced in this Division. | |
| | | IV | Wired Lt Jackson to meet me at HdQrs D.A.C. tomorrow 10.30. | J.R.C. |
| " | 15/12/16 | I | Inspected 8 animals prior to evacuation to the B.V.H. | |
| | | II | Requested O.C. D.A.C. to collect 2 L.D. for re issue from M.V.S. | |
| | | III | " No 1 Coy A.S.C. to collect 1 mule ( " ) " | |
| | | IV | " Lt Jackson to send no animals to Rest Station until Wednesday | |
| | | V | Wired Capt Atkinson to meet me HdQrs 252 Bde R.F.A. tomorrow 10.30 | |
| | | VI | Visited and inspected animals of the 151st Inf Bde & 2nd F.A. (48 Div) | J.R.C. |
| " | 16/12/16 | I | Instructed Capt Atkinson & Lt Jackson how many animals to send to "Rest Station" on Wednesday and what articles would be required for men & horses. | |
| | | II | Wired Q. if men still eligible for leave in M.V.S. | |
| | | III | Visited and inspected animals of the 5th Yks & 5th D.L.I. also those of Divisional HdQrs. The former have still no standings or head cover. | J.R.C. |

A5834 Wt. W4973/M687 750,000 8/16 D. D. & L. Ltd. Forms/C.2118/13.

Instructions regarding War Diaries and Intelligence Summaries are contained in F. S. Regs., Part II. and the Staff Manual respectively. Title pages will be prepared in manuscript.

# WAR DIARY
*or*
# INTELLIGENCE SUMMARY.
*(Erase heading not required.)*

Army Form C. 2118.

| Place | Date | Hour | Summary of Events and Information | Remarks and references to Appendices |
|---|---|---|---|---|
| BAIZIEUX | 17/12/16 | I | Wrote D.D.V.S. supporting his idea that if water carts were not available for M.V.S.'s collapsible canvas tanks would be useful and could be made in the Division. Failing the adoption of these petrol tins could be resorted to for water carrying. | |
| | | II | Inspected 29 animals prior to evacuation to the B.V.H. | |
| | | III | Reported to D.D.V.S. on results of injections of Anti tetanic serum as being the basis for treatment for Tetanus | |
| | | IV | Wired all units concerned to meet remounts next day. | |
| | | V | Visited and inspected horses of the 252nd Bde R.F.A. They had lately come out of action at the Battle of the Somme and many of them showed the effects of the hard work done. | |
| | 18/12/16 | I | Met and distributed 125 Remounts EDGEHILL for the Division | JRb |
| | | II | Submitted a detailed statement to D.A.Q.M.G. of all evacuation & fatal casualties (the later as reported by V.O.'s) of all Artillery from 28th Ult to 13th inst | |
| | | III | Wired to 250th & 251st Bdes R.F.A. to collect 34 & 24 light draught horses respectfully from the D.A.C. lines at FRICOURT. | |
| | | IV | Visited and inspected animals of the 150th Inf Bde | |
| | | V | Called to examine Camp Commandant's horse which had become very lame quite suddenly. | JRb |

A5834 Wt. W4973/M687 750,000 8/16 D. D. & L. Ltd. Forms/C.2118/13.

Instructions regarding War Diaries and Intelligence Summaries are contained in F. S. Regs., Part II. and the Staff Manual respectively. Title pages will be prepared in manuscript.

# WAR DIARY
*or*
# INTELLIGENCE SUMMARY.
*(Erase heading not required.)*

Army Form C. 2118.

| Place | Date | Hour | Summary of Events and Information | Remarks and references to Appendices |
|---|---|---|---|---|
| BAIZIEUX | 19/12/16 | I | Again wrote Capt Atkinson & Lt Jackson on further articles to accompany animals to "Rest Station" – eg. nosebags & haynets | |
| | | II | Reported D.A.Q.M.G. on horses I had inspected which were reported on for casting by Artillery. | |
| | | III | Wired to ask D.D.V.S. if the horse he had instructed this M.V.S to collect at MIRVAUX was a float case or not. | |
| | | IV | Visited and inspected animals of the 157th Inf Bde | JRC |
| " | 20/12/16 | I | Instructed Staff Capts 149 & 150 I. Bydes to collect mule & L.D. respectively from Artillery as they were unsuitable for Artillery work. | |
| | | II | C.R.A. applied again for an issue of portable field forges, correspondence was sent to D.A.Q.M.G. for his attention | |
| | | III | Visited Div. Sig Coy & found remount dying from pneumonia instructed unit to collect & to [illegible] from M.V.S. | |
| | | IV | Wrote to Lt Jackson to meet me at H.Q. D.A.C 10.15 tomorrow. | |
| | | V | Wired D.D.V.S. respecting a V.O. to replace Lt Brown evacuated "nervous debility". Wrote details later to him same day. | |
| | | VI | Informed D.D.V.S. that the animal he wished M.V.S. to collect from inhabitant at Mirvaux had already been collected by 2[illegible] M.V.S | |
| | | VII | Instructed all V.O's to arrange to give lectures on horse management | JRC |

A5834 Wt. W4973/M687 750,000 8/16 D. D. & L. Ltd. Forms/C.2118/13.

Instructions regarding War Diaries and Intelligence Summaries are contained in F. S. Regs., Part II. and the Staff Manual respectively. Title pages will be prepared in manuscript.

# WAR DIARY
*or*
# INTELLIGENCE SUMMARY.
*(Erase heading not required.)*

Army Form C. 2118.

| Place | Date | Hour | Summary of Events and Information | Remarks and references to Appendices |
|---|---|---|---|---|
| BAIZIEUX | 21/12/16 | I | Informed Q that there were no British Columbians in the M.V.S | |
| | | II | " O.C. M.V.S of the posting of Pte Wylde to M.V.S in place of a man evacuated sick & requested him to inform Records A.V.C direct and this office of the man's arrival | |
| | | III | Visited and inspected D.A.C. & 7th D.L.I. in forward area. | |
| | | IV | Wrote to V.O.s having A.V.C. sergts under their control to report by the end of the month the rate of Duty pay each showed in his pay book | JRC |
| " | 22/12/16 | I | Wrote Capt R K P[illegible] again for positions of his wagon lines | |
| | | II | Received memo from Staff Capt 150th Inf Bde asking for a lecture to be given to his officers & N.C.O's on 27th inst at Contay. | |
| | | III | Visited 151st Inf Bde & other units. | |
| | | IV | Visited D.A.D.O.S. re construction of Tanks for M.V.S | JRC |
| | 23/12/16 | I | Informed D.D.V.S. of arrival of Pte Wylde A.V.C. to M.V.S. | |
| | | II | Attended a conference at the D.D.V.S.'s office | |
| | 24/12/16 | I | Visited and inspected 5th Yorks & 6th D.L.I. transport, 151st Inf Bde | JRC |
| | 25/12/16 | I | Capt E. Heane arrived to take over the position of A.D.V.S. 50th Div | |
| | | II | Visited animals of Div Hd Qrs & M.M.P. | |
| | | III | Handed over to Capt E. Heane A.V.C. | JRC |

A5834 Wt. W4973/M687 750,000 8/16 D. D. & L. Ltd. Forms/C.2118/13.

Instructions regarding War Diaries and Intelligence Summaries are contained in F. S. Regs., Part II. and the Staff Manual respectively. Title pages will be prepared in manuscript.

# WAR DIARY
*or*
# INTELLIGENCE SUMMARY.
*(Erase heading not required.)*

ADVS 50(N) DIV

Army Form C. 2118.

| Place | Date | Hour | Summary of Events and Information | Remarks and references to Appendices |
|---|---|---|---|---|
| BAIZIEUX | 26.12 '16 | 11.0 am | Took over the duties of ADVS from Capt Crome acting ADVS. 50(N) DIV. Authority Director Vety No. DV. 1560 dated 22-12-16. Reported for duty HQ 50 DIV. Visited MVS of DIV and saw the men mounted for inspection, they looked smart and were well turned out. The Section horses were in good condition | EH |
| | 26th Dec '16 | | Inspected horses of Divl HQ. also inspected horses at MVS which were being evacuated to B.V.H. Visited Divl. Rest Station for horses at MILLENCOURT | EH |
| | 27th | | Saw Capt Atkinson and gave him instructions with regard to careful daily inspection of the horses in the Transport Lines where he was stationed, especially for mange also that he was to give further instruction to his Vety. Sergeants & see that they performed their duties thoroughly | EH |
| | 28th | | Went to FRESCHENCOURT to inspect animals that were being evacuated. Visited DDVS at HQ 4 Army reported my arrival, and received instructions with regard to Vety. matters | EH |
| | 29th | | Consultation with DADOS re canvas tanks for limbers. Informed units of horses transferring to BVH. Notified DDVS & Q of position of MVS | EH |
| | 30th | | Wrote DDVS re horse evacuated by 27 MVS at MIRVAUX. Sent copies of DDVS' letter re "rusty nails" to all V.O.s & OC MVS. Reading up back orders of DW. etc. so as to acquaint myself of all orders | EH |
| | 31st | | Visited MVS & Rest Station. Went to ALBERT to inspect horses being evacuated | |
| | | | E Kearne Capt AVC<br>ADVS 50 (N) DIV. | |

A5834 Wt. W4973/M687 750,000 8/16 D. D. & L. Ltd. Forms/C.2118/13.

Instructions regarding War Diaries and Intelligence Summaries are contained in F. S. Regs., Part II. and the Staff Manual respectively. Title pages will be prepared in manuscript.

# WAR DIARY
or
~~INTELLIGENCE SUMMARY.~~ ADVS 50 (N) DIV.

(Erase heading not required.)

Army Form C. 2118.

| Place | Date 1917 Jany | Hour | Summary of Events and Information | Remarks and references to Appendices |
|---|---|---|---|---|
| FRICOURT | 1st | | Arrived at FRICOURT FARM from BASIEUX. notified DDVS of my position. Instructed V.Os to send me positions of their wagon lines. Notified units of animals evacuated to Base. | E.H. |
| | 2nd | | Visited M.V.S. Inspected D.A.C. horses at FRICOURT. Had all suspicious skin cases separated. Capt Newton reported off leave from England. Instructed V.Os not to keep horses in a debilitated condition too long in their units, as many cases should have been evacuated earlier. Also that very careful inspection should be made re skin troubles. | E.H. |
| | 3rd | | Inspected debilitated horses at Rest station, visited MVS. and saw the horses at Div! Train | E.H. |
| | 4th | | Inspected horses and mules at 7th D.L.I. (Pioneer) Bn. Also B/250 Bde at BOTTOM WOOD. Sent 9 cases of mange from this unit to MVS and had stable disinfected. | |
| | | | Inspected horses at ALBERT prior to evacuation to Base. | E.H. |
| | 5th | | Attended MVS & gave instructions re horses with suspicious skin disease from DAC. Had scrapings taken and examined same under microscope. | E.H. |
| | 6th | | Attended conference of ADVS's at DDVS' office H.Q. 4th Army. Made arrangements with Capt Crone AVC re Veterinary lectures | E.H. |

Instructions regarding War Diaries and Intelligence Summaries are contained in F. S. Regs., Part II. and the Staff Manual respectively. Title pages will be prepared in manuscript.

# WAR DIARY
or
# ~~INTELLIGENCE SUMMARY.~~
(Erase heading not required.)

ADVS
50th (N) DIV

Army Form C. 2118.

| Place | Date | Hour | Summary of Events and Information | Remarks and references to Appendices |
|---|---|---|---|---|
| | 1917 Jany | | | |
| FRICOURT | 7th | | Inspected sick horses prior to evacuation to Base at ALBERT horses 12th S. Staffs (Pioneer) Bn. Gave Capt Newton AVC instructions to attend the horses of the 21st Cheshire Labour Bn | EH. |
| | 8th | | Met DDVS. 4th Army as arranged and had a consultation re skin disease amongst the horses of the DAC & 7DLI. L. Bn. Visited DIVl TRAIN & inspected horses & mules, ordered 5. mange cases to MVS. The other horses & mules were in splendid condition | EH. |
| | 9th | | Inspected horses at ALBERT prior to evacuation to Base. Proceeded to MVS. and inspected horses under treatment there | EH. |
| | 10th | | Consultation with V.O i/c DAC, examined suspected skin cases, gave orders to have the worst cases clipped and dressed. Informed Staff Captain 149 I Bde to have Sgt. Houghton AVC to be sent to No 2 Vety Hospital for further instruction, as this man was not satisfactory. Report to DDVS on debilitated & exhausted horses | EH. |
| | 11th | | Visited horselines A B D Batteries 252 Bde RFA also C/251 BOTTOM WOOD. Made arrangements at MILLENCOURT to make solution of Calcium Sulphide to wash some horses belonging to DAC. Examined several scrapings of the skin for mange parasites. | EH |

A5834 Wt. W4973/M687 750,000 8/16 D. D. & L. Ltd. Forms/C.2118/13.

Instructions regarding War Diaries and Intelligence Summaries are contained in F. S. Regs., Part II. and the Staff Manual respectively. Title pages will be prepared in manuscript.

# WAR DIARY
*or*
# ~~INTELLIGENCE SUMMARY.~~
*(Erase heading not required.)*

Army Form C. 2118.

ADVS
50. (N) DIV.

| Place | Date | Hour | Summary of Events and Information | Remarks and references to Appendices |
|---|---|---|---|---|
| | 1917 Jany. | | | |
| FRICOURT | 12th | | At MVS whilst horses of DAC were being washed, microscopical work in connection with skin disease | EH |
| | 13th | | Inspected all transport animals of the 150th Infy Bde also the animals of the 151st Infy. Bde at BOTTOM WOOD. These animals were in good condition, and appeared to be well cared for by Transport officers. except the M. G. Co 150th I Bde They seemed too crowded. I represented this matter to Bde Major. Visited suspected skin cases at DAC | EH |
| | 14th | | Did microscopical work at MVS. and pointed out to OC MVS. that the grooming of the horses at the Rest Station could be improved Reported to DDVS. that S/t Houghton had departed to the Base for further instruction, also arrival of S/t Hill AVC to replace this NCO. | EH |
| | 15th | | Visited DAC and inspected 24 horses sent there for a rest from A/250 – a very poor lot. one died and two horses had to be destroyed | EH |

Instructions regarding War Diaries and Intelligence Summaries are contained in F. S. Regs., Part II. and the Staff Manual respectively. Title pages will be prepared in manuscript.

# WAR DIARY
*or*
# ~~INTELLIGENCE SUMMARY.~~
*(Erase heading not required.)*

A D V S
50 (N) DIV.

Army Form C. 2118.

| Place | Date | Hour | Summary of Events and Information | Remarks and references to Appendices |
|---|---|---|---|---|
| | 1917 Jany | | | |
| FRICOURT | 16th | | Inspected horses that were being clipped at D A C. | |
| | | | Visited 24th Bde RFA for ADVS 48th Div made arrangements to have one horse tested for Glanders | EH |
| | 17th | | Visited HQrs A + B/251 Bde and D/252 Bde in back area. Called at Mob-Vety Section. Some poor horses amongst the Artillery | EH |
| | 18th | | Inspected L.D. Horse 24th Bde RFA. whilst the test for Glanders was in operation. Told V.O i/c that this was not a case of Glanders. The ADVS 48 Div was away and I was instructed to supervise this test | |
| | | | Visited D A C gave orders for 5 debilitated horses to be destroyed as they were beyond treatment | EH |
| | 19th | | Inspected sick animals at ALBERT prior to evacuation to Base. | |
| | | | Visited M.V.S. and inspected 100 poor horses of D A C which had been sent to back area for a rest. | |
| | | | Inspected 149th Infy Bde transport animals at BOTTOM WOOD These animals were in excellent condition - good stable management | EH |

A5834 Wt. W4973/M687 750,000 8/16 D. D. & L. Ltd. Forms/C.2118/13.

Instructions regarding War Diaries and Intelligence Summaries are contained in F. S. Regs., Part II. and the Staff Manual respectively. Title pages will be prepared in manuscript.

# WAR DIARY
or
~~INTELLIGENCE~~ SUMMARY.
(Erase heading not required.)

ADVS
50th (N) DIV

Army Form C. 2118.

| Place | Date 1917 Jany | Hour | Summary of Events and Information | Remarks and references to Appendices |
|---|---|---|---|---|
| FRICOURT | 20th | | Attended conference of ADsVS. at DDVS' office 4th Army | |
| | | | Visited 7 DLI Lab. Bn. and gave V.O. i/c. instructions re skin cases | |
| | | | Saw CRA re DAC horses | EH |
| | 21st | | Inspected horses of the 1st 2nd Nn Fd Cos RE, 7th Fd Co RE. | |
| | | | 3rd Nn Fd Ambulance & 21st Cheshire Lab. Bn. | EH |
| | 22nd | | Saw sick horses prior to evacuation to Base. | |
| | | | Circulated to all VOs instructions to carefully examine all animals | |
| | | | for contagious stomatitis | EH |
| | 23rd | | At MVS inspected horses at Rest Station to see if any were fit to | |
| | | | return to their units. Inspected horses of DAC which were resting | |
| | | | near MVS. on account of debility | EH |
| | 24th | | Inspected suspected cases of mange at DAC. and had scrapings | |
| | | | taken from their skins for microscopical examination | EH |
| | 25th | | Inspected mules of DAC. Microscopical work at MVS | |
| | | | Again impressed on VOs the necessity for careful examination | |
| | | | for contagious stomatitis | |
| | 26th | | Conference with all VOs in the Div. Went to EDGEHILL and met | |

Army Form C. 2118.

Instructions regarding War Diaries and Intelligence Summaries are contained in F. S. Regs., Part II. and the Staff Manual respectively. Title pages will be prepared in manuscript.

# WAR DIARY
*or*
# INTELLIGENCE SUMMARY.
*(Erase heading not required.)*

ADVS
50 (N) DIV

| Place | Date 1917 Jany | Hour | Summary of Events and Information | Remarks and references to Appendices |
|---|---|---|---|---|
| FRICOURT | 26th | | and distributed 208 Remounts to units of DIV. Returned to FRICOURT on completion of duty at 2.30 am 27.1.17. | EH |
| | 27th | | Capt Postems AVC returned off leave, I detailed this officer for duty with 250th Bde RFA. | EH |
| RIBEMONT | 28th | | Left FRICOURT FARM and proceeded to RIBEMONT. Informed DDVS of my move | EH |
| | 29th | | Visited MVS. and inspected sick horses, and gave orders for some debilitated and emaciated horses to be destroyed as further treatment of these animals would be waste of public monies. Visited horses DAC in Rest Station | EH |
| | 30th | | Inspected horses 1st Infy Bde | |
| | 31st | | Attended conference of ADsVS at DDVS office 4th Army. Reported to DAQMG necessity for a permanent Transport Officer for each Brigade of Artillery. | EH |

E Stearne
Major AVC
ADVS 50th (N) DIV

A5834 Wt. W4973/M687 750,000 8/16 D. D. & L. Ltd. Forms/C.2118/13.

Confidential

Vol 20

# War Diary

of

# A.D. of V.S. 50th Division

from February 1st 1917 to February 28th 1917

## Volume XVII.

Instructions regarding War Diaries and Intelligence Summaries are contained in F. S. Regs., Part II. and the Staff Manual respectively. Title pages will be prepared in manuscript.

# WAR DIARY
*or*
# INTELLIGENCE SUMMARY.
*(Erase heading not required.)*

ADVS 50th DIV

Army Form C. 2118.

| Place | Date | Hour | Summary of Events and Information | Remarks and references to Appendices |
|---|---|---|---|---|
| RIBEMONT | 1.2.17 | | Inspected horses & stables in RIBEMONT | E.H. |
| | | | Left for BOULOGNE on leave to LONDON 10 days | E.H. |
| " | 2.2.17 | | | |
| BOIS. ST MARTIN | 14.2.17 | | Returned off leave from England. Reported my return to DDVS | E.H. |
| | | | Informed Vety. Officers that horses could now be sent to M.V.S. in moderation for evacuation | |
| | | | Saw R.T.O. LA FLAQUE and made arrangements for evacuation of horses to Base from that Railhead | E.H. |
| " | 15.2.17 | | Visited French stables in area, met French V.O. and made inquiries as to infectious & contagious diseases amongst his horses, on account of Divisional animals would occupy these stables when evacuated | E.H. |
| | | | Reported to Divl. H.Q. and received instructions, to arrange with Town Major PROYART to move M.V.S. to LA BRIQUETTERIE. Instructed O.C. MVS to have stables at the latter place thoroughly disinfected before occupying. | E.H. |
| | | | MVS moved into stables & Hut at LA BRIQUETTERIE | E.H. |
| | 16.2.17 | | Attended a conference of A.Ds.V.S. at D.D.V.S office 4th Army | |
| | 17.2.17 | | Inspected 250 Bde Skin cases | |
| | | | Accompanied G.O.C. & C.R.A. at inspection of all animals not on duty, of the | |

A5834 Wt. W4973/M687 750,000 8/16 D. D. & L. Ltd. Forms/C.2118/13.

Instructions regarding War Diaries and Intelligence Summaries are contained in F. S. Regs., Part II. and the Staff Manual respectively. Title pages will be prepared in manuscript.

# WAR DIARY *or* INTELLIGENCE SUMMARY.

*(Erase heading not required.)*

ADVS 50 (N) DIV

Army Form C. 2118.

| Place | Date | Hour | Summary of Events and Information | Remarks and references to Appendices |
|---|---|---|---|---|
| BOIS ST MARTIN | 17.2.-17 | | DAC and those of the 250 + 251 Bdes RFA<br>Attended conference at D.A.C. HQ with CRA. V.Os i/c Artillery and DAC Section commanders with reference to mange + suspected skin cases. I suggest evacuating all bad cases, to clip treat + work in segregation slight cases. Also suggested that more attention should be paid to ordinary stable management | EH |
| " | 18/2/17 | | Inspected I + II Sections DAC for skin disease, and separated the animals into 3 classes I Mange II Suspected III Healthy.<br>Visited MVS. Instructed DAC to collect 2 LDs from MVS which were fit for issue | EH |
| " | 19/2/17 | | Visited + inspected animals of 150 + 151 Infy Bdes 7th DLI and 7th F.F. 60 RE | EH |
| " | 20/2/17 | | Office work. | EH |
| " | 21/2/17 | | Visited + inspected horses under treatment at MVS, also Divl Sig Coy RE.<br>Reported to DHQ absence in some units of nose-bags + hay nets, especially 9 DLI. Transport, and consequent waste of forage<br>Arranged for 6 TU men to be sent to MVS to help until sick men were replaced | EH |

A5834 Wt. W4973/M687 750,000 8/16 D. D. & L. Ltd. Forms/C.2118/13.

Instructions regarding War Diaries and Intelligence Summaries are contained in F. S. Regs., Part II. and the Staff Manual respectively. Title pages will be prepared in manuscript.

# WAR DIARY
*or*
# INTELLIGENCE SUMMARY.
*(Erase heading not required.)*

ADVS 50 (N) DIV

Army Form C. 2118.

| Place | Date | Hour | Summary of Events and Information | Remarks and references to Appendices |
|---|---|---|---|---|
| BOIS ST MARTIN | 22/2/17 | | Visited animals of Grenade Dumps. They looked well. Gave instructions to Transport Sgt of the necessity of good stable management, and that these animals when returned to their own units should be in good working condition. Visited M.V.S. inspected skin cases awaiting evacuation. Saw Veterinary cases at D.A.C. clipping of suspected cases was proceeding | EH |
| " | 23/2/17 | | Visited 574 (Cornwall) A.T. Co. RE reclassified horses for DHQ. Horses in good condition. Visited 446 + 447 Fd Cos RE. latter need closer supervision, reported on this to "Q" | EH |
| " | 24/2/17 | | Inspected 40 horses being evacuated at Railhead, visited MVS + 1st Sec DAC skin cases | EH |
| | 25/2/17 | | Saw 4 suspected skin cases at B Echelon DAC. " all animals Divl A.S.C. - in good condition | EH |
| | 26/2/17 | | Inspected all animals 149 Inf Bde + 7 DLI | EH |
| | 27/2/17 | | Inspected worst skin cases at DAC. met DDVS 4th Army | |
| | 28/2/17 | | Conference at DDVS office 4th Army | EH |

E Hearne Major AVC.
ADVS 50 DIV.

A5834 Wt. W4973/M687 750,000 8/16 D. D. & L. Ltd. Forms/C.2118/13.

ORIGINAL

Confidential

Vol 21

# War Diary
of
A. D. V. S, 50th Division

from 1st March 1917 to 31st March 1917.

Volume XVIII

Instructions regarding War Diaries and Intelligence Summaries are contained in F. S. Regs., Part II. and the Staff Manual respectively. Title pages will be prepared in manuscript.

# WAR DIARY
*or*
# INTELLIGENCE SUMMARY. A.D.V.S. 50th (N) Div

(*Erase heading not required.*)

Army Form C. 2118.

| Place | 1917 Date | Hour | Summary of Events and Information | Remarks and references to Appendices |
|---|---|---|---|---|
| St MARTIN'S WOOD | MARCH 1st | | Visited M.V.S. inspected animals under treatment, and picked out those for evacuation to Base. Called at D.A.C. 1st + 2nd Sections, to see suspected mange cases and gave instructions to V.O. | |
| | | | Saw AA + QMG with reference to Sgt Dyet's application for a commission | |
| | | | Applied for a man capable of skinning horses, to be attached to M.V.S. All horses which die or are destroyed in the Division, could have the hides taken off by this man. The hides to be sent down to the Base with sick horses and disposed of there. An average of 20 hides per month would mean a saving to the Government of £300 a year. | E.H. |
| | 2nd | | Interviewed V.O.s at my office, checked over their weekly returns, and gave each the necessary instructions to assist him in his Vety. duties | |
| | | | Visited suspected skin cases at D.A.C. | |
| | | | Instructed Capt Crone A.V.C. to inspect a horse of the 7th N.F. reported by M.M.P. as having been ill-treated – bit injury | E.H. |
| | 3rd | | Went to Rail-head to see animals being evacuated to Base. | |
| | | | Accompanied G.O.C. Div to see horses of 1st 2nd Sections D.A.C., 2 Cos A.S.C. + Mobile Vety. Section | |
| | | | Submitted to D.A.D.O.S. Div. my recommendations re: nose-bags | |
| | | | Instructed several units to collect bran at M.V.S. | E.H. |
| | 4th | | Met A.D.V.S. of Div taking over, took him to M.V.S. and Transport Lines of Div. Explained that we had some cases of mange, and | |

A5834 Wt. W4973/M687 750,000 8/16 D. D. & L. Ltd. Forms/C.2118/13.

Instructions regarding War Diaries and Intelligence Summaries are contained in F. S. Regs., Part II. and the Staff Manual respectively. Title pages will be prepared in manuscript.

# WAR DIARY
*or*
# INTELLIGENCE SUMMARY. ADVS 50 (N) DIV
(*Erase heading not required.*)

Army Form C. 2118.

| Place | Date 1917 | Hour | Summary of Events and Information | Remarks and references to Appendices |
|---|---|---|---|---|
| St MARTIN'S WOOD | MARCH | | gave him every possible help. | |
| | 4th | | Instructed V.O.s when going their rounds to give Transport Officers and drivers every help as regards stable-management, and prevention of disease, also to give practical demonstrations in 1st aid etc. | |
| | | | Drew up and issued to all V.O.s a uniform method in the treatment of slight cases of mange. | E.H. |
| " | 5th | | Inspected animals of the 1st Fd Amb & 2nd Fd Amb. | |
| | | | Picked out animals at M.V.S. for evacuation to Base. | E.H. |
| " | 6th | | Attended at Rail-head and saw 22 animals before evacuation. | |
| | | | Inspected horses under treatment for skin disease at 1st Sec. D.A.C. a good improvement was noticed | |
| | | | Saw C.R.A. with reference to debility cases | |
| | | | Examined skin cases and gave instructions as to their treatment at 7 D.L.I. | |
| " | 7th | | Visited M.V.S. and 2nd Action D.A.C. | E.H. |
| " | 8th | | Inspected horses in Transport lines of the 250 Bde RFA | E.H. |
| MERICOURT SUR SOMME | 9th | | M.V.S moved to MERICOURT-SUR-SOMME | E.H. |
| | | | Inspected animals 251 Bde RFA. horses looking much better except C/251. | E.H. |
| | 10th | | Met and detained 334 Remounts at CERISY | E.H. |

A5834 Wt. W4973/M687 750,000 8/16 D. D. & L. Ltd. Forms/C.2118/13.

Instructions regarding War Diaries and Intelligence Summaries are contained in F. S. Regs., Part II. and the Staff Manual respectively. Title pages will be prepared in manuscript.

# WAR DIARY
*or*
# INTELLIGENCE SUMMARY. ADVS. 50 (N) DIV
*(Erase heading not required.)*

Army Form C. 2118.

| Place | Date 1917 | Hour | Summary of Events and Information | Remarks and references to Appendices |
|---|---|---|---|---|
| MERICOURT SUR SOMME | MARCH 11th | | MVS moved to WARFUSSÉE, as it was more central for Infy Bdes also near Railhead. Wrote to V.O.s for a comparative statement as regards the prevalence of mange among horses clipped at the proper season and those that were not clipped | E.A. |
| " | 12th | | Visited IV Army Remount Section and chose a Charger for Brig. Gen. 149 I Bde and 5 draught horses for Divl Train. Capt. Atkinson AVC returned off leave. | E.A. |
| " | 13th | | Visited 7th DLI horses and mules. also visited M.V.S. and saw 15 sick animals for evacuation. Inspected animals of 149 M.G. Co, No 2 Co ASC. 1st N.F Ambulance and 1st + 2nd Sections DAC. Applied to DDVS for the return of Vety Capt. Wallon a/250 to the Base, as he was unsuitable for the job. too old, slow, and not satisfactory. | E.A. |
| " | 14th | | Visited 150 Infy Bde to select riders for Staff Captain + Interpreter. Visited 250 Bde RFA transport lines. | E.A. |
| " | 15th | | Visited MVS. saw horses of 7th DLI. 1+2 Sections DAC and No 1 Co. Div Train. Reported to DDVS on rough shunting of trains at ROMESCAMP containing animals evacuated on the 13th inst. | E.A. |

A5834 Wt. W4973/M687 750,000 8/16 D. D. & L. Ltd. Forms/C.2118/13.

Army Form C. 2118.

Instructions regarding War Diaries and Intelligence Summaries are contained in F. S. Regs., Part II. and the Staff Manual respectively. Title pages will be prepared in manuscript.

# WAR DIARY
*or*
# INTELLIGENCE SUMMARY.
*(Erase heading not required.)*

| Place | 1917 Date MARCH | Hour | Summary of Events and Information | Remarks and references to Appendices |
|---|---|---|---|---|
| MERICOURT SUR SOMME | 16th | | Conference with VOs checked their returns, and gave instructions as to thorough disinfection of stables on vacating. Instructed OC 33rd Reserve Park to comply with GRO 1810 and send into MVS a stray horse in their possession | E.A. |
| | 17th | | Visited MVS with DAQMG saw animals for evacuation visited 1/1st N.F. Amb. Asked OC MVS to endeavour to find if there was any one in the near neighbourhood who would buy carcases, so that I could credit the Public with the money. But the nearest buyer was in AMIENS. | E.A. |
| | 18th | | Visited 3 Batteries of the 251 Bde and 1 battery of the 250 Bde RFA. Submitted Remount demand to "Q" office | E.A. |
| | 19th | | Submitted nominal roll of men of the MVS who had no leave for 12 mths or over Conference at office of DDVS IV Army | E.A. |
| | 20th | | Inspected eleven animals before evacuation at MVS. | E.A. |
| | 21st | | Met DDVS at MVS and inspected animals in Section and 149 MGCo. | E.A. |
| | 22nd | | Visited animals of 151 MGCo No 360 ASC 7 DLI and all the horses of the 251 Bde RFA. Visited vacated stables of 1 & 2 Sections DAC re disinfection | E.A. |

A5834 Wt. W4973/M687 750,000 8/16 D. D. & L. Ltd. Forms/C.2118/13.

Army Form C. 2118.

Instructions regarding War Diaries and Intelligence Summaries are contained in F. S. Regs., Part II. and the Staff Manual respectively. Title pages will be prepared in manuscript.

# WAR DIARY
*or*
# INTELLIGENCE SUMMARY. ADVS. 50 (N) DIV.
(*Erase heading not required.*)

| Place | Date 1917 MARCH | Hour | Summary of Events and Information | Remarks and references to Appendices |
|---|---|---|---|---|
| MERICOURT SUR SOMME | 23rd | | Conference of all VOs Division. Inspected eleven animals for evacuation. Informed by wire all units as to arrival of remounts. | E.H. |
| | 24th | | Met and distributed 222 Remounts at CERISY and gave Remount Officer a receipt for DAQMG. Wired Staff Captain 150 I. Bde to collect a charger at DHQ. Wired Staff Captain RA. that I was visiting Artillery horses with DDVS. | E.H. |
| | 25th | | Visited with DDVS 250 Bde + B/251 Bde sent 18 animals to MVS at CORBIE (43rd MVS) for evacuation unable to march. | E.H. |
| | 26th | | Visited MVS. and personally had 18 horses destroyed. These animals were useless and were unfit to travel to Base. They were incurable too far gone, and some were in pain. Doing duty for OC MVS for 10 days while on leave. | E.H. |
| | 27th | | Visited Railhead + MVS. inspected 54 animals prior to evacuation | E.H. |
| | 28th | | Issued instructions with regard to their forthcoming move of the MVS | E.H. |
| | 29th | | Attended at MVS. + examined horses returned by chaplains. | E.H. |
| | 30th | | Visited Railhead + evacuated 11 horses to Base. MVsection | E.H. |
| | 31st | | Moved to St GRATIEN. by road with 151 Bde Infy. DHQ move to MOLIENS AU BOIS. E Hearne Major AVC. ADVS. 50th Div | E.H. |

A5834 Wt. W4973/M687 750,000 8/16 D. D. & L. Ltd. Forms/C.2118/13.

Confidential

Vol 22

# War Diary

of

A. D. of V. S. 50th Division

from 1st April 1917 to 30th April 1917.

Volume XIX

Instructions regarding War Diaries and Intelligence Summaries are contained in F. S. Regs., Part II. and the Staff Manual respectively. Title pages will be prepared in manuscript.

# WAR DIARY
*or*
# INTELLIGENCE SUMMARY. A D V S 50th (N.) DIV.

(*Erase heading not required.*)

Army Form C. 2118.

| Place | Date | Hour | Summary of Events and Information | Remarks and references to Appendices |
|---|---|---|---|---|
| MOLLIENS au BOIS | 1st May 1917 | | In charge of Mobile Vety Section from 1-4.17 to 8.4.17 until O.C. returned off leave from England. Collected two LD's from FLESSELS left there by 251 Bde RFA. Evacuated and sent to MVS 2 HDs (ASC) suffering from mange. These animals had been at School of Instruction at MONTIGNY. Reported the matter to "A" as I consider these animals should have been reported to V.O. earlier. | E.H. |
| BEAUVAL | 2nd May | | Marched to BEAUVAL with MVS and collected one mule at FLESSELS left behind by 1st Co. ASC. At BEAUVAL I heard that 1 HD was left behind at BERTANGLE. I went to this place and collected the horse that night by Horse Ambulance. | E.H. |
| BOUQUE-MAISON | 3rd | | Proceeded to BOUQUEMAISON and then collected 2 horses left at HEM by 250 Bde RFA, one walked and the other had to be brought in by Float. | E.H. |
| RAME-COURT | 4th | | Evacuated 7 animals from BOUQUEMAISON to the Base, and then proceeded to RAMECOURT on arrival there. I found that remounts for the Div were due in at FREVENT at 6.0 pm. I proceeded to FREVENT and waited until train arrived which came in at 4.0 am 5.4.17. Distributed remounts to their various units. | E.H. |

A5834 Wt. W4973/M687 750,000 8/16 D. D. & L. Ltd. Forms/C.2118/13.

Instructions regarding War Diaries and Intelligence Summaries are contained in F. S. Regs., Part II. and the Staff Manual respectively. Title pages will be prepared in manuscript.

# WAR DIARY
*or*
# INTELLIGENCE SUMMARY.
(*Erase heading not required.*)

ADVS 50th (N) DIV

Army Form C. 2118.

| Place | Date | Hour | Summary of Events and Information | Remarks and references to Appendices |
|---|---|---|---|---|
| RAMECOURT | 5/4/17 | | Returned from FREVENT at 8.0 a.m. visited MVS and attended sick animals attached. Instructed Capt Porteous VO i/c 250 Bde RFA to evacuate his sick animals through 56th MVS being the nearest mobile section available. | EH |
| RAMECOURT. | 6/4/17 | | Issued to all VOs resumé of "Vesicular Dermatitis" by J Gregg MRCVS. and requested them to be very particular in their inspection of horses for this disease. Asked for an explanation from VO i/c 149 I. Bde re' the death of a horse belonging to that Bde. Explanation satisfactory | EH |
| ROELLECOURT. | 7/4/17 | | Moved to ROELLECOURT. Inspected remounts on the way from BOULOGNE to DAC 50th DIV | EH |
| LE CAUROY | 8/4/17 | | Moved to LE CAUROY. Informed DDVS 4th ARMY that a sick animal belonging to DAC was left at CORBIE. and asked for arrangements to be made for its collection | EH |
| .. | 9/4/17 | | Requested V.O i/c DAC to furnish explanation as to why no notification had reached me re DAC animal left at CORBIE<br>OC MVS returned off leave. Met remounts at FREVENT and distributed them. | EH |
| BERNEVILLE | 10/4/17 | | Moved to BERNEVILLE. | EH |
| | | | Inspected for DDVS 3rd Army, the 47th Reserve Park horses. I forwarded a detailed report as to their condition | EH |

A5834 Wt. W4973/M687 750,000 8/16 D. D. & L. Ltd. Forms/C.2118/13.

Instructions regarding War Diaries and Intelligence Summaries are contained in F. S. Regs., Part II. and the Staff Manual respectively. Title pages will be prepared in manuscript.

# WAR DIARY
*or*
# INTELLIGENCE SUMMARY.
*(Erase heading not required.)*

ADVS. 50th (N) DIV

Army Form C. 2118.

| Place | Date | Hour | Summary of Events and Information | Remarks and references to Appendices |
|---|---|---|---|---|
| BERNEVILLE | 11/4/17 | | Stopped in BERNEVILLE | EH |
| ARRAS | 12/4/17 | | Moved to ARRAS left MVS at BERNEVILLE, as it was more convenient to railhead - GUOY, and asked O.C. MVS to have his advanced collecting post at ARRAS. This arrangement worked out well as the sick animals were inspected by me every night and collected by personnel of MVS the following morning. Notified DDVS of my position. | EH |
| ARRAS | 13/4/17 | | Visited horses of the A/251 B/251 C/251 & D/251 Bde RFA and picked out about 30 poor debilitated animals for evacuation, owing to the very severe weather, short rations, & lack of remounts. The Artillery horses suffered much, but for military reasons and the above this could not be helped. Informed DDVS that V.O. i/c 250 Bde had been admitted to Hospital. Instructed Capt. Crone to proceed to 250 Bde for duty, and arranged with O.C. MVS to attend to animals of the Train. | EH |
| ARRAS | 14/4/17 | | Visited MVS and inspected 12 animals before evacuation. " DAC at MONCHIET and selected several animals for evacuation. Instructed O.C. 7 DLI to collect 4 L.D. mules from 47th Reserve Park by order of DDR. 3rd Army | EH |

A5834 Wt. W4973/M687 750,000 8/16 D. D. & L. Ltd. Forms/C.2118/13.

Instructions regarding War Diaries and Intelligence Summaries are contained in F. S. Regs., Part II. and the Staff Manual respectively. Title pages will be prepared in manuscript.

# WAR DIARY
*or*
# INTELLIGENCE SUMMARY. ADVS 50. (N) DIV.

(*Erase heading not required.*)

Army Form C. 2118.

| Place | Date | Hour | Summary of Events and Information | Remarks and references to Appendices |
|---|---|---|---|---|
| ARRAS | 15/4/17 | | Eleven men attached to M.V.S from 14. DIV. to help the MVS to bring sick and wounded horses to the Base.<br>DDVS informed of their arrival<br>Inspected Transport lines of the 150 + 151 I. Bdes + 446. Fd Co RE<br>Visited MVS<br>Saw Adjt. of Train ref to purchase of straw for 2 lbs hay due to Artillery horses. Explained to CRA the condition of his horses | EH. |
| ARRAS | 16/4/17 | | Inspected 81 animals at MVS before evacuation to Base, and others that were too debilitated, and beyond treatment were humanely destroyed. The hides were taken off + sent to the Base Vety Hospital for sale. The proceeds to be credited to the Public. The carcases were properly buried, in a place selected by the Town Major BERNEVILLE | EH. |
| ARRAS | 17/4/17 | | Visited MVS + advanced collecting post<br>Animals of other Divisions were admitted to our collecting Post and disposed of by our MVS, as the men could not find their MVS.<br>Inspected horses of C Sqd. Northd Hussars | |
| ARRAS | 18/4/17 | | Visited advd collecting Post. D.H.Qrs horses + HQ CRA.<br>Inspected 62 horses for evacuation | EH. |

Army Form C. 2118.

Instructions regarding War Diaries and Intelligence Summaries are contained in F. S. Regs., Part II. and the Staff Manual respectively. Title pages will be prepared in manuscript.

# WAR DIARY
*or*
# INTELLIGENCE SUMMARY. ADVS. 50th (N) Div

(*Erase heading not required.*)

| Place | Date | Hour | Summary of Events and Information | Remarks and references to Appendices |
|---|---|---|---|---|
| ARRAS. | 19/4/17. | | Visited M.V.S. and inspected sick animals and selected animals for evacuation, treatment, and some for destruction, unfit to travel to Base and not worth treating<br>Called on ADVS. 14 Div and arranged to help him to evacuate his sick animals, as he was full up with sick and injured animals<br>Visited collecting Posts. Conferred with V.Os as to their duties<br>Applied to D.D.V.S. to replace a Sergeant in Sgt. Walton's place Vety Sgt. to A/250. R.F.A. Requested adjt D.A.C. to forward 12 mules' nosebags which he brought from Boulogne to send them to M.V.S. so that I could distribute them to their respective units. | EH |
| ARRAS. | 20/4/17 | | Visited adv.d coll.g Posts and gave instructions as to animals collected<br>Inspected all animals of the D.A.C. | EH |
| ARRAS | 21/4/17 | | Visited M.V.S. + adv.d coll.g Posts. Examined 65 animals before evacuation | EH |
| ARRAS | 22/4/17 | | Consultation with DDVS 3rd Army<br>Attended at adv.d Remount Squadron FREVENT to select animals with O.C. Squadron for Division | EH |

Instructions regarding War Diaries and Intelligence Summaries are contained in F. S. Regs., Part II. and the Staff Manual respectively. Title pages will be prepared in manuscript.

# WAR DIARY
*or*
# INTELLIGENCE SUMMARY.
*(Erase heading not required.)*

ADVS 50th Div.

Army Form C. 2118.

| Place | Date | Hour | Summary of Events and Information | Remarks and references to Appendices |
|---|---|---|---|---|
| ARRAS. | 23/4/17 | | Examined 30 animals for evacuation to Base Vety Hospital | |
| | | | Again saw animals of DAC | |
| | | | Vety serjeant 149 I Bde brought before me for being slow and lazy at his work. I told this NCO that I would give him just one more chance and if he did not give satisfaction that he would be severely dealt with. | |
| | | | Submitted to DDVS roll of Vety serjeants doing duty with Division. | E.H. |
| ARRAS | 24/4/17 | | Visited and inspected all horses of the 250 Bde RFA. | |
| | | | Capt Porleins' 2 riders returned to MVS. One issued to V.O. DAC who had no horse, and one to V.O. 250 Bde RFA to replace one much too heavy for a rider. The latter was issued as an LD to Sigl Co HQrs Div. under instructions from DAQMG | E.H. |
| ARRAS | 25/4/17 | | Visited advd Coll. Post and arranged to send 5 wagon loads of wounded & sick horses to Base from Arras, and 51 horses at MVS to be sent to Base from Gouy | |
| | | | Visited 4 Cos ASC with OC Train 10 animals unfit for duty | |
| | | | Requested VOs to examine all vety equipment under their charge & report. | E.H. |
| COUTURELLE | 26/4/17 | | Moved to COUTURELLE, and handed over to MVS 14 Div. all cases unable to move | |
| | | | Inspected Bde Amm Col. horses of 46 Bde for DDVS at RONVILLE | E.H. |

A5834 Wt. W4973/M687 750,000 8/16 D. D. & L. Ltd. Forms/C.2118/13.

Instructions regarding War Diaries and Intelligence Summaries are contained in F. S. Regs., Part II. and the Staff Manual respectively. Title pages will be prepared in manuscript.

Army Form C. 2118.

# WAR DIARY
*or*
# INTELLIGENCE SUMMARY. ADVS 50th DIV.

*(Erase heading not required.)*

| Place | Date | Hour | Summary of Events and Information | Remarks and references to Appendices |
|---|---|---|---|---|
| COUTURELLE | 27/4/17 | | M.V.S. moved into COUTURELLE. | |
| | | | Inspected transport animals of 7 DLI & 151 Bde Infantry | |
| | | | Handed over 11 attached AVC men to 14 DIV on coming out of the Line. | |
| | | | Informed VOs artillery, that they could evacuate their sick through 14 DIV MVS at BERNEVILLE | EH. |
| | 28/4/17 | | Visited MVS and men's billets | |
| | | | " DAC at MONCHIET and inspected mules which were returned from Infy Bdes. They were in good working condition and showed that good care was taken of them whilst they were under the charge of the Infantry | EH. |
| | | | Submitted report to DDVS that there were 320 animals evacuated to base of which many were cases of shell wounds. | |
| | | | No animals were refused at Collecting Post no matter which formation they belonged to | EH. |
| | 29/4/17 | | Office duties. | EH. |
| | 30/4/17 | | Visited CRA and A. B. C. D Batteries 250 Bde RFA C Battery in poor condition, and the shoeing was bad, stable management could be improved. explained this to CRA and DADMG | EH |
| | | | E. Hearne. Major AVC ADVS 50 DIV. | |

A5834 Wt. W4973/M687 750,000 8/16 D. D. & L. Ltd. Forms/C.2118/13.

Vol 23

Confidential

# War Diary

of

## A. D. of V. S., 50th Division

from 1st May 1917 to 31st May 1917

## Volume XX

Instructions regarding War Diaries and Intelligence Summaries are contained in F. S. Regs., Part II. and the Staff Manual respectively. Title pages will be prepared in manuscript.

# WAR DIARY
or
# INTELLIGENCE SUMMARY. ADVS 50 DIV.
(Erase heading not required.)

Army Form C. 2118.

| Place | Date May | Hour | Summary of Events and Information | Remarks and references to Appendices |
|---|---|---|---|---|
| COUTURELLE | 1st | | Visited M.V.S. at MONCHIET. Inspected horses for evacuation and horses under treatment. Gave orders for issue of animals cured. | |
| | | | Inspected 7 D.L.I. Pioneer Battalion. Animals improving. | E.H. |
| BASSEUX | 2nd | | D.H.Qrs moved to BASSEUX. Saw sick horses being entrained at GUOY | E.H. |
| | | | Informed DDVS of my move | |
| | | | Wrote to Capt Crowe & Capt Atkinson for explanation why they omitted to show two missing animals on previous A.F. A 2000. | E.H. |
| BASSEUX | 3rd | | Inspected 5th Border transport, shoeing not good, drew O.C.s attention to it. | |
| | | | Inspected 8th Durham Light Infantry transport. Animals which were tied in dirty sheds, I ordered to have them picketed out in the open. 2 Officers' chargers were tied in one shed which was far too small for them and the horses could not possibly lie down. Nails all about the billets, I told the transport officer to have them picked up | |
| | | | Inspected 6th D.L.I. transport, animals looked well - Stable-management very good. Great care seemed to be taken of animals in this transport. | |
| | | | Inspected 2nd/2nd North[n] Field Ambulance horses - grooming good - ~~...~~ officers and Co.s riders packed too closely in stable, this was altered whilst I was there | E.H. |
| COUTURELLE | 4th | | Inspected 9th D.L. Infy Transport. The animals were in fair condition, shoeing not so good, instructed the shoeing smiths to be more careful in future, and pointed out their mistakes. | |

A5834 Wt. W4973/M687 750,000 8/16 D. D. & L. Ltd. Forms/C.2118/13.

Instructions regarding War Diaries and Intelligence Summaries are contained in F. S. Regs., Part II. and the Staff Manual respectively. Title pages will be prepared in manuscript.

# WAR DIARY
*or*
# INTELLIGENCE SUMMARY. A.D.V.S. 50. DIV.

(*Erase heading not required.*)

Army Form C. 2118.

| Place | Date May | Hour | Summary of Events and Information | Remarks and references to Appendices |
|---|---|---|---|---|
| COUTURELLE | 4th | | Inspected 151 Infy Bde M. G. Co. Picketing arrangements bad. Site chosen was too near "refuse dumps" nails and cartridge cases lying about. Animals picketed in buildings, should be picketed out in the open. Stable-management not so good. | |
| | | | Inspected animals 151 Bde HQrs | |
| | | | Treated two civilian horses, one horse was injured by British grenade whilst the horse was ploughing. | E.H. |
| | | | Moved to COUTURELLE. | |
| " | 5th | | Visited M.V.S. at MONCHIET and inspected animals collected | |
| | | | Dispatched 3 AVC men to advanced post ACHICOURT to assist in collecting sick horses from Divl Artillery still in the Line. | E.H. |
| | | | Advanced posts from M.V.S. do good work, and are most convenient for the Artillery, and consequently the M.V.S. is always in touch with the Artillery | |
| " | 6th | | Called on DDR 3rd Army for DAQMG with reference to remounts | |
| | | | Visited DDVS 3rd Army | |
| | | | Instructed VO i/c + Vety Sgts attached DAC, to attend a demonstration at M.V.S. in the use of the new anti-gas appliance for animals | E.H. |
| " | 7th | | Inspected Transports of the 4th 5th 6th + 7th Northd Fusiliers. Also 1st N. Fd Amb. | |
| | | | Instructed OC M.V.S. to have two sick animals collected from 151 Infy Bde | |
| | | | Provided Vety attendance for 3rd + 12th Labour Bn dets situated in my area | E.H. |

A5834 Wt. W4973/M687 750,000 8/16 D. D. & L. Ltd. Forms/C.2118/13.

Army Form C. 2118.

Instructions regarding War Diaries and Intelligence Summaries are contained in F. S. Regs., Part II. and the Staff Manual respectively. Title pages will be prepared in manuscript.

# WAR DIARY
*or*
# INTELLIGENCE SUMMARY. ADVS. 50. Div

*(Erase heading not required.)*

| Place | Date May | Hour | Summary of Events and Information | Remarks and references to Appendices |
|---|---|---|---|---|
| COUTURELLE | 8th | | Suggested to "Q" how the anti-gas appliances should be distributed | |
| | | | Inspected animals H.Qrs 150 Bde 4th Yorks, 4 E Yorks 5th Yorks 5th DLI and 150 Infy Bde M. G. Co. Also the 149 Infy Bde M.G. Co. and 447 Fd Co. RE | Ed |
| " | | | Applied to DDVS for a Vety Sgt to replace Vety Sgt. Walton evacuated sick from A Baty 250 Bde | |
| | | | Rider cured at MVS issued to OC Salvage Coy. | |
| | | | Forwarded to 150 M.G. Coy result of inquiries at ordnance re nosebags As this Coy. was short of nosebags, + consequently waste of forage | |
| " | 9th | | Visited MVS. + inspected 24 animals before their evacuation to Base | |
| | | | Inspected animals of Labour Bns at SAULTY + GOMBREMETZ | |
| | | | Instructed VOs + Vety Sgts Artillery Brigades to attend a demonstration in the use of the new anti-gas appliance for animals | |
| | | | Reported to "Q" and O.C. Train that bad straw was being issued to artillery horses | |
| | | | Saw DDR about shortage of horses in the Division, and explained that this entailed double work on the other horses | |
| | | | Called on Town Major SAULTY and gave instructions as to disinfecting stables which were recently occupied by horses affected with mange | Ed |

A5834 Wt. W4973/M687 750,000 8/16 D. D. & L. Ltd. Forms/C.2118/13.

Instructions regarding War Diaries and Intelligence Summaries are contained in F. S. Regs., Part II. and the Staff Manual respectively. Title pages will be prepared in manuscript.

# WAR DIARY
*or*
# INTELLIGENCE SUMMARY.
*(Erase heading not required.)*

A DVS 50 DIV

Army Form C. 2118.

| Place | Date May | Hour | Summary of Events and Information | Remarks and references to Appendices |
|---|---|---|---|---|
| COUTURELLE | 11th | | Assisted a French farmer, by operating on a colt which was bleeding after castration. Instructed OC MVS to collect a horse of the 29 DIV left with a farmer at GOUY | EA |
| " | 12th | | Visited MVS. MONCHIET. inspected those under treatment, and selected 9 for evacuation<br>Inspected 100 Remounts at DAC<br>Informed DDR of the issue of a chargr animal which had been put in Div<sup></sup>l orders, 7 days previously. | EA |
| " | 13th | | Inspected horses of A C + D Batteries 250 Bde at RONVILLE These animals have improved and the stable management was good<br>Discussed question of hiring some grazing for thin animals of DAC<br>Gave DDVS further information on Sgt Wallins unsuitability as a Vety Sgt. with a battery of artillery. | EA |
| " | 14th | | Instructed Sgt Dyet AVC to proceed to England to take up a commission<br>Requested an issue of bran to DAC mules | EA |
| " | 15th | | At FREVENT to see Eye Specialist<br>Applied to DDVS for a Vety. Sgt to replace Sgt Dyet at C/250 Bde | EA |
| " | 16th | | Visited MVS at MONCHIET inspected 13 animals for evacuation<br>Called on DDVS 3rd Army | EA |

A5834 Wt. W4973/M687 750,000 8/16 D. D. & L. Ltd. Forms/C.2118/13.

Instructions regarding War Diaries and Intelligence Summaries are contained in F. S. Regs., Part II. and the Staff Manual respectively. Title pages will be prepared in manuscript.

# WAR DIARY
*or*
# INTELLIGENCE SUMMARY.
(*Erase heading not required.*)

ADVS 50 DIV.

Army Form C. 2118.

| Place | Date May | Hour | Summary of Events and Information | Remarks and references to Appendices |
|---|---|---|---|---|
| COUTURELLE | 17th | | Inspected mange stables at GOUCHES, at request of Town Major. Disinfection had been properly carried out. | Est |
| " | 18th | | Reported a case to A.P.M. & DDVS of an Govt. horse having been handed over to a civilian farmer at COULLAMONT. No receiving Form No 1 left. It appears the farmer gave a sergeant 30 francs. Asked DDVS if I could collect this horse. The animal was collected later and is now in MVS. to await further instructions | |
| | | | Wrote to CRA ~~that~~ a Vety sgt would replace Sgt Wallis AVC | Est |
| BEAUMETZ | 19th | | Moved to BEAUMETZ-les-LOGES | |
| | | | Met and distributed at AUBIGNEY 70 LD mules for artillery and 10 LD mules for other units of Division. | Est |
| | 20th | | Received instructions to select 12 Riders & 19 HD horses at FREVENT and distributed these to units of Division | Est |
| | | | Wrote to Salvage officer to find out if any Vety stores had been collected by him – | |
| | 22nd | | Visited MVS and horses of HQ CRA | Est |
| COUIN. | 23rd | | Moved to COUIN. Made arrangements for a collecting post to be stationed at St AMAND to collect sick animals from Infantry. | Est |

A5834 Wt. W4973/M687 750,000 8/16 D. D. & L. Ltd. Forms/C.2118/13.

Instructions regarding War Diaries and Intelligence Summaries are contained in F. S. Regs., Part II. and the Staff Manual respectively. Title pages will be prepared in manuscript.

# WAR DIARY
*or*
# INTELLIGENCE SUMMARY. ADVS 50 DIV
*(Erase heading not required.)*

Army Form C. 2118.

| Place | Date May | Hour | Summary of Events and Information | Remarks and references to Appendices |
|---|---|---|---|---|
| COUVIN. | 24th | | Visited 4th + 4th E York's Transport. The latter were tied in dirty sheds. I had them picketed outside. All manure which was left by previous units was covered with earth as it was impossible to cart it all away | |
| | | | Inspected 22 horses at DOULLENS coming from ABBEVILLE for Infantry. | EH |
| " | 25th | | Visited horses of Labour dets at HENU HALLOY | |
| | | | Instructed Capt Newton to report on Vety. Sgt Hill 149 Inf/Bde. | |
| | | | Collecting post fixed at St AMAND | |
| | | | Collected at COULLEMONT rider left by an unknown unit | EH |
| " | 26th | | Sgts Smith + Holmes reported here for duty with Artillery. | |
| | | | Inspected animals of 6th 8th D.L.I. No 3 + 4 Coys ASC and 447 Fd Co RE | |
| | | | Took up the question of water supply at SOUASTRE. Reported to "Q" and had the matter put right | |
| | | | Wrote to DDR for authority to return one HD as unfit for work or further training | |
| " | 27th | | Visited + inspected animals of DAC. and MVS. | EH |
| | | | Asked OC MVS to have as many men as possible inoculated | |
| | | | Reported to DDVS destruction of a rider left with a broken leg by 4th Cav. Bde M.G. Coy. in COIGNEUX | EH |

A5834 Wt. W4973/M687 750,000 8/16 D. D. & L. Ltd. Forms/C.2118/13.

Instructions regarding War Diaries and Intelligence Summaries are contained in F. S. Regs., Part II. and the Staff Manual respectively. Title pages will be prepared in manuscript.

# WAR DIARY
*or*
# INTELLIGENCE SUMMARY.
*(Erase heading not required.)*

ADVS 50 DIV.

Army Form C. 2118.

| Place | Date May | Hour | Summary of Events and Information | Remarks and references to Appendices |
|---|---|---|---|---|
| COUIN | 28th | | Inspected at BEAURAINS + NEUVILLE VITASSE A. B + D Batteries 251 Bde RFA. These animals were much improved. Called at Advd Post ACHICOURT. Notified O.C. 14 Vety Hospital that Major Cornwall Advd GHQ wished to have his charger (recently evacuated) returned to him when fit | Est |
| " | 29th | | Visited + inspected 149 Infy Bde animals except 149 M G Coy. Lt. Jackson departure on leave. at MVS. | Est |
| | 30th | | Inspected A/250 + C/251 Batteries. At FISCHEUX; animals looking much better. Inspected 149 M. G. Coy. at MONCHY au BOIS | Est |
| | 31st | | Inspected animals of 9 DLI. 5th Borders 447 Fd Co RE. Called at collecting post St AMAND. Examined Sgt Hill AVC attd 149 Infy Bde and reported him as inefficient for his duties as Vety Sgt. and requested that this NCO be returned for further training | Est |
| | | | E Kearne Major AVC ADVS 50th Division | |

A5834 Wt. W4973/M687 750,000 8/16 D. D. & L. Ltd. Forms/C.2118/13.

Vol 24

Confidential

# War Diary

of

A. D. V. S., 50th North'bn Division

from 1. June 1917. to 30 June 1917

Volume XXI

Instructions regarding War Diaries and Intelligence Summaries are contained in F. S. Regs., Part II. and the Staff Manual respectively. Title pages will be prepared in manuscript.

# WAR DIARY
or
# ~~INTELLIGENCE SUMMARY.~~

(Erase heading not required.)

ADVS 50. DIVISION

Army Form C. 2118.

| Place | Date June | Hour | Summary of Events and Information | Remarks and references to Appendices |
|---|---|---|---|---|
| COUIN | 1st | | Visited 4th Yorks 1/3rd Nn Field Ambulance & 446 Fd Co RE's transport lines | |
| | | | Reported to DDVS 3rd Army & DDR on the different types of animals in the field as regards stamina & suitability | |
| | | | Inspected 21 animals at MVS prior to their evacuation to Base | |
| " | 2nd | | Visited 5th DLI & 5th Yorks transport at COIGNEUX | E.H. |
| | | | Circulated through medium of DRO's instructions on prevention of colic and "kicks" in lines | E.H. |
| " | 3rd | | Met and distributed from SAULTY 102 Remounts for artillery & 46 for other units. These animals were a good lot and looked well | |
| | | | Attended conference of ADsVS at 3rd Army | |
| | | | Visited MVS at MONCHIET. | E.H. |
| " | 4th | | Inspected all animals of 149 Infy Bde at MONCHY AU BOIS | |
| | 5th | | Inspected Batteries wagon lines of the A. B. & D/250 Bde near BEAURAINS. also inspected 1st & 2nd Sections D.A.C. 50 Div. a great improvement was noticed in the latter | E.H. |
| | | | Visited MVS MONCHIET. | E.H. |
| | 6th | | Visited HQ Divl Train, HQ DAC & B Echelon DAC | E.H. |
| | | | Inserted notice in DRO of a stray mule in MVS | |
| | | | Instructed Capt [illegible] to attend 1 & 2 Secs DAC in relief of Capt Wright | E.H. |
| " | 7th | | Office work, and attendance on HQ [illegible] Div | E.H. |

A5834 Wt. W4973/M687 750,000 8/16 D. D. & L. Ltd. Forms/C.2118/13.

Army Form C. 2118.

# WAR DIARY
*or*
~~INTELLIGENCE SUMMARY.~~ ADVS. 50 DIV.
*(Erase heading not required.)*

Instructions regarding War Diaries and Intelligence Summaries are contained in F. S. Regs., Part II. and the Staff Manual respectively. Title pages will be prepared in manuscript.

| Place | Date June | Hour | Summary of Events and Information | Remarks and references to Appendices |
|---|---|---|---|---|
| COUIN. | 8th | | Visited A Battery 250 Bde 7th Fd Co RE & MVS. MONCHIET and inspected animals before evacuation to Base. | EH. |
| " | 9th | | Inspected horses of 4th Yorks 5th Yorks. 5th DLI. & 1st/1st No 7d Ambulance. Received report from 8th DLI. that dandy brushes were not being supplied in sufficient quantity for grooming, reported matter to "Q" Report to DDVS 3rd Army on the advantage of an intermediate mule shoe between sizes 15 & 16 being introduced. | |
| " | 10th | | Applied to DDR re two vicious mules as to their disposal for further training Informed "Q" re accommodation for horses and men at MVS. | EH |
| " | 11th | | Inspected all animals of 250 Bde RFA A/251 and two Sections DAC Brought to notice of Q two cases of "Kicks" which necessitated destruction, drawing attention to D.R.O. re prevention of "Kicks" | EH |
| " | 12th | | Visited No 1 2 3 & 4 Cos ASC & MVS Selected site for MVS at FISCHEUX Reported to DDR of a vicious mule at 149 Bde MG Co Recommended the promotion of Lt Jackson V.O. i/c DAC to the temporary rank of Capt on completion of his 12 months service | EH |
| " | 13th | | Visited 7th Fd Co RE. HQrs 151 Inf Bde 446 Fd Co RE & 150 MG. Co | EH EH |

A5834 Wt. W4973/M687 750,000 3/16 D. D. & L. Ltd. Forms/C.2118/13.

Army Form C. 2118.

Instructions regarding War Diaries and Intelligence Summaries are contained in F. S. Regs., Part II. and the Staff Manual respectively. Title pages will be prepared in manuscript.

# WAR DIARY
*or*
# ~~INTELLIGENCE~~ SUMMARY.
(*Erase heading not required.*)

ADVS 50 DIV

| Place | Date JUNE | Hour | Summary of Events and Information | Remarks and references to Appendices |
|---|---|---|---|---|
| COUIN | 14th | | Inspected 22 animals for evacuation to Base at MONCHIET | |
| | | | Instructed OCMVS to send a man to take over from 30th MVS | |
| | | | Detailed 4 men for duty at 7th Corps Vety Det[t] | E.H. |
| | 15th | | Interview with ADVS 18th DIV re taking over his Artillery horses | E.H. |
| | 16th | | Interview with ADVS VII Corps, visited MVS and inspected animals for evacuation. Saw 3 French horses suffering from mange. | E.H. |
| | 17th | | Placed a field close to COIGNEUX out of bounds for British horses also a farm in COIGNEUX owing to the above having 3 horses with mange. Informed DDR of the issue of a stray to DAC after 7 days notice in orders | E.H. |
| Nr BOISLEUX au MONT | 18th | | Div HQ moved to S17 a 9.4 and MVS to FISCHEUX notified ADVS VII Corps. | E.H. |
| | 19th | | Visited 149 Infy Bde & 150 Infy Bde transport lines | |
| | | | Visited ~~five~~ Batteries 50 DIV with Staff Capt. RA. The C/251 Battery still needs more careful stable management, explained to CRA. | E.H. |
| | 20th | | Visited MVS inspected 3 Batteries near FISCHEUX | E.H. |
| | 21st | | MVS moved to S16 a 4.8. | E.H. |
| | 22nd | | Interview with DDVS 3rd Army. | E.H. |

E Hearne Major ADVS 50 DIV

Instructions regarding War Diaries and Intelligence Summaries are contained in F. S. Regs., Par. II. and the Staff Manual respectively. Title pages will be prepared in manuscript.

# WAR DIARY
*or*
# ~~INTELLIGENCE SUMMARY.~~ ADVS. 50(N) Division

*(Erase heading not required.)*

Army Form C. 2118.

| Place | Date | Hour | Summary of Events and Information | Remarks and references to Appendices |
|---|---|---|---|---|
| | 23.6.17 | | ADVS on leave, I (A.A. Wright Capt AVC) acting. Visited with ADVS VII Corps 251 Bgde RFA inspecting the horses for mange. One brigade of the 250 RFA also visited. Visited O/c Ammunition Railhead BOISLEUX-au-MONT to arrange for SAA cases to be temporarily lent to MVS (for journey down to Base only) to carry water for animals evacuated. On arrival at destination they would be handed into Ordnance. Informed DDVS Army of ADVS having gone on leave. Inspected twenty one animals for evacuation. | AAW |
| | 24.6.17 | | Arranged for MVS to have on loan a Soyer Stove from 1/1 N Field Amb. Reported to Q that all winter underclothing had been returned to Ordnance Stores. Visited with ADVS VII Corps 250 Bgde RFA horses | AAW |
| | 25.6.17 | | Visited and inspected the horses and mules of the DAC with ADVS VII Corps. Inspected twenty four horses suffering for mange previous to evacuation | AAW |
| | 26.6.17 | | Informed DDR Army of having issued stray mule to DAC. Information re Shell Cases forwarded to ADVS VII Corps. Arrangements made for the disinfection of the horse rugs of the Divisional Artillery. ADVS VII Corps visited Headquarters | AAW |
| | 27.6.17 | | Inspected sixteen animals for evacuation. Visited all batteries of the 251 Bgde. Case of horse lost by Captain Newton AVC placed in the hands of Divisional APM. Visited 47 Bgde RFA inspected horse with mange. | AAW |

A5834 Wt. W4973/M687 750,000 8/16 D. D. & L. Ltd. Forms/C.2118/13.

Instructions regarding War Diaries and Intelligence Summaries are contained in F. S. Regs., Part II. and the Staff Manual respectively. Title pages will be prepared in manuscript.

# WAR DIARY
*or*
# INTELLIGENCE SUMMARY.
*(Erase heading not required.)*

Army Form C. 2118.

ADVS 50N Division

| Place | Date | Hour | Summary of Events and Information | Remarks and references to Appendices |
| --- | --- | --- | --- | --- |
| | 28.6.17 | | Visited the batteries of the 250 Bde RFA. | SHW |
| | 29.6.17 | | Met and distributed remounts at SAULTY 4AM. Informed Q types of revolvers in possession of Veterinary Officers. S.H. Wright Capt AVC appointed D.A.D.V.S. 9th Division. Issued Remount at M.V.S. 8th D.L.I. Informed Q of stores taken over by M.V.S. from 18th Division | SHW |
| | 30.6.17 | | A.D.V.S. VII Corps at D.H.Q. Informed by letter A.D.V.S. VII Corps that the disinfection of horse rugs of the Divisional Artillery was in progress. | SHW |
| | | | S.H. Wright Capt AVC<br>Officer Commanding<br>1/1 North. Mobile Vet. Section<br>for<br>A.D.V.S.<br>50 (N) Division | |

CONFIDENTIAL.

# WAR DIARY

OF THE

DADVS

50th (N) DIVISION

JULY 1917

VOL XXII

Instructions regarding War Diaries and Intelligence Summaries are contained in F. S. Regs., Part II. and the Staff Manual respectively. Title pages will be prepared in manuscript.

# WAR DIARY
*or*
# INTELLIGENCE SUMMARY.
(*Erase heading not required.*)

A.D.V.S 50th Division

Army Form C. 2118.

| Place | 1917 Date | Hour | Summary of Events and Information | Remarks and references to Appendices |
|---|---|---|---|---|
| BOISLEUX au MONT | July 1st | | Capt Wright acting ADVS. visited 1st/3rd N. F. Amb. Capt Newton AVC (TF) took over duties of O.C. 1st/1st N. Mob. Vety. Section | E.H. |
| " | 2nd | | a/ADVS attended inspection with ADVS VII Corps of 250 + 251 Bdes RFA | E.H. |
| " | 3rd | | a/DADVS inspected 1st + 2nd Sections + B Echelon 50th D.A.C. | E.H. |
| " | 4th | | I returned from leave and took over duties of DADVS from Capt Wright AVC. Informed ADVS Corps that all rugs of Divl Artillery had been disinfected | E.H. |
| " | 5th | | Visited M.V.S. Major J H Wright AVC (TF) left Division to take up his appointment of DADVS 9th Division | E.H. |
| " | 6th | | Visited 250 + 251 Bdes R F A. Inspected horse lines of 149 + 151 Infy Bdes. As Major Wright AVC was not replaced by a Vety Officer I detailed Artillery V.Os to take Vety charge of a brigade of Infantry each | E.H. |
| | 7th | | Conference of DADsVS at ADVS' office VII Corps. Visited all Companies of Divl Train. Reported to D.D.R. Army that there were 3 animals for casting | E.H. |

A5834 Wt. W4973/M687 750,000 8/16 D. D. & L. Ltd. Forms/C.2118/13.

Instructions regarding War Diaries and Intelligence Summaries are contained in F. S. Regs., Part II. and the Staff Manual respectively. Title pages will be prepared in manuscript.

# WAR DIARY
*or*
# INTELLIGENCE SUMMARY. ADVS. 50th Division

(*Erase heading not required.*)

Army Form C. 2118.

| Place | 1917 Date | Hour | Summary of Events and Information | Remarks and references to Appendices |
|---|---|---|---|---|
| BOISLEUX AU MONT | July 8th | | Inspected 149 + 151 Infy Bdes with ADVS VII Corps. | |
| | | | Inspected suspected mange cases at 251 Bde R.F.A. | E.H. |
| " | 9th | | Forwarded request of OC Train for drawing his full forage ration as grazing was of a poor quality. | |
| | | | Detailed one Cpl from MVS for duty with Dipping Bath MONDICOURT | |
| | | | Visited MVS 7th D.L.I. (Pioneers) 447 RE Fd Co. + 250 Bde RFA. | E.H. |
| " | 10th | | Met + distributed remounts at BEAUMETZ. I inspected horses and found 3 cases of mange. Reported the matter + had horses sent to MVS. 500 horses dipped at MONDICOURT. | |
| | | | Visited MONDICOURT + MVS | |
| | 11th | | Visited all the animals of DAC, 149 Infy Bde + suspected mange cases of 250 + 251 Bde | E.H. |
| | 12th | | Visited 7th RE Fd Co. 446 + 447 RE Fd Cos and 150 Infy Bde | E.H. |
| | 13th | | Visited 4 Cos Train + Divl Signals | E.H. |
| | 14th | | At Conference of ADVS VII Corps. Inspected 1st/3rd N.Fd Amb at GOUY + BARLEY | E.H. |
| | 16th | | Inspected Infantry horses + ASC horses with ADVS VII Corps | E.H. |

A5834 Wt. W4973/M687 750,000 8/16 D. D. & L. Ltd. Forms/C.2118/13.

Instructions regarding War Diaries and Intelligence Summaries are contained in F. S. Regs., Part II. and the Staff Manual respectively. Title pages will be prepared in manuscript.

# WAR DIARY
*or*
# INTELLIGENCE SUMMARY.
*(Erase heading not required.)*

Army Form C. 2118.

A DVS 50th Division

| Place | 1917 Date | Hour | Summary of Events and Information | Remarks and references to Appendices |
|---|---|---|---|---|
| BOISLEUX AU MONT | July 17th | | Inspected 39 Remounts at BEAUMETZ and distributed same to units | EH. |
| " | 18th | | Visited 7 DLI. (Pioneers) 447 Fd Co RE, 149 + 151. Infy Bdes | EH. |
| " | 19th | | Visited MVS. Divl. HQ horses. Conference with V.Os Division | EH. |
| " | 20th | | Visited horse lines 250+251 Bdes RFA and DAC. 1/1. N Fd Amb. | EH. |
| " | 21. | | Visited suspected skin cases of 3 sections DAC. Ordered special iodoform for special sp-cases. | EH. |
| " | 22nd | | Inspected skin cases 250 + 251 Bdes RFA. | EH. |
| " | 23rd | | Visited 149 Infy Bde. At MONDICOURT Bath. Called at MVS | EH. |
| " | 24th | | Saw skin cases of A B.D Batteries RFA at BEAURAINS + C Battery at DOUCHY-AYETTE | EH. |
| " | 25th | | Visited 149 MGC. 4 NF 5 NF 6 N.F. 7 N.Fusiliers + 447 Fd Co RE | EH. |
| " | 26th | | Visited 4 Cos Train and 150, 151. Infy Transport | EH. |
| | 27. | | Conference with V.Os Division. Inspected DAC mules | EH. |
| | 28. | | Conference with ADVS VII Corps. Picked out horses for evacuation at MVS | EH. |
| | 29th | | Inspected with CRE. 7th Fd Co. 446. 447. Fd Co. + Divl Signals | EH |

A5834 Wt. W4973/M687 750,000 8/16 D. D. & L. Ltd. Forms/C.2118/13.

Instructions regarding War Diaries and Intelligence Summaries are contained in F. S. Regs., Part II. and the Staff Manual respectively. Title pages will be prepared in manuscript.

# WAR DIARY
*or*
# INTELLIGENCE SUMMARY.
*(Erase heading not required.)*

ADVS 50. Division

Army Form C. 2118.

| Place | Date 1917 | Hour | Summary of Events and Information | Remarks and references to Appendices |
|---|---|---|---|---|
| BOISLEUX AU MONT. | July 30. | | Visited MVS inspected animal under treatment | E.H. |
| | 31st. | | Inspected all horses of 250 Bde. RFA with ADVS VII Corps. | E.H. |
| | | | E Stearne. Major. | |
| | | | 1st August 1917. DADVS 50th Division | |

A5834 Wt. W4973/M687 750,000 8/16 D. D. & L. Ltd. Forms/C.2118/13.

Confidential



# War Diary

of

# D. A. D. V. S., 50th Division

from August 1st. 1917

to August 31st. 1917.

Volume XXIII.

Instructions regarding War Diaries and Intelligence Summaries are contained in F. S. Regs., Part II. and the Staff Manual respectively. Title pages will be prepared in manuscript.

# WAR DIARY ~~or~~ ~~INTELLIGENCE SUMMARY.~~

(Erase heading not required.)

Army Form C. 2118.

D.A.D.V.S, 50th Division

| Place | Date August 1917 | Hour | Summary of Events and Information | Remarks and references to Appendices |
|---|---|---|---|---|
| BOISLEUX au MONT | 1/8/17 | | Inspected 27 animals for evacuation at Mobile Vety. Secn. Mange cases amongst animals of 50th Divl. Train A.S.C. were dipped in bath at MONDICOURT. | E.H. |
| | 2/8/17 | | Inspected A. B. C. Batteries 251 Bgde R.F.A. especially for mange. All four batteries of 250 Bgde R.F.A visited for same purpose. | E.H. |
| | 3/8/17 | | 200 horses of First Line Infantry Transport dipped in bath at MONDICOURT. Infected horses of R.F.A. also dipped. Inspected again, mange cases of 251 Bgde. R.F.A. | E.H. |
| | 4/8/17 | | Attended conference of D.A.D.s V.S. at Corps HQrs. at office of A.D.V.S. Inspected 9 animals at M.V.S. before their evacuation. Examined A.S.C animals which had been dipped in mange bath on 1st inst. Conducted an experiment with sulphur fumes chamber on 3 animals at M.V.S. | E.H. |
| | 5/8/17 | | Visited M.V.S with A.D.V.S. Corps. Inspected B Echelon 50th D.A.C and skin cases of 1st + 2nd sections 50th D.A.C. | E.H. |
| | 6/8/17 | | Visited M.V.S. with A.D.V.S Corps. Met + distributed, after examination, 18 Remounts at MIRAUMONT. | E.H. |
| | 7/8/17 | | Met D.D. Remounts at M.V.S. + accompanied him during his inspection of surplus horses. Inspected animals of 58th D.A.C + 290 Bgde R.F.A. recently attached for administration. | E.H. |
| | 8/8/17 | | Inspected 24 animals at M.V.S. before their evacuation. Routine Work. | E.H. |
| | 9/8/17 | | Visited M.V.S and issued several of the surplus animals to units deficient. Visited + inspected 245 M.G. Coy. 150 Inf. Bgde. + 50th Divl Train A.S.C | E.H. |
| | 10/8/17 | | Held conference of executive V.O's. at my office. Visited M.V.S. + selected animals for Inf. Transport + Artillery. Visited 2 Batteries of 290 Bgde R.F.A. 58th Division (attached) | E.H. |

Instructions regarding War Diaries and Intelligence Summaries are contained in F. S. Regs., Part II. and the Staff Manual respectively. Title pages will be prepared in manuscript.

# WAR DIARY
or
## ~~INTELLIGENCE SUMMARY.~~ D.A.D.V.S, 50th Division

(Erase heading not required.)

Army Form C. 2118.

| Place | Date | Hour | Summary of Events and Information | Remarks and references to Appendices |
|---|---|---|---|---|
| BOISLEUX au MONT | 11/8/17 | | Attended conference of D.A.D.V.S at office of A.D.V.S. Corps<br>Inspected 27 animals at M.V.S before their evacuation. | E.H. |
| | 12/8/17 | | Visited all sections and HdQrs 50th D.A.C. Selected 2 mules for 149 M.G. Coy at M.V.S.<br>Informed A.D.V.S. Corps that no complaints had been lodged about Zinc collar pads producing galls. | E.H. |
| | 13/8/17 | | Inspected animals of all batteries 250 Bgde R.F.A. Routine Work. Submitted to A.D.V.S. Corps list of men in M.V.S. for replacement, if necessary, by older men. | E.H. |
| | 14/8/17 | | Visited & inspected animals of 3 Coy. 50th Divl Train A.S.C. Selected site for winter standings for M.V.S. Selected a ridel for 245 M.G. Coy. Visited several Labour Coys & Pontoon Parks to arrange veterinary attendance on their animals. | E.H. |
| | 15/8/17 | | Inspected 39 animals at M.V.S before their evacuation. Visited moto detachments of Labour Coys. to secure for them veterinary attendance providing they were within reasonable distance. Of those for whom I was unable to arrange attendance I informed A.D.V.S. Corps, who provided for them. | E.H. |
| | 16/8/17 | | Visited & inspected B & C Batteries 250 Bgde R.F.A, B.C & D. Batteries 251 Bgde R.F.A, No 1 Secn. 27th Reserve Park and 149 M.G. Coy<br>Inspected a mule - float case at GOUY and ordered M.V.S. to remove it. Submitted my report to A.D.V.S Corps on the disadvantages of the Turner-Bitty Horse Shoe Pads after having experimented with a set in M.V.S. Requested A.D.V.S. Corps to give permission for the stabling to be commenced with, on winter standings, selected on 14th inst. | E.H. |
| | 17/8/17 | | Held conference with V.Os at my office. Visited transport lines of 150 Inf Bgde. Reported to A.D.M.S on the falling off in condition of the H.D. water cart horses in 3rd Fd Ambce, the bad condition of standings and occupation of unhealthy village stables by riders of this Ambulance. | E.H. |

A5834 Wt. W4973/M687 750,000 8/16 D. D. & L. Ltd. Forms/C.2118/13.

Instructions regarding War Diaries and Intelligence Summaries are contained in F. S. Regs., Part II. and the Staff Manual respectively. Title pages will be prepared in manuscript.

# WAR DIARY
~~or~~
## ~~INTELLIGENCE SUMMARY.~~
(Erase heading not required.)

D.A.D.V.S. 50th Division

Army Form C. 2118.

| Place | Date | Hour | Summary of Events and Information | Remarks and references to Appendices |
|---|---|---|---|---|
| BOISLEUX au MONT | 18/8/17 | | Inspected 34 animals at M.V.S before their evacuation. Issued 2 H.D. Horses to 5th Border and 4th Yorks Regt. Arranged for the casting of a mule belonging to 58th Div. Amm. Col. when visiting unit today. | B.H. |
| | 19/8/17 | | Visited & inspected 1st section D.A.C. and reported on their mules being dirty and falling off in condition. Submitted to 'Q' recommendations & scale for the issue of chaff cutters to units – these cutters to be held by units permanently. | B.H. |
| | 20/8/17 | | Visited A/251 Bgde R.F.A., 150 Inf. Bgde, 2/2 Northbn Fld Ambce and 3 Fld Coy. RE. | B.H. |
| | 21/8/17 | | Selected 2 H.D. horses for 7th NF and 2 L.D. horses for Artillery. Visited Mob. Vety. Secn. | B.H. |
| | 22/8/17 | | Inspected 43 animals at M.V.S before their evacuation. Visited 149 Inf Bgde HQrs. Submitted to D.D.V.S Army a report on Impalpable Iodoform as a treatment for Ophthalmia. Instructed V.O. i/c 58th Div. Artillery (attached this Div.) to evacuate all his worst skin cases to this Division's M.V.S. before the Artillery rejoined its own Div. | B.H. |
| | 23/8/17 | | Corps General visited M.V.S to see horses under treatment for mange in sulphur gas chamber. Instructed V.O. i/c D.A.C. to furnish a certificate that all animals that were handed over from unit under his charge to 23 A. Bgde R.F.A were workably sound and free from contagious or infectious disease. | B.H. |
| | 24/8/17 | | Conference of V.Os in my office. Inspected with A.D.V.S Corps all mares in Division for breeding purposes, minutely examining all those selected to ensure their being free from hereditary disease. Distributed remounts to Infantry Bgdes. Evacuated through this M.V.S. 78 riders of South Irish Horse. Issued 3 riders to 251 Bgde R.F.A & 2 riders to 250 Bgde R.F.A. | B.H. |

A5834 Wt. W4973/M687 750,000 8/16 D. D. & L. Ltd. Forms/C.2118/13.

Instructions regarding War Diaries and Intelligence Summaries are contained in F. S. Regs., Part II. and the Staff Manual respectively. Title pages will be prepared in manuscript.

# WAR DIARY
or
# ~~INTELLIGENCE SUMMARY.~~

(Erase heading not required.)

Army Form C. 2118.

D.A.D.V.S, 50th Division

| Place | Date | Hour | Summary of Events and Information | Remarks and references to Appendices |
|---|---|---|---|---|
| BOISLEUX au MONT | 25/8/17 | | Inspected 26 more rides of South Irish Horse before their evacuation through M.V.S. | |
| | | | Inspected 14 animals of Divn + units attached before their evacuation | |
| | | | Admitted 8 Riders from Corps Cavalry into M.V.S for retesting for glanders - all having been doubtful reactors when previously tested. | EA |
| | 26/8/17 | | Visited + inspected animals of Div. HQrs + Divl. Signal Coy. RE. | EA |
| | 27/8/17 | | Inspected 24 animals at M.V.S. before their evacuation. Routine Work. | EA |
| | 28/8/17 | | Visited and inspected animals of all 4 Coys. 50th Divl Train A.S.C. Searched neighbourhood of BOISLEUX au MONT for a more suitable site for winter standings for M.V.S. Called for monthly mange charts from all VOs of Division. | EA |
| | 29/8/17 | | ROUTINE Work. | EA |
| | 30/8/17 | | Visited all Batteries of 250 Bde RFA. and M.V.S. | EA |
| | | | Issued L.D. horse to 251 Bde RFA. | |
| | 31/8/17 | | Held conference with VOs. of Division in my office. | EA |
| | | | DDVS. Army visited M.V.S. to inspect horse lines + billets. | |
| | | | Issued 1 L.D horse to 6th DLI. | |

1st Sept. 1917

E. Hearne Maj. AVC.
D.A.D.V.S, 50th Division

A5834 Wt. W4973/M687 750,000 8/16 D. D. & L. Ltd. Forms/C.2118/13.

Confidential

Vol 27

# War Diary

of

D.A.D.V.S. 50th Division

from Sept. 1st 1917 to Sept 30th 1917

Volume 24.

Instructions regarding War Diaries and Intelligence Summaries are contained in F. S. Regs., Part II. and the Staff Manual respectively. Title pages will be prepared in manuscript.

# WAR DIARY
~~or~~
## ~~INTELLIGENCE SUMMARY~~.
(*Erase heading not required.*)

Army Form C. 2118.

D.A.D.V.S., 50th Divn

| Place | Date | Hour | Summary of Events and Information | Remarks and references to Appendices |
|---|---|---|---|---|
| BOISLEUX-au-MONT | 1 9/17 | | Inspected 30 animals at M.V.S. prior to their evacuation to Base Veterinary Hospital. | |
| | | | Attended conference of D.A.Ds.V.S. at office of A.D.V.S. VI Corps. Third Army. | |
| | | | Held conference with all V.Os of Division on the subject of skin disease amongst animals of Divn. Authority having been given to evacuate mange & suspected mange I informed them it was my intention to give units a thorough cleaning out before winter set in. | E.H. |
| | 2 9/17 | | Visited and inspected 7th, 446th & 447th Fd Coys. R.E., Inspected 72 animals at M.V.S. before their despatch to Base | E.H. |
| | 3 9/17 | | Accompanied A.D.V.S. VI Corps on a tour of inspection round all Artillery, D.A.C. & Infantry Transport Lines. Again impressed on V.Os the importance of securing as many hides from carcases as possible, & of attending to urgent veterinary cases when requested in cases where animals belonged to units of some other Formation. | E.H. |
| | 4 9/17 | | Inspected 20 animals at M.V.S. before their evacuation to Base. | |
| | | | Made veterinary arrangements for the attendance of Labour Coys RE in Divisional Area. | |
| | | | Submitted to A.D.V.S. Corps a report on the arrangements existing in the Division for the issue of Bran & Linseed & recommended their issue, on a suggested scale, from M.V.S. | |
| | | | Attended Conference on "Clipping during winter months". | E.H. |
| | 5 9/17 - 16 9/17 | | Acting A.D.V.S. at Corps H.Qrs for 12 days during absence of A.D.V.S. on leave. | E.H. |
| | | | | E.H. |
| | 17 9/17 | | Inspected 33 animals before their despatch to Base Vety. Hospital from M.V.S. | |
| | | | Distributed 113 remounts which arrived by road - 42 to other units, 71 to Artillery units. | E.H. |
| | | | Returned to Division from Corps, on the return from leave of A.D.V.S. Corps. | |

A5834 Wt. W4973/M687 750,000 8/16 D. D. & L. Ltd. Forms/C.2118/13.

Instructions regarding War Diaries and Intelligence Summaries are contained in F. S. Regs., Part II. and the Staff Manual respectively. Title pages will be prepared in manuscript.

# WAR DIARY
*or*
# ~~INTELLIGENCE~~ SUMMARY.
*(Erase heading not required.)*

Army Form C. 2118.

D.A.D.V.S., 50th Division

| Place | Date | Hour | Summary of Events and Information | Remarks and references to Appendices |
|---|---|---|---|---|
| BOISLEUX-au-MONT | 18/9/17 | | Visited Corps H.Qrs. handed over to A.D.V.S. returned from leave. | Est. |
| | | | Inspected Mob. Vety. Secn. | |
| | | | Arranged vety. attendance for the units attended to by one of V.Os who had been evacuated with broken clavicle due to throw from horse. | |
| | 19/9/17 | | Visited some units with D.D.R. inspecting animals for casting. | Est. |
| | | | Inspected animals, lines of 150 Inf. Bgde. Transport | |
| | 20/9/17 | | Inspected 16 animals at M.V.S before their evacuation to Base Vety. Hosp. | |
| | | | Visited M.V.S & saw 8 Doubtful Reactors to MALLEIN test after being retested. All showed negative reaction and one was returned to its unit. | Est. |
| | 21/9/17 | | Held conference with V.Os and made inventory of all Stewart Clippers under their charge & available for use in view of the coming clipping season. | |
| | | | Visited animals of 151 Inf. Bgde. DHQ, Divl Sig. Coy & M.V.S. | Est. |
| | 22/9/17 | | Inspected 22 animals before their evacuation to Base Vety. Hosp. | |
| | | | Visited lines of 1/3 N'th Fld. Ambce & ordered the removal of a skin case to M.V.S. | |
| | | | Reported the inefficiency of the Shoeing Smith on D.H.Q. to Camp Commandant & suggested his return to Base for further training. | Est. |
| | 23/9/17 | | Inspected lines of D.A.C. | |
| | | | Visited Corps HQ. found a case of mange amongst animals of a civilian residing in zone of Army – prescribed treatment and placed buildings out of bounds. | Est. |
| | 24/9/17 | | Inspected 20 animals at M.V.S before their evacuation to Base Vety. Hosp. | |
| | | | Posted the V.O. sent from Base vice the V.O. evacuated sick, to duty with Infantry Bgdes. | Est. |
| | | | Visited 251 Art. Bgde R.F.A | |

A5834 Wt. W4973/M687 750,000 8/16 D. D. & L. Ltd. Forms/C.2118/13.

Army Form C. 2118.

Instructions regarding War Diaries and Intelligence Summaries are contained in F. S. Regs., Part II. and the Staff Manual respectively. Title pages will be prepared in manuscript.

# WAR DIARY
*or*
# ~~INTELLIGENCE SUMMARY~~. D.A.D.V.S., 50th Divn.

(*Erase heading not required.*)

| Place | Date | Hour | Summary of Events and Information | Remarks and references to Appendices |
|---|---|---|---|---|
| BOISLEUX-au-MONT | 25/9/17 | | Instructed by DDR to collect 15 HDs. from 20th Reserve Park A.S.C. Collected same & distributed them to representatives of units in need. Dispatched another collecting party to ALBERT (Fiel Remount Section) to draw 7 L.D.H. & 10 L.D.M. distributed these on their arrival. 3 to D.A.C. and 14 to other units. | EH |
| | 26/9/17 | | Visited DHQ Divl. Sig. Coy. M.M.P. & CRE'S horse lines. Routine Work. | EH |
| | 27/9/17 | | Visited M.V.S. and 2 Batteries of 250 Bgde R.F.A. wagon lines. | EH |
| | 28/9/17 | | Conference of V.O's in my office. Inspected some of the standings in proposed new Divisional Rest Area. Visited B/250 Bgde. R.F.A. | EH |
| | 29/9/17 | | Conference of D.A.D.V.S. at A.D.V.S. Office Corps H.Qrs. Inspected animals of 3 Batteries 250 Bgde. R.F.A. Inspected 38 animals at M.V.S. before their evacuation to Base Vety. Hosp. Made an inventory of all tooth rasps in charge in Division. | EH |
| | 30/9/17 | | Visited HQ, DAC, 1/1st N.F. Ambce. horse lines | EH |

DHQ
30. 9. 17

E. Shaw (?) Maj. AVC
D.A.D.V.S., 50th Division

A5834 Wt. W4973/M687 750,000 8/16 D. D. & L. Ltd. Forms/C.2118/13.

Confidential

# War Diary

of

D.A.D.V.S., 50th Division

from 1st Oct 1917 to 31st Oct. 1917

Vol. 25.

75

Army Form C. 2118.

Instructions regarding War Diaries and Intelligence Summaries are contained in F. S. Regs., Part II. and the Staff Manual respectively. Title pages will be prepared in manuscript.

# WAR DIARY
or
~~INTELLIGENCE SUMMARY.~~
(Erase heading not required.)

D.A.D.V.S. 50th Division

| Place | Date | Hour | Summary of Events and Information | Remarks and references to Appendices |
|---|---|---|---|---|
| BOISLEUX-au-MONT | 1/10/17 | | i Visited and inspected animals of 4 Coy. Divl. Train A.S.C. | E.H. |
| | | | ii Made rearrangement of duties for V.O's during the absence of one on leave. | |
| | | | iii Submitted to Q a new suggested scale for the issue of Smoke Helmets for Horses. | |
| " | 2/10/17 | | i Visited 20th Reserve Park to make arrangements for the evacuation of some of their surplus horses and to provide an A.V.C. man to be in attendance in case required. | E.H. |
| | | | ii Attended at Office of A.D.V.S. Corps. | |
| | | | iii Inspected animals of Divl. Sigl. Coy. R.E. | |
| | | | iv Called for a report from V.O's. on the quality of searching knives — previously reported as being of inferior quality | |
| | | | v Made provision for lamps for M.V.S during winter months | |
| | 3/10/17 | | i Inspected 19 animals at M.V.S prior to their evacuation. | E.H. |
| | | | ii Conducted D.A.D.V.S. of incoming Division over M.V.S winter standings, almost completed & ready for relieving unit. | |
| | | | iii Inspected animals of 20th Reserve Park — one evacuated as being a suspected mange case. | |
| | 4/10/17 | | i Malleined 11 animals (mules) and 1 Rider recently come from overseas for 245 M.G. Coy. | E.H. |
| | | | ii Visited 3 Batteries of the 251 Bgde R.F.A. | |
| | | | iii Made arrangements for the vety. attendance of units during the move, and informed O's. Cmdg units where attendance was to be obtained in case of mishap during the journey. | E.H. |
| | 5/10/17 | | i Held conference with V.O's. in my office. | |
| | | | ii Established an advanced collecting post at COURCELLES-le-COMTE to admit cases from Inf. Transport in RESERVE Area. | |
| | | | iii Left M.V.S in same position to admit cases from Artillery still in the line. | |
| ACHIET-le-PETIT | 6/10/17 | | i D.H.Q. moved to ACHIET-le-PETIT. | E.H. |
| | | | ii Attended conference of D.A.D's V.S. at Corps H.Q. | |
| | 7/10/17 | | i Went round lines of infantry transport to see how they had settled & fared during the move. | E.H. |
| | | | ii Handed over administration of 23 Army Bgde R.F.A. to D.A.D.V.S. 51st Division | |

A5834 Wt. W4973/M687 750,000 8/16 D. D. & L. Ltd. Forms/C.2118/13.

Instructions regarding War Diaries and Intelligence Summaries are contained in F. S. Regs., Part II. and the Staff Manual respectively. Title pages will be prepared in manuscript.

# WAR DIARY
*or*
# ~~INTELLIGENCE SUMMARY.~~

(*Erase heading not required.*)

Army Form C. 2118.

D.A.D.V.S. 50th Division

| Place | Date | Hour | Summary of Events and Information | Remarks and references to Appendices |
|---|---|---|---|---|
| ACHIET le PETIT | 8/10/17 | | i Informed D.A.D.V.S. of incoming Division of the number & location of small units (Labour Corps etc) in his new area which would require attendance, and instructed V.Os. under my administration to hand over sick to officers of the incoming relieving Division. | |
| | | | ii Visited M.V.S. and advanced posts. | EH |
| " | 9/10/17 | | i Visited and inspected 149 Inf. Bgde, 2/2 N.F. Ambce & Mob. Vety. Sec. | EH |
| | | | ii Submitted to Corps a report on the inferior quality of searching knives – too brittle & would take "no edge" | EH |
| " | 10/10/17 | | i Visited lines of 151 Inf. Bgde. | EH |
| | | | ii Issued instructions for 7 men from Infantry transport lines under the charge of 1 N.C.O. A.V.C. to proceed to ABBEVILLE to collect 15 Remounts & return by road. A.V.C. man sent in case of need. | |
| " | 11/10/17 | | i Attended at Corps H.Qrs. | EH |
| | | | ii Submitted to A.D.V.S. Corps, mallein return for 12 animals of 245 M.G. Coy going overseas. | |
| | | | iii Impressed on O.C., M.V. & V.O.s the importance of giving correct markings age etc when sending animals for evacuation. Incorrect descriptions cause great inconvenience at B.V.Hs. | |
| " | 12/10/17 | | i Issued instructions to O.C. M.V.S. & V.Os on their duties immediately before and during the move by rail. V.Os left behind with Art. were instructed to send their sick cases to the nearest M.V.S., i.e., 51st Divn. | EH |
| | | | ii Collected and distributed 6 R. from Advanced Fd. Remount Section. | |
| " | 13/10/17 | | i Issued instructions for the malleining of animals of the 347 Road Construction Coy. newly arrived from overseas | EH |
| | | | ii Visited all 3 Fd. Coys RE. & ASC. | |
| " | 14/10/17 | | i Visited M.V.S. | EH |
| | | | ii Distributed to Art. 6 L.D.H. & 6 L.D.Ms which had arrived by road from ABBEVILLE. | |
| | | | iii Inspected lines of 151 Inf. Bgde. | |

A5834 Wt. W4973/M687 750,000 8/16 D. D. & L. Ltd. Forms/C.2118/13.

Instructions regarding War Diaries and Intelligence Summaries are contained in F. S. Regs., Part II. and the Staff Manual respectively. Title pages will be prepared in manuscript.

# WAR DIARY
*or*
~~INTELLIGENCE SUMMARY.~~
*(Erase heading not required.)*

Army Form C. 2118.

D.A.D.V.S., 50th Div

| Place | Date | Hour | Summary of Events and Information | Remarks and references to Appendices |
|---|---|---|---|---|
| ACHIET-le-PETIT | 15/10/17 | | Collected & issued the following Remounts 7 Riders to M.M.P., 83 for Infantry units. | E.H. |
| | | | Visited 150 Inf. Bgde. & 2 Coy. A.S.C. | |
| | | | Issued instructions to the 2 V.O.S. with Artillery in old area, with regard to their weekly returns. | |
| | 16/10/17 | | Preparing to leave Third Army | E.H. |
| | | | Inspected all R.E. & 149 Inf. Bgde. | E.H. |
| LEDERZEELE | 17/10/17 | | D.H.Q. moved to LEDERZEELE | |
| | 18/10/17 | | Was present at detraining of Infantry, R.E.s. & A.S.C. transport, & Fld Ambces. | E.H. |
| | 19/10/17 | | Visited Corps H.Qrs. and arranged for vety. attendance on small units around PROVEN. | E.H. |
| | | | Present at further detraining of Infantry, R.E.s. & A.S.C. transport & M.V.S. | |
| PROVEN | 20/10/17 | | D.H.Q. at PROVEN. | E.H. |
| | | | Instructed O.C. to bring up his section with rear of forward area after the last unit had moved, thus being able to pick up any casualty on the way. | |
| | 21/10/17 | | Established M.V.S. at PROVEN and had half the M.V.S. personnel sent there to take over the site | E.H. |
| | | | Visited XIV Corps H.Qrs. | |
| | 22/10/17 | | Present during detraining of 250 Bgde R.F.A. & part D.A.C. | E.H. |
| | | | Visited M.V.S. now properly established at PROVEN. | |
| | 23/10/17 | | Sent 9 men from M.V.S to V.C.C.S to conduct 51 animals by road to B.V.H. | E.H. |
| | | | Investigated and reported to Corps on a case of contagious stomatitis belonging to 9th Div which had been evacuated to M.V.S. | |
| ELVERDINGE 28/a.18 b 2.8 | 24/10/17 | | D.H.Q. moved to ELVERDINGE | E.H. |
| | | | Sent float for duty with V.C.C.S from M.V.S. and 4 men also to be attached to V.C.C.S. for duty. | |

A5834 Wt. W4973/M687 750,000 8/16 D. D. & L. Ltd. Forms/C.2118/13.

Army Form C. 2118.

Instructions regarding War Diaries and Intelligence Summaries are contained in F. S. Regs., Part II. and the Staff Manual respectively. Title pages will be prepared in manuscript.

# WAR DIARY
or
~~INTELLIGENCE SUMMARY.~~ D.A.D.V.S. 50th Div

(*Erase heading not required.*)

| Place | Date | Hour | Summary of Events and Information | Remarks and references to Appendices |
|---|---|---|---|---|
| ELVERDINGE 28/A.18.b.2.8 | 25/10/17 | | Adopted the method of evacuation recommended by A.D.V.S. Corps. | |
| | | | Informed V.Os. of this method, giving them locations of all V.C.C.Ss. Advanced Collecting Posts, Forward & Rear M.V.Ss. | |
| | | | Instructions on same subject also communicated to Sgts A.V.C. with Units. | Est |
| | 26/10/17 | | Conference with V.O.s | |
| | | | Visited Advanced Collecting Posts to see how evacuations were carried out. | |
| | | | Visited & inspected Art. Wagon lines. | Est |
| | 27/10/17 | | Attended conference of D.A.Ds.V.S. at Corps H.Q. | |
| | | | Was present at entrainment of sick from V.C.C.S. | |
| | | | Wired 12 bomb casualties amongst animals in Divn. | |
| | | | Detailed driver & float for duty with Forward M.V.S. | Est |
| | 28/10/17 | | Met & distributed 18 remounts to Artillery. | |
| | | | Visited M.V.S. with D.D.V.S. Army | Est |
| | 29/10/17 | | Met & distributed 19 remounts to other units of Divn. | |
| | | | Visited 149 I. Bgde. | |
| | | | Took over Vety. administration of 33rd Reserve Park & visited their lines. | Est |
| | | | Issued 2 riders to 149 I. Bgde to replace casualties by gun shot. | |
| | 30/10/17 | | Wired 33 animals wounded by bombs. (26 eventually dying or having to be destroyed) Unit, 33rd Reserve Park. | |
| | | | Visited 33rd Reserve Park to see wounded animals & made arrangements for skinning the dead and evacuating 7 to V.C.C.S. | |
| | | | Took over 34th Div. Art. & visited their lines. | Est |

A5834 Wt. W4973/M687 750,000 8/16 D. D. & L. Ltd. Forms/C.2118/13.

Instructions regarding War Diaries and Intelligence Summaries are contained in F. S. Regs., Part II. and the Staff Manual respectively. Title pages will be prepared in manuscript.

# WAR DIARY

~~or~~

# ~~INTELLIGENCE SUMMARY.~~

*(Erase heading not required.)*

Army Form C. 2118.

D.A.D.V.S. 50th Div

| Place | Date | Hour | Summary of Events and Information | Remarks and references to Appendices |
|---|---|---|---|---|
| ELVERDINGE 28/A.18 b2.8 | 31/10/17 | | Visited all units in Div. having casualties from Bombs during raid night 30/31. Conducted several of cases to M.V.S made arrangements for evacuation of others. Wired 40 casualties by bombs to A.D.V.S Corps. | EH |

E. [illegible] Maj AVC
D.A.D.V.S, 50th Div

A5834 Wt. W4973/M687 750,000 8/16 D. D. & L. Ltd. Forms/C.2118/13.

Confidential

War Diary

of

D.A.D.V.S. 50th Division.

from 1. XI. 17 to 30. XI. 17.

Volume XXVII

Instructions regarding War Diaries and Intelligence Summaries are contained in F. S. Regs., Part II. and the Staff Manual respectively. Title pages will be prepared in manuscript.

# WAR DIARY
or
~~INTELLIGENCE SUMMARY.~~
(Erase heading not required.)

Army Form C. 2118.

D.A.D.V.S, 50th Division.

| Place | Date | Hour | Summary of Events and Information | Remarks and references to Appendices |
|---|---|---|---|---|
| EIVERDINGHE 28/A 18 b.2.8 | 1 xi/17 | | Visited XIX Corps Veterinary Casualty Clearing Station with A.D.V.S. Corps. | |
| | | | Inspected A.S.C. units having casualties from bombs. | LH. |
| | | | Saw D.A.Q.M.G. with view to having several animals replaced which had been hit and evacuated. | |
| | 2 xi/17 | | Held conference of V.Os at my Office. | |
| | | | Visited animals of 34th D.A.C. attached for administration. | |
| | | | Had 2 animals evacuated to Vety. Hospital by motor ambulance. | LH. |
| | | | Kept A.D.V.S. Corps informed of further losses from enemy bombs. | |
| | 3 xi/17 | | Attended conference of D.A.D.s V.S. at Corps A.D.V.S. Office. | |
| | | | Inspected sick and wounded animals of D.H.Q. at M.V.S. where I had sent them after they were exposed to bombing raid. | LH. |
| | | | Visited animals of 310 Coy 33rd Reserve Park. | |
| | 4 xi/17 | | Inspected animals of 149. Inf. Bgde. | |
| | | | Ordered removal of an animal of 57 Div. into M.V.S. - too lame to proceed. | |
| | | | Evacuated 14 animals to B.V.H. - 9 of other Formations. - | |
| | | | Submitted to Corps a statement showing nos. of animals evacuated to rear by road, rail & motor float. | LH. |
| | 5 xi/17 | | Inspected. Div. Sig. Coy R.E. & No. 4 Coy. A.S.C | |
| | | | Visited M.V.S. at PROVEN. | |
| | | | Provided Corps A.D.V.S. with list of units detached, coming under this Division for Veterinary administration. | |
| | | | Reported to Q on the sufficient number of cold shoes and shoeing smiths with units of Division. | LH. |

A5834 Wt. W4973/M687 750,000 8/16 D. D. & L. Ltd. Forms/C.2118/13.

Instructions regarding War Diaries and Intelligence Summaries are contained in F. S. Regs., Part II. and the Staff Manual respectively. Title pages will be prepared in manuscript.

# WAR DIARY
~~or~~
## ~~INTELLIGENCE SUMMARY~~.
*(Erase heading not required.)*

Army Form C. 2118.

D.A.D.V.S., 50th Division

| Place | Date | Hour | Summary of Events and Information | Remarks and references to Appendices |
|---|---|---|---|---|
| ELVERDINGHE 28/A18b.2.8 | 6/XI/17 | | Inspected 150 M.G. Coy. 4th Yorks. | |
| | | | Attended conference of D.A.D.s V.S. at Corps. | |
| | | | Requested D.D.R. to inspect a H.D. with Div! Train with a view to casting. | |
| | | | Inspected an animal abandoned by some unit & found in this Divn's. Artillery Wagon lines. Left instructions with V.O. i/c Artillery as to its treatment & if necessary, removal. | |
| | | | Issued instructions to V.Os on the disposal of Cellulitis Cases, and animals too much debilitated & recovery of which seemed almost hopeless. | E.H. |
| | 7/XI/17 | | Visited Div. Sig. Coy. R.E. and M.V.S. PROVEN. | |
| | | | Saw 9 animals - all from other Formations - before their evacuation to Base. | |
| | | | Visited Art. units having casualties from bombs. | |
| | | | Instructed M.V.S. to collect a mule, which had been left by a unit, with an inhabitant in PROVEN. | E.H. |
| | 8/XI/17 | | Inspected animals of D.H.Q. & 33rd Reserve Park 310 Coy. A.S.C. | |
| | | | Arranged with D.A.D.V.S. 35th Divn. on handing over M.V.S. site to his M.V.S. on 12th inst. | |
| | | | Arranged for skinners to be sent to skin animals destroyed in Artillery units. | E.H. |
| | 9/XI/17 | | Held conference of V.Os in my Office. | |
| | | | Visited M.V.S. & gave O.C. instructions on moving. | |
| | | | Saw 10 animals - all other Formations - before their evacuation. | |
| | | | Issued to V.Os instructions on the sale of animals for slaughter & consumption. | E.H. |
| EPERLECQUES | 10/XI/17 | | Div. H.Q. moved to EPERLECQUES and units to outlying area. | E.H. |
| | | | Visited M.V.S. and gave instructions to evacuate all sick before leaving on 12th. | E.H. |

A5834 Wt. W4973/M687 750,000 8/16 D. D. & L. Ltd. Forms/C.2118/13.

Instructions regarding War Diaries and Intelligence Summaries are contained in F. S. Regs., Part II. and the Staff Manual respectively. Title pages will be prepared in manuscript.

# WAR DIARY
*or*
# ~~INTELLIGENCE SUMMARY~~.
*(Erase heading not required.)*

Army Form C. 2118.

D.A.D.V.S. 50th Div

| Place | Date | Hour | Summary of Events and Information | Remarks and references to Appendices |
|---|---|---|---|---|
| EPERLECQUES | 11 XI/17 | | Met and distributed 56 Remounts from PROVEN Railhead | |
| | | | Saw 45 animals before their evacuation – 43 belonged to other Formations. | E.H. |
| | 12 XI/17 | | Chose site nr. EPERLECQUES for M.V.S. | |
| | | | Suggested to 'Q' a more liberal supply of field forges on the grounds that they would be more economical in the long run, considering the no. of shoes pulled off by the mud and fascines. | E.H. |
| | 13 XI/17 | | Saw A.D.V.S. XVIII Corps and reported arrival of Divn in this area. | |
| | | | Met & distributed 96 remounts for Artillery from PROVEN Railhead and 6 for A.S.C. Coy. remaining in forward area. | |
| | | | Reported to ADVS. Corps on a complaint of shortage of horse shoe nails. | E.H. |
| | 14 XI/17 | | Visited No. 3 Coy. A.S.C. & sent H.D to M.V.S. suffering from mange. | |
| | | | " 2/2 Fld Ambce. 6th N.F. 5th D.L.I. 4th Yorks. 150 M.G. Coy. Div. Sig. Coy. & D.H.Q.. | |
| | | | Instructed VOs. i/c Artillery to report to D.A.D.V.S. 18th Divn. so long as they remained in forward area. | E.H. |
| | | | Submitted to 'Q' a return of superlative brood mares – marked for breeding purposes – & at present in M.V.S. | |
| | 15 XI/17 | | Visited M.V.S., 1st Canadian Reserve Park, 25 Aux. H.T. Coy., 85 Labour Coy., 3 Forestry Coy., D.H.Q. | |
| | | | Impressed on V.Os the importance of having hopeless cases destroyed in their own unit lines, and not sent to M.V.S., where their destruction & burial entail extra work on A.V.C. personnel. | E.H. |
| | 16 XI/17 | | Visited 15 Reserve Park, 29 P.O.W. Coy., 45 Labour Coy., DHQ, 65 Labour Group. 4.5.&6th N.F., No. 2 Coy. A.S.C. and M.V.S. | E.H. |
| | 17 XI/17 | | Visited Corps H.Q.rs & assumed command of M.V.S. during absence on leave of O.C. M.V.S. | |
| | | | Evacuated 15 animals – (6 of this Divn. & 9 of other Formations) | |
| | | | Issued a surplus mule in 149 Bgde. to 5th Border Regt. | |
| | | | Reported to D.D.R. a L.D. in Artillery too small for that type of work. | E.H. |
| | | | Arranged to commence "standings" for animals in M.V.S. | |

A5834 Wt. W4973/M687 750,000 8/16 D. D. & L. Ltd. Forms/C.2118/13.

# WAR DIARY
*or*
~~INTELLIGENCE SUMMARY~~.
*(Erase heading not required.)*

Instructions regarding War Diaries and Intelligence Summaries are contained in F. S. Regs., Part II. and the Staff Manual respectively. Title pages will be prepared in manuscript.

Army Form C. 2118.

D.A.D.V.S., 50th Div.

| Place | Date | Hour | Summary of Events and Information | Remarks and references to Appendices |
|---|---|---|---|---|
| EPERLECQUES | 18 XI/17 | | Issued surplus mule in 149 Bde. to 6th N.F. | |
| | | | " stray mule to 245 M.G.Coy | |
| | | | Visited and inspected 150 Inf. Bde. | E.H. |
| | 19 XI/17 | | Inspected 7 N.F., 9th D.L.I., + 5th Border - ordered an animal of 9th D.L.I. into M.V.S with debility. | |
| | | | Collected animal from an inhabitant - float case - left behind by an outgoing Division. | E.H. |
| | 20 XI/17 | | Visited 1/1 N.F. Ambce. + evacuated 1 horse blind | |
| | | | Placed a local Brewery at MOULLE 'out of bounds' to British Horses owing to mange existing amongst civilian's horse. Informed Area Commandant + A.D.V.S. Corps of proceedings taken. | |
| | | | Visited 4th Yorks, 1 evacuated 1 for debility + 1 with an abscess. | |
| | | | " 3rd Aux. H.T. Coy., 6th NF, 1st Canadian Reserve Park + sent 1 to M.V.S. broken winded, also 1 with mange from No. 4 Coy. ASC | E.H. |
| | 21 XI/17 | | Visited 23 Vety Hospital St. OMER in connection with animals evacuated there from this Division | |
| | | | " 151 Bde HQ., No 2 Coy ASC, 245 M.G.Coy, 1st Reserve Park + sent 3 animals to M.V.S from latter with mange. | |
| | | | Had animal in ASC cast by DDR's authority. | E.H. |
| | 22 XI/17 | | Inspected + evacuated 14 horses + 4 mules from M.V.S. | |
| | | | Visited 5th Yorks, 2 Coy ASC, 151 Bde HQ, 12th K.O.Y.L.I. (Pioneers), 149 M.G. Coy + sent 1 debility case from latter to M.V.S. | E.H. |
| | 23 XI/17 | | Inspected Nos. 3 + 4 Coys. ASC, + 4th Yorks. | E.H. |
| | 24 XI/17 | | Visited ADVS. Corps | |
| | | | Inspected 1/3 N.F. Ambce. | |
| | | | Evacuated Rider from DHQ. with mange - discovered after dipping. | E.H. |
| | 25 XI/17 | | Visited 7th Yorks + Lancs (Pioneers). | E.H. |

Instructions regarding War Diaries and Intelligence Summaries are contained in F. S. Regs., Part II. and the Staff Manual respectively. Title pages will be prepared in manuscript.

# WAR DIARY
*or*
# ~~INTELLIGENCE~~ SUMMARY.
*(Erase heading not required.)*

D.A.D.V.S. 50th Div.

Army Form C. 2118.

| Place | Date | Hour | Summary of Events and Information | Remarks and references to Appendices |
|---|---|---|---|---|
| EPERLECQUES | 26.xi.17 | | Evacuated 14 animals to Base – 5 of other Formations | |
| | | | Visited 11th Pontoon Park, 245 Machine G. Coy, 12th K.O.Y.L.I (sent 2 to M.V.S.), 151 M.G. Coy (sent 1 to M.V.S). | E.H. |
| | 27.xi.17 | | Visited & inspected Canadian Reserve Park (sent 1 case to M.V.S) 6th N.F., Div. Sig. Coy RE, M.M.P, No. 4 Coy. A.S.C. 5th D.L.I., 4th Yorks, 25 Aux. H.T. Coy. & 151 I Bgde. | E.H. |
| | 28.xi.17 | | Inspected 151 Inf. Bgde. | |
| | | | Arranged to collect 42 Remounts from No. 5 Base Remount Depot on 1st. prox. | E.H. |
| | 29.xi.17 | | Evacuated XI animals to Base – (5 of other Formations) | |
| | | | Again visited cases of civilian, at MOULLE, infected with mange. Every possible precaution taken to prevent infection of British Army horses. | E.H. |
| | 30.xi.17 | | Conference of V.Os in my office. | |
| | | | Visited Nos. 2 & 3 Coy. A.S.C., 5th D.L.I. | |
| | | | " Vety Hosp. St OMER in connection with animals evacuated there from Div. H.Qrs. | E.H. |

[signature]
Maj A.S.C.
D.A.D.V.S, 50th Division

D.H.Q.
1. XII. 17

A5834 Wt. W4973/M687 750,000 8/16 D. D. & L. Ltd. Forms/C.2118/13.

Confidential

WA 30

War Diary

of

D. A. D. V. S. 50th Division

from 1st Decr. 1917 to 31st Decr. 1917

Volume. XXVII

Army Form C. 2118.

# WAR DIARY
~~or~~
~~INTELLIGENCE~~ ~~SUMMARY~~. D.A.D.V.S. 50th Division

(Erase heading not required.)

Instructions regarding War Diaries and Intelligence Summaries are contained in F. S. Regs., Part II. and the Staff Manual respectively. Title pages will be prepared in manuscript.

| Place | Date | Hour | Summary of Events and Information | Remarks and references to Appendices |
|---|---|---|---|---|
| EPERLECQUES | 1 XII 17 | | Visited 5 Remount Depot CALAIS and collected 42 Remounts for Division. Commanding Mobile Veterinary Section during absence of O.C. on leave. | EH. |
| | 2 XII 17 | | Inspected mules of 447 Fd.Coy. reported as being too light + small for drawing heavy pontoon wagons. Reported this matter to "Q". and suggested an exchange for mules of a larger type. Visited 15th Reserve Park A.S.C and evacuated 1 H.D to M.V.S. suffering from mange. | EH. |
| | 3 XII 17 | | Inspected 1st Canadian Reserve Park and examined carcase of an animal which died from internal haemorrhage. Visited 25 Aux H.T. Coy, 5th N.F. and 4th E. Yorks. | EH. |
| | 4 XII 17 | | Inspected 15 animals (4 of Div and 11 of other units) before their evacuation to Base. Visited No. 1 Coy ASC. ELVERDINGHE and instructed V.O. 4 to evacuate 6 cases suspected of mange. | EH. |
| | 5 XII 17 | | Relinquished command of Mobile Vety. Secn. O.C. having returned from leave. Inspected animals of 7th D.L.I (Pioneers) 7th Yorks Lancs (Pioneers attached) Div. Sig Coy RE, No 4 Coy. A.S.C, 4th Yorks 1/3 N'bn. Fld. Ambce. and sent 2 Riders from Div. H.Qrs. into M.V.S. | EH. |
| | 6 XII 17 | | Visited No. 3 Coy. A.S.C – 6 very slight cases of suspected mange. Went to No 23 Vety. Hospital for calcium sulphide for their treatment and sent N.C.O. A.V.C to apply the solution. | EH. |
| | 7 XII 17 | | Inspected all animals of Nos. 2. 3 + 4 Coys A.S.C. Examined 10 animals prior to their evacuation from M.V.S to Vety. Hosp. All from this Div. except one. | EH. |
| | 8 XII 17 | | Evacuated 1 animal of 65 Labour Coy. to M.V.S. Visited Nos. 2 + 3 Coys A.S.C again and 446 Fd.Coy RE. Instructed Staff Capt 50th D.A as to distribution of remounts being drawn on 12th for Artillery units. Instructed units concerned to send on 12th to CALAIS to collect remounts. Made arrangements with B.G.C. 150 I. Bgde. to have remounts for that Bgde collected seeing that Transport of Bgde. was on the move and no men were available. | EH |

Instructions regarding War Diaries and Intelligence Summaries are contained in F. S. Regs., Part II. and the Staff Manual respectively. Title pages will be prepared in manuscript.

# WAR DIARY

~~or~~

~~INTELLIGENCE SUMMARY.~~

(Erase heading not required.)

Army Form C. 2118.

D.A.D.V.S. 50th Div

| Place | Date | Hour | Summary of Events and Information | Remarks and references to Appendices |
|---|---|---|---|---|
| EPERLECQUES | 9.12.17 | | Visited and inspected 150 Bgde animals. | |
| | | | Collected D.A.Q.M.G's rider from No. 23 Vety. Hosp. where it had been for a short time under treatment and issued instructions for its treatment - light duty & feeding re re. for a few days. | |
| | 10.12.17 | | Exchanged 22 mules from 447 Fd. Coy for larger mules, and arranged for the collection of a Rider for the Senior A.D.C. to G.O.C. Division from No. 23 Vety. Hospital | [initials] |
| | | | Inspected [illegible] animals (2 of other formations) before their evacuation. | [initials] |
| | 11.12.17 | | The Division preparing to move again into forward area I inspected Inf Transport before entraining. | [initials] |
| | 12.12.17 | | Visited No. 5 Base Remount Depot to collect 101 Remounts for Division - 63 being for Artillery. | [initials] |
| BRANDHOEK | 13.12.17 | | D.H.Q. moved to BRANDHOEK (H 7c. 8.5 Sheet 28). Saw last of Inf. Transport + R.E.s entraining. | [initials] |
| | 14.12.17 | | Visited 5 Yorks & evacuated 2 badly wounded mules to M.V.S. | |
| | | | Inspected 3 Coy. A.S.C. | |
| | | | Notified A.D.V.S. Corps for information of DADVS Division going into area this Divn. had just vacated, of mange existing amongst civilian horses at MOULLE. | |
| | | | Instructed O.C. M.V.S. to establish an Advanced Collecting and Dressing Station through YPRES at POTIJZE (I 3 d 8.6 Sheet 28) for animals in advanced area. | [initials] |
| | 15.12.17 | | Attended conference of D.A.Ds.V.S. at office of A.D.V.S. VIII Corps. | |
| | | | Visited No. 3 Coy. A.S.C. | |
| | | | Issued Rider to V.O. i/c D.A.C. and Rider to Chaplain 5th D.L.I (on loan) | |
| | | | Examined a rider of 39th D.A.C. lent to an officer of a Chinese Labour Coy. supposed to have been ill treated due to indifferent horsemanship. Reported on case to A.D.V.S. VIII Corps. | |
| | | | Inspected 39 Div. Art. animals now attached to this Divn. for Vety. administration. | [initials] |

A5834 Wt. W4973/M687 750,000 8/16 D. D. & L. Ltd. Forms/C.2118/13.

Instructions regarding War Diaries and Intelligence Summaries are contained in F. S. Regs., Part II. and the Staff Manual respectively. Title pages will be prepared in manuscript.

# WAR DIARY
or
~~INTELLIGENCE SUMMARY.~~

(Erase heading not required.)

Army Form C. 2118.

D.A.D.V.S., 50th Division

| Place | Date | Hour | Summary of Events and Information | Remarks and references to Appendices |
|---|---|---|---|---|
| BRANDHOEK | 16/12/17 | | Visited M.V.S. and 3 sections D.A.C. Latter having only just returned from command of 18th Division and animals looked well. | |
| | | | Applied to A.D.V.S. II Corps for permission to dip about 30 animals of A.S.C in [struck] Cps bath. | |
| | | | Requested D.D.R. Army to inspect 6 Artillery horses with a view to their being cast - useless for Art.y work | |
| | | | Inspected animals of 50 Div. Sig. Coy & evacuated one to M.V.S. - severe contused wound O.F. | Est |
| | 17/12/17 | | Inspected animals of 251 Bgde RFA recently rejoined Division. Animals in good condition. | |
| | | | Advanced Collecting & Dressing Station at POTIJZE opened. | |
| | | | Instructed VO i/c Inf. Bgdes to keep the Vety. Sgt. attached to which-ever Bgde was doing duty in the line also attached to this Collecting Station to be in readiness to attend casualties in his Bgde. transport going to & from the forward dumps. | |
| | | | Visited M.V.S. and inspected 40 animals (29 of other formations) before their evacuation. | Est |
| | 18/12/17 | | Major E Hearne D.A.D.V.S. goes on leave. Capt H Newton, AVC. OC No 9 M.V.S. acting during his absence. | HN |
| | | | Made arrangements for vety. attendance on 2nd Army Troops Coy. RE. & 306 Road Construction Coy. | |
| | 19/12/17 | | Evacuated 40 animals seen by DADVS on 17th inst. | |
| | | | Made arrangements to have about 30 A.S.C. horses and 2 mules from D.A.C. put through Corps Dipping bath. | HN |
| | | | Visited 3 Coy. [struck] Divisional Train A.S.C. | |
| | 20/12/17 | | Attended Corps Dipping Bath, but severity of weather did not permit the horses being dipped. | |
| | | | Instructed VOs. of 39 D.A. left behind in the line to render returns of sick & injured to this office. | HN |
| | | | Informed O.C. 5 Army Field Remount Section that I was sending 6 animals to them, cast by D.D.R. Army. | |
| | | | Wired [struck] ADVS 8th Corps for an allotment of trucks to convey 60 animals to Base _ congestion on line did not permit evacuation today. | |
| | 21/12/17 | | Conference of VOs. in DADVS Office. | |
| | | | Wired ADVS 9th Corps for accommodation, not obtained the previous day, to evacuate about 60 animals and informed ADVS. that I had complied with his suggestion. | HN |

Instructions regarding War Diaries and Intelligence Summaries are contained in F. S. Regs., Part II. and the Staff Manual respectively. Title pages will be prepared in manuscript.

# WAR DIARY
or
~~INTELLIGENCE SUMMARY.~~
(Erase heading not required.)

Army Form C. 2118.

DADVS. 50th Div.

| Place | Date | Hour | Summary of Events and Information | Remarks and references to Appendices |
|---|---|---|---|---|
| BRANDHOEK | 22 12/17 | | Attended conference of D.A.D.V.S Divisions at office of 8th Corps A.D.V.S. | |
| | | | Received complaint from this Divl. Art. of several cases of mange having been left behind by an outgoing unit. Wired back that I had arranged to see these animals, which C.R.A. considered were a source of danger as they were in too close proximity to this D.A's wagon lines. | NN |
| | 23 12/17 | | Visited this D.A. wagon lines and found mange cases left behind by another unit were isolated. Left further instructions for the prevention of spread and informed C.R.A. of action taken. | NN |
| | | | Arranged vety. attendance for the following detached units:- 11th Fld Coy. R.E., 212 Fld Coy R.E. & No. 1 Troop 3rd Traffic Control Squadron. | |
| | 24 XII/17 | | Evacuated 51 animals to Base (34 of other Formations). | |
| | | | Arranged to return to No. 43 M.V.S. (33rd Divn) 4 mules lent by them to a unit of this Divn, but on receiving word that they were no longer required by this M.V.S. they were absorbed into this Divn. | NN |
| | | | On A.D.V.S. VIII Corps instructions I despatched 15 O.R. of a Corps Mobile Detachment to No. 23 Vety. Hospital, using them on the downward journey as a railway conducting party for sick animals. | |
| | 25 XII/17 | | Distributed 24 Remounts to Infantry Transport & A.S.C. | NN |
| | | | Visited 2 Coy A.S.C. | |
| | 26 XII/17 | | Wired A.D.V.S. IX Corps for truck accommodation for 56 animals, & informed A.D.V.S. VIII Corps how many animals I intended evacuating. | |
| | | | Visited & inspected DHQ animals. | NN |
| | | | Notified D.A.D.O.S. of the distribution, (and authority for same), of protective plates for the soles of horses' feet. | |
| | | | Discussed the question of an increased ration of bran for DHQ horses. | |
| | 27 XII/17 | | Instructed 5 Yorks to send 4 surplus mules to M.V.S. for inspection prior to redistribution. | |
| | | | Forwarded to C.R.A. authority from DDR 4th Army for the evacuation of 6 animals unsuitable for Art. work. | NN |
| | | | Wrote O.C. Divl. Train requesting a report in due course on the protective value, or otherwise, of the plates for horses feet issued to Train for trial purposes. | |

Instructions regarding War Diaries and Intelligence Summaries are contained in F. S. Regs., Part II. and the Staff Manual respectively. Title pages will be prepared in manuscript.

# WAR DIARY

~~or~~

~~INTELLIGENCE SUMMARY.~~

(Erase heading not required.)

D.A.D.V.S, 50 Div.

Army Form C. 2118.

| Place | Date | Hour | Summary of Events and Information | Remarks and references to Appendices |
|---|---|---|---|---|
| BRANDHOEK | 28/12/17 | | Visited entraining Station & evacuated 36 animals (25 belonging to other Formations)<br>At D.H.Q. as usual on daily visit during absence of D.A.D.V.S. | H.N. |
| | 29/12/17 | | Attended conference of D.A.D.V.S Divisions at office of A.D.V.S. Corps.<br>Requested DDR to sanction the reissue of a rider, now recovered from mange, to V.O. of this Division whose rider it had been. | H.N. |
| | 30/12/17 | | Issued instructions to units concerned on collection of Remounts on Jan. 1. 1918 from No 5. Base Remount Depot.<br>Visited No 3 Coy. A.S.C.<br>Called on Staff Capt. 50 D.A. with instructions for Art. to collect 58 Remount from No 5 B.R.D. on Jan. 1. 1918 | H.N. |
| | 31/12/17 | | Absorbed into Divn. 10 stray mules after having malleined them.<br>Issued further instructions to unit concerned for the collection of Remounts from No 5 B.R.D. on Jan. 1. 1918<br>Wired A.D.V.S. VIII Corps for truck accommodation for 38 animals on train leaving forward area on 2nd prox.<br>Examined animals brought forward by D.A. for casting – several proved to be veterinary cases & were retained for evacuation as such.<br><br>H. Newton Capt. AVC.<br>A/D.A.D.V.S. 50 Division<br><br>D.H.Q.<br>31. 12 17 | H.N. |

A5834 Wt. W4973/M687 750,000 8/16 D. D. & L. Ltd. Forms/C.2118/13.

CONFIDENTIAL

WO 95/2831

# WAR DIARY

OF

D.A.D.V.S 50TH. DIVISION.

FROM 1. 1. 18 TO 31. 1. 18.

VOLUME XXVIII.

Instructions regarding War Diaries and Intelligence Summaries are contained in F. S. Regs., Part II. and the Staff Manual respectively. Title pages will be prepared in manuscript.

# WAR DIARY

~~or~~

~~INTELLIGENCE SUMMARY.~~

*(Erase heading not required.)*

Army Form C. 2118.

D.A.D.V.S.
50 Division

| Place | Date | Hour | Summary of Events and Information | Remarks and references to Appendices |
|---|---|---|---|---|
| BRANDHOEK | 1/8/18 | | Visited all Coys. 50 Div. Train A.S.C. | |
| | | | Informed O.C. 23 Vety. Hospital that arrangements were being made to return a detachment of A.V.C. personnel tomorrow to the Hospital. They had been attached for duty with M.V.S. | |
| | | | Notified C.R.A. that animals brought forward to be cast were really veterinary cases and would be evacuated in the ordinary way. | Int. |
| | 2/8/18 | | Called for reports from Vety. Officers on Sgts. A.V.C. attached for duty to field units. | |
| | | | Visited 3 Fd. Coy. R.E. and 3 Fd. Ambulances. Inspected 38 animals at M.V.S. before evacuation – 22 of other formations | Int. |
| | 3/8/18 | | Arranged with D.A.D.V.S. of Division coming forward to relieve this Div. the handing over of M.V.S. location | |
| | | | Made further arrangements with Officer i/c Corps Dipping Bath for the dipping of several animals of the Division before the 9th inst. as Division would be moving back then to Reserve Rest area. | Int. |
| | 4/8/18 | | Inspected animals & transport horse lines of 3 Infantry Bgdes. | Int. |
| | | | Arranged for the disposal of remounts which were arriving by road. | Int. |
| | 5/8/18 | | D.A.D.V.S. Division returned from leave and resumed duty. | |
| | | | Inspected 65 animals at M.V.S before their evacuation, 46 belonged to other Formations | |
| STEENVOORDE | 6/8/18 | | D.H.Q. moved to STEENVOORDE. | |
| | | | Wrote to A.V.C. Records to have 3 Sgts A.V.C. sent up to Bgdes R.F.A to replace 3 evacuated sick. | Int. |
| | | | Had M.V.S moved further back to WATOU | |
| | 7/8/18 | | Visited and inspected animals of 150. I. Bgde. | Int. |
| | | | Visited and inspected M.V.S at WATOU and arranged to inspect 13 brood mares | |
| | 8/8/18 | | Attended at Office of A.D.V.S. Corps & arranged veterinary attendance on Fd. Coy. R.E. and No. 1 Coy. A.S.C. | |
| | | | Inspected animals of 4 Yorks. M.M.P. & arranged veterinary attendance on 3 Fd. Coy. R.E. and No. 1 Coy. A.S.C. | |
| | | | Despatched from M.V.S. for duty at a V.E.C.S. one N.C.O. and 3 men. | |
| | | | Inspected animals of 151 Inf. Bgde. 1/1 N.F. Ambulance. No. 3 Coy A.S.C. | |
| | | | Communicated with D.A.D.V.S. 33rd Divn. re the destruction of a Stray Draught horse belonging 33rd Div. Train left with No. 3 Coy A.S.C. 50 Div. Train with an open joint (kick). D.A.D.V.S. 33rd informed me of his intention to see it before it was destroyed. | Int. |

A5834 Wt. W4973/M687 750,000 8/16 D. D. & L. Ltd. Forms/C.2118/13.

Instructions regarding War Diaries and Intelligence Summaries are contained in F. S. Regs., Part II. and the Staff Manual respectively. Title pages will be prepared in manuscript.

# WAR DIARY
or
~~INTELLIGENCE SUMMARY.~~
(Erase heading not required.)

D.A.D.V.S. 50 Div.

Army Form C. 2118.

| Place | Date | Hour | Summary of Events and Information | Remarks and references to Appendices |
|---|---|---|---|---|
| STEENVOORDE | 9/8/18 | | Sent 2 Riders from DHQ. to 23 Veterinary Hospital for further treatment<br>Made a redistribution of work on account of one V.O. being on leave<br>Accompanied DADVS 33rd Div. to see animal of that Division brought to his notice yesterday. He decided to have it destroyed and skinned and I detailed M.V.S personnel to carry out these instructions | Est. |
| | 10/8/18 | | Sent instructions to O.C. M.V.S. to have animals numbers clipped on quarters instead of stencilled when they were evacuated<br>Inspected animals of 150 M.G. Coy + 245 M.G. Coy. 1/3 N'bn Fld. Ambce. 3 Coy. ASC<br>Submitted to 'Q' a report on frost cogs + shoes. Had no complaint to make on the way in which holes were drilled<br>Examined + evacuated 25 animals left by 43 M.V.S. 33rd Division | Est. |
| | 11/8/18 | | Conference of V.O.s at my office. Visited 3 Fld Coy RE.<br>Again accompanied Corps Horsemaster to inspect Broodmares and had one mare branded which belonged to M.M.P. | Est. |
| | 12/8/18 | | Issued further instructions to V.O.s + Sgts A.V.C. on economising in drugs + veterinary equipment.<br>Attended conference of D.A.D.V.S. at Office of A.D.V.S. Corps.<br>Inspected animals for evacuation at M.V.S.<br>Visited 3 Coy. ASC. | Est. |
| | 13/8/18 | | Inspected animals of 250. 251 Bgdes RFA. and 3 stray mules sent into M.V.S<br>Issued further instructions to V.O.s. on the injection of Lugol's solution in ophthalmia cases (doses + dates when injections were made to be stated) | Est. |
| | 14/8/18 | | Accompanied G.O.C during his inspection of 151 Bgde. Transport.<br>Inspected prior to their evacuation to Base 21 animals - 17 of which belonged other formations<br>As M.V.S was moving next day to reserve rest area I arranged with DADVS incoming Division to take over sick animals. There were 13 in all - 9 of which belonged to other formations. | Est. |
| | 15/8/18 | | M.V.S moving to new area had to stay one night at STEENVOORDE! I arranged billeting accommodation<br>Inspected DHQ horses prior to the march<br>Collected 2 animals from an inhabitant. left by the D.A.C. | Est. |

A5834 Wt. W.973/M687 750,000 8/16 D. D. & L. Ltd. Forms/C.2118/13.

Instructions regarding War Diaries and Intelligence Summaries are contained in F. S. Regs., Part II. and the Staff Manual respectively. Title pages will be prepared in manuscript.

# WAR DIARY
or
~~INTELLIGENCE SUMMARY.~~
(Erase heading not required.)

Army Form C. 2118.

D.A.D.V.S., 50 Div.

| Place | Date | Hour | Summary of Events and Information | Remarks and references to Appendices |
|---|---|---|---|---|
| STEENVOORDE | 16.4/18 | | Despatched M.V.S from STEENVOORDE to reserve rest area | |
| | | | Submitted reports to A.D.V.S. Corps on the advantages & disadvantages of Horse Respirators & Protective metal plates for feet. | Ist |
| | 17/4/18 | | Inspected animals of 2/2 N'bn F.C.S. Ambce. & 149 M.G. Coy | Ist |
| | 18/4/18 | | Visited horse lines of Div Sig. Coy. and 150 I. Bgde. | |
| | | | Conference of V.Os. at my office | Ist |
| WIZERNES | 19/4/18 | | D.H.Q. moved to WIZERNES | |
| | | | Attended conference at office of A.D.V.S VIII Corps. | |
| | | | Received a report from one of my V.Os. of mange existing among horses belonging to a civilian living in the billeting area near THIEMBRONNE. Investigated, and found he has already placed one farm out of bounds to British horses. | Ist |
| | 20/4/18 | | Received instructions from A.D.V.S. VIII Corps to provide vety. attendance for 25th & 101st Squadrons RFC. I personally visited 101 Squadron but found no horses and O.C. M.V.S found none with 25th Squadron. It appears they are entitled to 9 animals between them but so far they have not arrived. | |
| | | | Inspected 251 Bgde R.F.A at MERCKE | Ist |
| | 21/4/18 | | Inspected animals of 250 Bgde R.F.A and 6 units of the Special Bgde R.E. | |
| | | | Requested O.C. 23 Vety. Hospital to supply me with some Calcium Sulphide Solution | Ist |
| | 22/4/18 | | Inspected all animals in H.Qrs & 3 sections D.A.C. | Ist |
| | 23/4/18 | | Visited Div. Sig. Coy R.E. 446 & 447 Fd Coy R.E. 2 Fd Ambces, 1 Coy A.S.C. and 5th N.F. | Ist |
| | | | Inspected 9 animals before their evacuation to 23 Vety. Hospital | |
| | | | Arranged to have 1 man from each M.G. Coy's horse lines attached to M.V.S for a short period for training in dressing & stable management. | Ist |
| | 24/4/18 | | Visited M.V.S & inspected all animals in 3 Fd Ambces. & A.S.C. | |
| | | | Destroyed an animal belonging to a Fr. civilian at BOISDINGHEM that had been wounded by a bomb dropped from a British Aeroplane. Provided the usual vety. certificates to parties concerned. | Ist |

A5834 Wt. W4973/M687 750,000 8/16 D. D. & L. Ltd. Forms/C.2118/13.

Instructions regarding War Diaries and Intelligence Summaries are contained in F. S. Regs., Part II. and the Staff Manual respectively. Title pages will be prepared in manuscript.

# WAR DIARY
or
~~INTELLIGENCE SUMMARY.~~
(Erase heading not required.)

D.A.D.V.S, 50th Divn

Army Form C. 2118.

| Place | Date | Hour | Summary of Events and Information | Remarks and references to Appendices |
|---|---|---|---|---|
| WIZERNES | 25.1.18 | | Conference of V.Os in my office | |
| | | | Inspected 28 animals at M.V.S before their evacuation to Base Vety. Hospitals. | |
| | | | Requested D.D Remounts to inspected 2 H.Ds of 1/1 N.Z. Ambce. with a view to their being cast | |
| | | | Issued instructions to O.C. M.V.S. for move to forward area on 29th inst | Wt. |
| | 26.1.18 | | Inspected animals of 7th DLI., No. 4 Coy. ASC, & No. 1 Coy. ASC. | |
| | | | Visited 23 Vety. Hospital to see 2 riders from D.H.Q under treatment there. | Wt. |
| | 27.1.18 | | Inspected Art. units as they were moving past for forward area. | |
| | | | Saw an animal of HQs 251 Bde R.F.A which had had its leg broken by colliding with a motor lorry. Ordered its destruction. | |
| | | | Arranged with D.A.D.V.S. of relieving Division for the exchange of locations of the 2 M.V.Ss. | |
| | | | Forwarded to DADVS relieving Division a list of units which would come under his administration when relief was completed. | Wt. |
| | 28.1.18 | | Saw two stray mules which had been admitted into M.V.S. | |
| | | | Inspected 24 animals in M.V.S before their evacuation – one was a stray, remainder belonged to Division | Wt. |
| | | | Reported to Records A.V.C the arrival of 3 Vety. Sgts. to replace 3 evacuated sick. | |
| | 29.1.18 | | Despatched M.V.S to new forward position, with instructions to establish a forward collecting & dressing station if absolutely necessary. | |
| | | | Received instructions from ADVS Corps to collect 2 mules left by an Australian Artillery unit with inhabitants. As this Divn. M.V.S had already left area DADVS relieving Division undertook their collection. Together we visited & inspected the animals. Though they were stabled several miles away we concluded they could easily travel the distance. I informed A.D.V.S. Corps what arrangements had been made. | Wt. |

A5834 Wt. W4973/M687 750,000 8/16 D. D. & L. Ltd. Forms/C.2118/13.

Army Form C. 2118.

Instructions regarding War Diaries and Intelligence Summaries are contained in F. S. Regs., Part II. and the Staff Manual respectively. Title pages will be prepared in manuscript.

# WAR DIARY
~~or~~
~~INTELLIGENCE SUMMARY.~~

(*Erase heading not required.*)

D.A.D.V.S. 50 Division

| Place | Date | Hour | Summary of Events and Information | Remarks and references to Appendices |
|---|---|---|---|---|
| BRANDHOEK | 30.1.18 | | D.H.Q. moved to BRANDHOEK. | [initials] |
| | 31.1.18 | | Attended at office of A.D.V.S. Corps and reported arrival of Division in area. Inspected animals of DHQ, Signal Coy. RE, & CRA. Informed D.D. Remounts where it would be most convenient to inspect Fld. Ambces. horses with a view to having some cast, and requested him to examine 3 others from the Divl. Art. which were unsuitable. | [initials] |

DHQ
31. 1. 18

[signature]
Maj. AVC.
D.A.D.V.S., 50th Division.

A5834 Wt. W4973/M687 750,000 8/16 D. D. & L. Ltd. Forms/C.2118/13.

Confidential

# WAR DIARY

OF

D.A.D.V.S. 50th DIVISION

from 1. 2. 18 to 28. 2. 18

Vol. XXIX.

Vol 32

7

Instructions regarding War Diaries and Intelligence Summaries are contained in F. S. Regs., Part II. and the Staff Manual respectively. Title pages will be prepared in manuscript.

# WAR DIARY
~~or~~
# INTELLIGENCE ~~SUMMARY~~.
*(Erase heading not required.)*

D.A.D.V.S., 50th Division

Army Form C. 2118.

| Place | Date | Hour | Summary of Events and Information | Remarks and references to Appendices |
|---|---|---|---|---|
| BRANDHOEK | 1/2/18 | | Visited M.V.S. and 3 Coy. A.S.C. | |
| | | | Attended animal of civilian farmer - animal had a punctured wound, foot. I had shoe removed, wound dressed and administered anti-tetanic injection. | E.H. |
| | 2/2/18 | | Attended Conference at VIII Corps H.Qrs. of D.A.Ds.V.S. at office of A.D.V.S. | E.H. |
| | | | Inspected animals of 3 Field Coys. R.E. | |
| | 3/2/18 | | Inspected at M.V.S. 24 animals before their evacuation - 16 of this Division & 8 belonging to other formations. | E.H. |
| | | | Visited 3 Field Ambulances. | |
| | 4/2/18 | | Inspected transport animals of 4 Battalions of No I. Bgde. & D.H.Q. | E.H. |
| | 5/2/18 | | Visited 251 Bgde R.F.A. | E.H. |
| | 6/2/18 | | Visited 1/1 N.M.V.S. No 1 Coy. A.S.C. & 4 Machine Gun Corps. | E.H. |
| | | | Made arrangements with O.C. A.S.C. to inspect all N.C.Os. rides some of which reported to be too light to carry weights of their riders. | |
| | 7/2/18 | | Inspected in M.V.S before their evacuation 25 animals all of other formations. | |
| | | | Reported on inferior stable management of M.G. Coys & demonstrated to T.Os on how it may be improved. | |
| | | | Inspected N.C.Os. rides in A.S.C. and condemned 5 as unsuitable to perform the work demanded of them, as they were really only pack ponies. Informed 'Q' with a view to affecting an exchange. | |
| | | | Arranged with D.A.D.O.S for a further early supply of haynets for 1/1 N.M.V.S | E.H. |
| | 8/2/18 | | Inspected 1/1 N.F.A., 1/3 N.F.A., & D.H.Q animals. | |
| | | | Ordered destruction of a horse of 86 A. Bgde F.A - open joint, and notified unit of action taken. | E.H. |
| | | | Arranged by redistributing rides in A.S.C. to have N.C.O. more suitably mounted. | |

A5834 Wt. W4973/M687 750,000 8/16 D. D. & L. Ltd. Forms/C.2118/13.

Instructions regarding War Diaries and Intelligence Summaries are contained in F. S. Regs., Part II. and the Staff Manual respectively. Title pages will be prepared in manuscript.

# WAR DIARY
~~OF~~
# INTELLIGENCE ~~SUMMARY~~. D.A.D.V.S., 50 Div.

(Erase heading not required.)

Army Form C. 2118.

| Place | Date | Hour | Summary of Events and Information | Remarks and references to Appendices |
|---|---|---|---|---|
| BRANDHOEK | 9/2/18 | | Attended conference of D.A.D's V.S. at office of A.D.V.S. VIII Corps. | |
| | | | Inspected animals of 7.N.F. 5 Border. 9.D.L.I. prior to their being withdrawn from their respective Brigades. | |
| | | | Wrote II Corps A.D.V.S. to arrange to have animals of D/250 Bgde. all dipped in II Corps Dipping Bath as this unit were occupying standings where mange has existed. | E.H. |
| | 10/2/18 | | Inspected animals of 3 7th. Corps. R.E. | |
| | | | Reissued several surplus animals from Div. Train to other units of Divn. | E.H. |
| | 11/2/18 | | At M.V.S. and inspected before their evacuation 16 animals (10 of other formations) | |
| | | | Suggested to 'Q' the issue of an order that all clipped animals sent to M.V.S. sick, should be accompanied with rugs, as they may have to stand in M.V.S. for a few days awaiting evacuation. | E.H. |
| | | | Inspected all animals of 4 Machine Gun Corps. | |
| | 12/2/18 | | At M.V.S. | |
| | | | Met A.D.V.S. Corps at V.C.C.S. to make arrangements for engineers to effect alterations in premises. | E.H. |
| | | | Visited & inspected 8. D.L.I. | |
| | | | Arranged with 'Q' to have 58 Remounts for units of Divn. | |
| | 13/2/18 | | Inspected animals of M.M.P., Div. Sig. Coy. 4 Yorks. 4 E. Yorks. 3 Fd. Ambces. 5 D.L.I. | E.H. |
| | | | Informed 'Q' that permission had been obtained from II Corps to have animals of D/250 Bgde. F.A. dipped in II Corps Dipping Bath. | |
| | | | Instructed O.C. 1/1 N.M.S. & V.O. i/c A.S.C. units to select any cases they might have for dipping also. | |
| | | | Brought a rider of A.S.C. to notice of D.D.R. with a view to its being cast. | |
| | | | Transferred a surplus Rider from 149 Bgde. to 150 Bgde. | |
| | | | Reissued to 1/3 Fd. Ambce. a stray animal in M.V.S. claimed by them. | |

A5834 Wt. W4973/M687 750,000 8/16 D. D. & L. Ltd. Forms/C.2118/13.

Instructions regarding War Diaries and Intelligence Summaries are contained in F. S. Regs., Part II. and the Staff Manual respectively. Title pages will be prepared in manuscript.

# WAR DIARY

~~or~~

~~INTELLIGENCE~~ SUMMARY.

(Erase heading not required.)

Army Form C. 2118.

D.A.D.V.S, 50 Div.

| Place | Date | Hour | Summary of Events and Information | Remarks and references to Appendices |
|---|---|---|---|---|
| BRANDHOEK | 14/2/18 | | Interview with CRA re dipping of D/250 horses on 16th inst. Inspected all 4 M.G. Coys horses again – improvement shown. Submitted report to 'Q' on the effect of the reduction of oats.. no appreciable difference in condition noticed during the good weather though the severe weather expected later would be almost certain to affect condition if reduced ration was continued. | [initials] |
| | 15/2/18 | | Inspected 3 Battys 250 Bgde RFA. Conference of V.Os in my office. Reported to ADVS. Corps a case of neglect in 28 A. Bgde F.A. where an animal of that unit had been detained in M.V.S. suffering from mange. Issued instructions to units collecting remounts on 16th inst from Army Fld. Remount Section. | [initials] |
| | 16/2/18 | | Attended conference at office of ADVS. VIII Corps. Saw animals of D/250 Bgde at II Corps dips. Drew 58 Remounts for Divn. from Army Field Remount Section. | [initials] |
| | 17/2/18 | | Visited 3 Fld Coys. RE. & 3/2 Fld Ambce. Saw at M.V.S. 85 animals before their evacuation – 42 of this Divn. & 43 of other formations. | [initials] |
| | 18/2/18 | | Accompanied Corps Horse Adviser during his inspection of animals of 3 Fld. Coys RE. 3 Fld Ambces. DHQ & Sig Coy. CRA HQrs, ASC HQrs. 149 Inf Bgde. & HQrs of 150 & 151 Inf. Bgdes. Wrote Officer i/c Signal Sec. attd to 149 Bgde HQrs. on the inefficiency of the NCO i/c section animals and suggested his removal & replacement by a more capable man. | [initials] |
| | 19/2/18 | | Visited M.V.S. & 2 Coys. ASC. Received notification from DADVS 33 Div. of mange existing in their units and whose standings this Division was about to take over. Informed Q & CRA, & V.O i/c Art. as artillery were most probably taking over these standings. | [initials] |

Instructions regarding War Diaries and Intelligence Summaries are contained in F. S. Regs., Part II. and the Staff Manual respectively. Title pages will be prepared in manuscript.

# WAR DIARY
or
~~INTELLIGENCE SUMMARY.~~
(Erase heading not required.)

D.A.D.V.S., 50 Div.

Army Form C. 2118.

| Place | Date | Hour | Summary of Events and Information | Remarks and references to Appendices |
|---|---|---|---|---|
| BRANDHOEK | 20/2/18 | | Inspected animals of 149. I. Bgde. | |
| | | | Wired Corps ADVS. asking if DADVS 33 Div. was having standings - mange infected - disinfected before that Div. left the area to be occupied by this Div. | Est. |
| | 21/2/18 | | Inspected DAC, Sig Coy's animals attached to Artillery. | Est |
| | 22/2/18 | | Accompanied Corps Horse Adviser to see Art. horses on the march to new area. | Est |
| WIZERNES | 23/2/18 | | DAC moved to WIZERNES | Est |
| | 24/2/18 | | Visited Div. HQ. animals. Div. Sig. Coy. RE. and new area occupied by Art. to see what disinfection had been carried out in standings occupied by outgoing units. | Est |
| | 25/2/18 | | Called at Vety Hosp. ST. OMER to arrange with O.C. for a further supply of disinfectant for Artillery standings. | Est |
| | | | Instructed M.V.S. to collect an animal left behind by outgoing Division. | |
| | 26/2/18 | | Inspected 17 animals at M.V.S. before their evacuation - all belonged to Division with one exception. | Est |
| | | | Requested 39 Div. to collect an animal belonging to A.S.C. of this Div. left behind on line of march | Est |
| | 27/2/18 | | Visited & inspected Div. Sig. Coy. RE. & 150. I. Bgde. | |
| | 28/2/18 | | Visited artillery standings and had stables & standings occupied by mange cases in outgoing Division disinfected, and all litter burnt. | |
| | | | Reported to "Q" on the general dirty condition in which standings had been left by outgoing Division. | Est |
| | | | Established a collecting post for the reception of Art. horses. midway between the M.V.S. & Art. units locations. | |

[signature] Maj. A.V.C.
D.A.D.V.S., 50 Div.

DAQ
1. 3. 18.

A5834 Wt. W4973/M687 750,000 8/16 D. D. & L. Ltd. Forms/C.2118/13.

CONFIDENTIAL

WO 95/33

# WAR DIARY

OF

D. A. D. V. S., 50th Division

From 1st. March 1918 to 31st. March 1918.

VOLUME XXX

29

Instructions regarding War Diaries and Intelligence Summaries are contained in F. S. Regs., Part II. and the Staff Manual respectively. Title pages will be prepared in manuscript.

# WAR DIARY
or
~~INTELLIGENCE~~ SUMMARY.
(Erase heading not required.)

Army Form C. 2118.

D.A.D.V.S., 50th Division

| Place | Date | Hour | Summary of Events and Information | Remarks and references to Appendices |
|---|---|---|---|---|
| WIZERNES | 1.3.18 | | Conference of V.O.s in my office.<br>Visited MERCK-ST-LIEVIN where a Battery of the 33rd Divn has been billetted, and as there has been mange in that unit I arranged for disinfection of standings and reported to Q what has been done to prevent further contagion | E.H. |
| | 2.3.18 | | Inspected animals of No. 1 Coy. A.S.C.<br>Visited M.V.S. and examined 7 animals before their evacuation to Base.<br>Submitted to D.A.D.O.S. a suggested scale for the allotment of protective plates for horses' feet. | E.H. |
| | 3.3.18 | | Visited and inspected 446 Fd Coy RE., and 4th E. Yorks. Instructed O.C. M.V.S. to establish collecting post at CLÉTY. | E.H. |
| | 4.3.18 | | Attended Vety. Hospital ST. OMER and obtained further supplies of Calcium Sulphide for the treatment of a few itchy horses in ASC. | E.H. |
| | 5.3.18 | | Inspected all animals in the 4 Machine Gun Corps.<br>Visited M.V.S.<br>Instructed one of my V.O.s to examine several surplus animals in 7 D.L.I before they were issued to other units. | E.H. |
| | 6.3.18 | | Inspected animals of 2 Coy. A.S.C.<br>Issued the 12 animals surplus to 7 D.L.I. and examined the previous day, to units of the Division who were mostly in need of them. | E.H. |
| | 7.3.18 | | Inspected 2 Coy A.S.C.<br>Wrote A.D.V.S. VIII Corps, requesting, if possible, that a Sgt. A.V.C. be posted for duty with the Machine Gun Battalion which has an establishment of about 230 animals in the 4 Coys. In the meantime & during the move I posted a Cpl A.V.C. from the M.V.S for duty with the Battalion.<br>On instructions received from A.D.V.S. VIII Corps I had A.V.C. personnel from this M.V.S. withdrawn from 22nd Corps V.E.C.S and despatched them to V.C.C.S. VIII Corps. | E.H. |
| | 8.3.18 | | Issued 3 L.D.H. & 2 L.D.M. to 150 I. Bgde.<br>Was present at the entraining of Inf. Transport from WIZERNES, ARQUES, & ST. OMER. | E.H. |
| MOREUIL | 9.3.18 | | D.H.Q. moved to MOREUIL en route for PERONNE front. | E.H. |
| | 10.3.18 | | Division concentrating in MOREUIL area. | E.H. |

A5834 Wt. W4973/M687 750,000 8/16 D. D. & L. Ltd. Forms/C.2118/13.

Instructions regarding War Diaries and Intelligence Summaries are contained in F. S. Regs., Part II. and the Staff Manual respectively. Title pages will be prepared in manuscript.

# WAR DIARY

~~or~~

## ~~INTELLIGENCE SUMMARY.~~

(Erase heading not required.)

Army Form C. 2118.

D.A.D.V.S. 50. Divn.

| Place | Date | Hour | Summary of Events and Information | Remarks and references to Appendices |
|---|---|---|---|---|
| HARBONNIERES | 11.3.18 | | DHQ moved & arrived HARBONNIERES preparatory to moving into forward area - PERONNE front. Artillery already east of canal under administration of 19th Corps. | Est |
| | 12.3.18 | | Inspected animals of DHQ. 151 M.G. Coy. 2/2 N.F. Ambce. 447 Fd Coy R.E. | Est |
| | 13.3.18 | | Reported arrival in area to D.D.V.S. Fifth Army. | |
| | | | Inspected 151 Bgde HQ 5th 6th & 8th D.L.I. Examined animals of M.M.P. Found shoeing very satisfactory. Reported this to Q as complaint had been made about indifferent shoeing. | Est |
| | 14.3.18 | | Examined all animals of 150 Inf. Bgde. | Est |
| | | | Instructed M.V.S. to collect an Art. horse left behind on line of march - at HOURGES | |
| | | | Instructed units concerned to collect remounts arriving on 15th inst. | Est |
| | 15.3.18 | | Met & distributed 128 Remounts from station LA CHAPELLETTE. | |
| | 16.3.18 | | Visited & inspected 149. I. Bgde. | Est |
| | | | Made arrangements for the attendance of Field Coy R.E. in forward area. | |
| | | | At M.V.S. and inspected 4 animals before their evacuation to Base. | |
| | 17.3.18 | | Routine work. Supported a charge made by A.P.M. against a driver for unnecessarily trotting mules attached to vehicle on hard roads. | Est |
| | 18.3.18 | | In company with Divisional Gas Officer I inspected the fitting of Horse Respirators in Artillery Units | Est |
| | | | Instructed VOs. as to what M.V.Ss. in forward area they could evacuate to if necessary. | |
| | 19.3.18 | | Examined Horse respirators with Inf. Bgdes. | Est |
| | | | Inspected 11 animals at M.V.S (3 of which belonged to other Formations) before their evacuation. | |
| | 20.3.18 | | Examined all animals of the 3 Field Ambces. Suggested to Q that antigas drill for drivers be taken occasionally with that for animals, in order to accustom the animals, mules especially, to seeing men thus equipped, as well as to make the men more adept at the adjustment of the respirators on the horses. | Est |
| BEAUMETZ | 21.3.18 | | DHQ moved to BEAUMETZ - east of the Canal & south east of town of PERONNE. | Est |
| | | | Reported to D.D.V.S. 5th Army a mange case which had arrived in batch of remounts for the Division on 15th inst. | |

A5834 Wt. W4973/M687 750,000 8/16 D. D. & L. Ltd. Forms/C.2118/13.

Instructions regarding War Diaries and Intelligence Summaries are contained in F. S. Regs., Part II. and the Staff Manual respectively. Title pages will be prepared in manuscript.

# WAR DIARY
or
~~INTELLIGENCE SUMMARY.~~
(Erase heading not required.)

D.A.D.V.S. 50th Div.

Army Form C. 2118.

| Place | Date | Hour | Summary of Events and Information | Remarks and references to Appendices |
|---|---|---|---|---|
| LE MESNIL-BRUNTEL | 22.3.18 | | Owing to rapid German advance DHQ & M.V.S. retired on LE MESNIL BRUNTEL. Formulated a scheme for evacuation of sick during retreat. Arranged by making use of all available railheads in rear to keep M.V.S. always fairly empty of sick so as not to interfere with its mobility. | E.H. |
| FOUCAUCOURT | 23.3.18 | | Retired on VILLERS CARBONNEL and left same day for FOUCAUCOURT. Reported to "Q" on the shortage of water in this area. This was fully realised by Corps & some points were developed. In other cases animals were kept scattered as much as possible. | E.H. |
| " | 24.3.18 | | DHQ moved to school of instruction near FOUCAUCOURT. Wired to D.D.V.S. Fifth Army for motor ambulance to remove cases from M.V.S unable to walk. Visited M.V.S. and inspected 20 (11 of which were from other formations) before their evacuation to Base from railhead at VILLERS BRETONNEUX. | E.H. |
| HARBONNIERES | 25.3.18 | | DHQ & M.V.S. retired on HARBONNIERES. Inspected 28 animals at M.V.S (16 of which were from other formations) before their evacuation to Base from railhead at VILLERS BRETONNEUX | E.H. |
| MARCELCAVE | 26.3.18 | | DHQ retired on MARCELCAVE – M.V.S was sent about 4 miles further back to CACHY. A.D.V.S. 19th Corps informed me of his inability to find a Railhead for evacuating purposes. | E.H. E.H. |
| VILLERS BRETONNEUX | 27.3.18 | | DHQ retired on VILLERS BRETONNEUX. M.V.S. remained at CACHY admitting walking wounded cases. | |
| HANGARD | 28.3.18 | | DHQ retired on HANGARD and left same day for SOURDON. Inspected 16 animals at M.V.S (11 of which were of other formations). These were evacuated at Railhead SALEUX, after attempts to entrain at VILLERS BRETONNEUX & BOVES were made. | E.H. E.H. |
| BOVES | 29.3.18 | | DHQ & M.V.S. retired on BOVES. | |
| SAINS-en-AMIENOIS | 30.3.18 | | DHQ moved to SAINS-en-AMIENOIS. M.V.S was sent to HÉBÉCOURT. | E.H. |

A5834 Wt. W4973/M687 750,000 8/16 D. D. & L. Ltd. Forms/C.2118/13.

Instructions regarding War Diaries and Intelligence Summaries are contained in F. S. Regs., Part II. and the Staff Manual respectively. Title pages will be prepared in manuscript.

# WAR DIARY

~~or~~

## ~~INTELLIGENCE SUMMARY.~~

*(Erase heading not required.)*

D.A.D.V.S. 50 Div

Army Form C. 2118.

| Place | Date | Hour | Summary of Events and Information | Remarks and references to Appendices |
|---|---|---|---|---|
| DOURIEZ | 31.3.18 | | D.H.Q. arrives DOURIEZ<br>I personally conducted all infantry transport along roads from BOYES to area round DOURIEZ and despatched them to the respective areas they were to occupy. | [illegible] |
| | | | D.H.Q. 3.4.18<br>[signature] Maj A.V.C.<br>D.A.D.V.S. 50 Division | |

A5834 Wt. W4973/M687 750,000 8/16 D. D. & L. Ltd. Forms/C.2118/13.

Confidential

WO 95/2834

# WAR DIARY

OF

D.A.D.V.S. 50TH DIVISION

FROM 1st April 1918 to 30th April 1918

VOLUME XXXI



14

Instructions regarding War Diaries and Intelligence Summaries are contained in F. S. Regs., Part II. and the Staff Manual respectively. Title pages will be prepared in manuscript.

# WAR DIARY
~~or~~
~~INTELLIGENCE~~ ~~SUMMARY.~~
*(Erase heading not required.)*

Army Form C. 2118.

Vol 3

D.A.D.V.S. 50th Division

| Place | Date | Hour | Summary of Events and Information | Remarks and references to Appendices |
|---|---|---|---|---|
| DOURIEZ | 1.4.18 | | D.H.Q. at DOURIEZ. In charge of all Divisional Transport (less Artillery) en route for DOURIEZ area by road. Detailed various units to the respective areas they were to occupy. | E.H. |
| | 2.4.18 | | Visited M.V.S at BERNAY-en-PONTHIEU and inspected transport lines of Inf. Bgdes. | E.H. |
| | 3.4.18 | | Inspected Div. HQ Riders & Sig. Coy R.E. - before they set out to ROBECQ. | E.H. |
| ROBECQ | 4.4.18 | | DHQ moved to ROBECQ | E.H. |
| | 5.4.18 | | Met Infantry transports on march - inspected animals & conducted them to their respective areas. | E.H. |
| | 6.4.18 | | Visited M.V.S. at LALEU near ROBECQ. | E.H. |
| | | | Inspected SAASec. DAC, No 4 Coy. ASC 245 M.G. Coy. 151 Bgde. and 1/3 N. Fld. Ambce. | E.H. |
| | 7.4.18 | | Routine Work. Informed ADVS XI Corps of M.G. Battn. having left a horse behind in old area with civilian at DOMINOIS. | E.H. |
| MERVILLE | 8.4.18 | | D.H.Q. moved to Chateau on outskirts of MERVILLE. my office in centre of town, and M.V.S. at LE SART | E.H. |
| | 9.4.18 | | moved office to chateau, MERVILLE on account of being shelled. M.V.S remained at LE SART. | E.H. |
| | 10.4.18 | | Visited ASC. and Fld. Coy. R.E. & attended an animal belonging to civilian which had been wounded by shrapnel. | E.H. |
| La MOTTE au BOIS | 11.4.18 | | Retired on La Motte au Bois - shelled out of MERVILLE Chateau. Moved M.V.S. back always arranging to have it within easy reach of all transport lines though not unduly exposed to shell fire. | E.H. |
| | | | Inspected 18 animals at M.V.S. before their evacuation. All belonged to units of this Division. | E.H. |
| THIENNES | 12.4.18 | | DHQ moved on night 11/12 to THIENNES. Inspected animals of DHQ. Signal Coy. R.E. and M.M.P. | E.H. |
| | 13.4.18 | | Visited 3 Coys. ASC. Routine Work. | E.H. |
| WITTES | 14.4.18 | | DHQ. moved to WITTES | |
| | 15.4.18 | | attended at office of ADVS. XI Corps. & informed him of Artillery having left an animal behind in old area with a civilian at CONTEVILLE. Visited M.V.S at WITTES and inspected 8 animals before evacuation - 4 belonging to units of this Div. Detailed O.C. M.V.S. to ~~and~~ see that 2 AVC personnel were sent to V.C.C.S at AIRE. | E.H. |

Instructions regarding War Diaries and Intelligence Summaries are contained in F. S. Regs., Part II. and the Staff Manual respectively. Title pages will be prepared in manuscript.

# WAR DIARY
or
# ~~INTELLIGENCE SUMMARY.~~
*(Erase heading not required.)*

DADVS. 50th Div

Army Form C. 2118.

| Place | Date | Hour | Summary of Events and Information | Remarks and references to Appendices |
|---|---|---|---|---|
| ROCQUETOIRE | 16.4.18 | | DHQ moved to ROCQUETOIRE | |
| | | | Visited M.V.S. & inspected before their evacuation 5 animals – 4 belonging to this Division. | E.H. |
| | | | Visited 1st Army Field Remount Section MARLES-les-MINES with a view to obtaining Remounts for Division. | |
| | 17.4.18 | | Saw 3 animals at M.V.S. before their evacuation. Instructed O.C. M.V.S. to keep M.V.S. fairly clear of sick animals in case of orders for a quick move. | E.H. |
| | 18.4.18 | | Distributed 6 Riders, 19 L.D.H. 21 L.D.W. to units of Division. Reported to A.D.V.S. XI Corps on the indifferent type of remount sent up as Riders for Infantry Officers. | E.H. |
| | | | Saw 9 animals at M.V.S. prior to their evacuation – 8 belonging to this Division | |
| | 19.4.18 | | Inspected all animals of 151 Inf. Bgde. Wrote D.D.R. 1st Army for instructions as to disposal of Portuguese stray animals. | E.H. |
| AIRE. | 20.4.18 | | DHQ moved to AIRE | E.H. |
| | | | Inspected animals of 150 & 245 M. Gun Coy. 149 Inf Bgde. 7 Fd. Coy. RE. 1/1 N'bn Fd. Ambce. | |
| | 21.4.18 | | Met & distributed 7 Riders & 30 H.D. at THEROUANNE. | E.H. |
| | | | Visited 446 & 447 Fd. Coys. & 3/2 N'bn Fd Ambce. | |
| | 22.4.18 | | Inspected 8 animals for evacuation at M.V.S. | E.H. |
| | | | Visited lines of 3 Coy ASC. | |
| | 23.4.18 | | Collected from 1st Army Fd. Remount Secn. 13 R. 10 L.D.H. & 8 L.D.W. | E.H. |
| | | | Attended conference of D.A.D.V.S at XI Corps. H.Qrs. – office of A.D.V.S. | |
| | 24.4.18 | | Saw 20 animals at M.V.S. before their evacuation – 2 belonged to other Formations. | |
| | | | Issued to units of Div. all strays & other cured animals in M.V.S. which were suitable for reissue as Div. under orders to move. | E.H. |
| | 25.4.18 | | Left AIRE for French Army area round FISMES (Sheet SOISSONS 22) to see some of the standings before being taken over by this Division | E.H. |
| | 26.4.18 | | DHQ entrained CALONNE-RICQUART for FISMES arriving there noon 28th. | E.H. |
| FISMES | 27.4.18 | | | E.H. |
| ARCIS LE PONSART | 28.4.18 | | " moved from FISMES to ARCIS-le-PONSART. | E.H. |

A5834 Wt. W4973/M687 750,000 8/16 D. D. & L. Ltd. Forms/C.2118/13.

Instructions regarding War Diaries and Intelligence Summaries are contained in F. S. Regs., Part II. and the Staff Manual respectively. Title pages will be prepared in manuscript.

# WAR DIARY

~~or~~

## ~~INTELLIGENCE SUMMARY~~.

*(Erase heading not required.)*

Army Form C. 2118.

D.A.D.V.S. 50th Division

| Place | Date | Hour. | Summary of Events and Information | Remarks and references to Appendices |
|---|---|---|---|---|
| ARCIS le PONSART. | 29.4.18 | | Reported arrival to ADVS. IX Corps. Found billets for & established M.V.S. on outskirts of ARCIS le PONSART. | E.H. |
| | 30.4.18 | | Visited M.V.S. and 151 Inf. Bgde. transport lines. Saw animals of No 4 Coy ASC & 150 Inf Bgde. Wrote ADVS IX Corps on the question of posting a Sgt. A.V.C. for duty with a Machine Gun Corps. As this formation has an establishment of horses over 200 a Sgt. A.V.C. would be most useful. | E.H. |

D.H.Q.
30.4.18.

[illegible] Maj. A.V.C.
D.A.D.V.S., 50th Division

G.S.O.I
Pen

Gx 19/8/4
23. 6. 18

Confidential

# WAR DIARY

OF.

35 D.A.D.V.S., 50th DIVISION

from MAY 1st to MAY 31st 1918

VOLUME XXXII

Vol

30/

Vol 32.

Instructions regarding War Diaries and Intelligence Summaries are contained in F. S. Regs., Part II. and the Staff Manual respectively. Title Pages will be prepared in manuscript.

# WAR DIARY

~~or~~

# ~~INTELLIGENCE SUMMARY~~

*(Erase heading not required.)*

Army Form C. 2118.

D.A.D.V.S., 50th Division

| Place | Date | Hour | Summary of Events and Information | Remarks and references to Appendices |
|---|---|---|---|---|
| ARCIS-le-PONSART | 1/5/18 | | Made a careful inspection of stabling in the new area, and had several stables and water troughs carefully cleaned and disinfected. | [illegible] |
| | | | Visited 149 Inf Bgde Transport | |
| | 2/5/18 | | Inspected stabling arrangements and sick at M.V.S. | [illegible] |
| | | | Examined animals of 3 Fd. Coy. R.E. | |
| | 3/5/18 | | Arranged for collection and distribution of quicklime for stable disinfection. | [illegible] |
| | | | Inspected all animals of 151 Inf. Bgde. | |
| | 4/5/18 | | Visited M.V.S. and accompanied A.D.V.S. Corps and Horse master on their inspection of Artillery horses & lines. | [illegible] |
| BEAURIEUX | 5/5/18 | | H.Q. moved to BEAURIEUX | |
| | | | Inspected 26 horses & 5 mules at M.V.S. before their evacuation to No 9 V.E.S. and 4 horses & 1 mule before their evacuation as Remount cases. | |
| | | | Arranged with a horse butcher in FISMES for the sale of carcases fit for human consumption, and examined one animal at M.V.S. before it was destroyed for sale. | [illegible] |
| | 6/5/18 | | Inspected 50 Battn. M.G. Corps and all Divl Ambulances. | [illegible] |
| | 7/5/18 | | Had M.V.S. moved to BAULIEUX | [illegible] |
| | | | Inspected D.A.C. & No 1 Coy. A.S.C. | [illegible] |
| | 8/5/18 | | Visited all Infantry transport in MAIZY area, and recommended that animals would do better if picketted in open, and run less risk of infection than if stabled. | [illegible] |
| | | | Had several stables placed out of bounds as they had previously been occupied by mange cases of French Army | |
| | 9/5/18 | | Inspected all animals of 250 Bgde R.F.A. | |

2449 Wt. W14957/M90 750,000 1/16 J.B.C. & A. Forms/C.2118/12.

Army Form C. 2118.

Instructions regarding War Diaries and Intelligence Summaries are contained in F. S. Regs., Part II. and the Staff Manual respectively. Title Pages will be prepared in manuscript.

# WAR DIARY
~~or~~
# ~~INTELLIGENCE SUMMARY~~

*(Erase heading not required.)*

D.A.D.V.S.
50th Division

| Place | Date | Hour | Summary of Events and Information | Remarks and references to Appendices |
|---|---|---|---|---|
| BEAURIEUX | 10/5/18 | | Attended conference at A.D.V.S. office Corps HQrs. | |
| | | | Inspected 7 D.L.I. (pioneer battalion) and 150 Bgde transport | [illegible] |
| | 11/5/18 | | Visited M.V.S. and reissued 3 H.D. cured to M.G. Corps. | |
| | | | Examined all animals of [illegible]ty Coy RE. | [illegible] |
| | 12/5/18 | | Again visited 37 Fd Coy RE especially for the purpose of inspecting feet & shoeing in these units. | [illegible] |
| | 13/5/18 | | Inspected 3 Coys. A.S.C. | [illegible] |
| | | | Routine Work. | |
| | 14/5/18 | | Visited M.V.S. and fixed a more central position for this unit ~~nr.~~ MAIZY on MAIZY - MUSCOURT Road. | [illegible] |
| | | | Inspected all animals of 251 Bgde R.F.A. | |
| | 15/5/18 | | Visited site for a Vety. Evacuating Station near COURLANDON, and arranged to have men from the M.V.S. to disinfect it previous to being taken over by the British. | [illegible] |
| | 16/5/18 | | Sent several lice cases from 150 Bgde into M.V.S. to be washed and returned to their units. | [illegible] |
| | | | Inspected 151 Inf. Bgde & 2/2 Nth ? Fd Ambce. | |
| | 17/5/18 | | Visited M.V.S. and inspected 17 H and L.D.W. before their evacuation to Base. | [illegible] |
| | | | Inspected D.A.C. & No. 1 Coy. A.S.C. | |
| | 18/5/18 | | Routine Work & conference at office of A.D.V.S. Corps. | [illegible] |
| | 19/5/18 | | Visited M.V.S. and inspected 15 H & 1 L.D.W. before their evacuation to Base | [illegible] |
| | | | Inspected 250 Bgde R.F.A. | |
| | 20/5/18 | | Accompanied A.D.V.S. IX Corps on inspection of infantry transport and M.V.S., and reissued 4 horses & 1 mule as fit for duty. | [illegible] |

Instructions regarding War Diaries and Intelligence Summaries are contained in F. S. Regs., Part II. and the Staff Manual respectively. Title Pages will be prepared in manuscript.

# WAR DIARY
or
# ~~INTELLIGENCE SUMMARY~~

*(Erase heading not required.)*

Army Form C. 2118.

D.A.D.V.S.
50th Division

| Place | Date | Hour | Summary of Events and Information | Remarks and references to Appendices |
|---|---|---|---|---|
| BEAURIEUX | 21/5/18 | | Rec'd & distributed after examination 91 Remounts, from Railhead COURLANDON, to units of Division. | [illegible] |
| | 22/5/18 | | Inspected animals of Fd. Ambces and had 2 or 3 exchanged as they were becoming debilitated. Instructed M.V.S. to collect a mule left by some unit unknown with a civilian at GRAND HAMEAU. | [illegible] |
| | 23/5/18 | | Examined 13 horses & 3 mules at M.V.S. before their evacuation & 1 vicious mule before its evacuation to Remounts. | [illegible] |
| | 24/5/18 | | Visited Artillery Bgdes. with a view to weeding out debility cases before too advanced. | [illegible] |
| | 25/5/18 | | Inspected D.A.C. & No. 1 Coy. A.S.C. | [illegible] |
| | 26/5/18 | | Examined No. 9 Corps animals and 7 D.L.I. (Pioneers) | [illegible] |
| ST. GILLES | 27/5/18 | | Morning of GERMAN attack. D.H.Q. retired on REVILLON & ST GILLES via BAULIEUX. - had M.V.S. withdrawn to COHAN. | [illegible] |
| LHÉRY | 28/5/18 | | D.H.Q. retired to LHÉRY via SAVIGNY and M.V.S. moved to ROMIGNY. | [illegible] |
| IGNY le JARD | 29/5/18 | | D.H.Q. moved to IGNY le JARD via CUISLES, and M.V.S. stayed at MEILLERAI to admit animals of Inf. & Art. showing signs of exhaustion & distress consequent on long marches. | [illegible] |
| LE BREUIL | 30/5/18 | | D.H.Q. moved to LE BREUIL, and M.V.S. moved on to IGNY le JARD moving as much as possible in rear of column to render necessary assistance & relieve units of animals unfit to proceed with units. | [illegible] |
| VERT. la GRAVELLE | 31/5/18 | | D.H.Q. retired to VERT la GRAVELLE and M.V.S. was brought on to GONGY. Visited M.V.S. and returned 6 animals to their units as fit, and ordered the destruction of 5 others suffering from incurable gunshot wounds. | [illegible] |

[illegible signature]
Major A.V.C.
D.A.D.V.S., 50th Division

D.H.Q.
31.5.18.

2449 Wt. W14957/M90 750,000 1/16 J.B.C. & A. Forms/C.2118/12.

Confidential.

# WAR DIARY



OF

# D.A.D.V.S., 50TH DIVISION

from 1st June 1918 to 30th June 1918.

VOLUME 33.

17

Vol 3/3

Instructions regarding War Diaries and Intelligence Summaries are contained in F. S. Regs., Part II. and the Staff Manual respectively. Title pages will be prepared in manuscript.

# WAR DIARY
or
~~INTELLIGENCE SUMMARY.~~
(Erase heading not required.)

D.A.D.V.S., 50th Division

Army Form C. 2118.

36

| Place | Date | Hour | Summary of Events and Information | Remarks and references to Appendices |
|---|---|---|---|---|
| VERT-la-GRAVELLE | 1/6/18 | | Attended conference of D.A.D.V.S. at office of A.D.V.S. Corps. Visited 3 Coys ASC at La CHAPELLE FARM – all animals in the open. | [initials] |
| | 2/6/18 | | Inspected animals of RES. – all 3 Field Coys. | [initials] |
| | 3/6/18 | | Moved M.V.S. from CONGY to La CHAPELLE farm to a more central position for units as well as being nearer railhead, and Veterinary Evacuation Station. Visited and inspected 149 Inf Bgde. | [initials] |
| | 4/6/18 | | Inspected all animals of 50th Battn. M.G. Corps & 2/2 Nth. Ambce at CHATEAU CHAPTON. Sent 1 HD from No.1 Coy ASC to M.V.S. for treat in harness – as it was considered by Coy to be unmanageable. | [initials] |
| | 5/6/18 | | Visited animals of 150 I. Bgde and 1/1 N. Field Ambce. | [initials] |
| | 6/6/18 | | Inspected animals of D.A.C. at VERDY. | [initials] |
| | 7/6/18 | | Capt Woods AVC reported for duty with Division in relief of Capt H. Newton transferred to 7 Vety Hospital. Inspected 24 animals at M.V.S. before their evacuation to Base – 2 were from units unknown. | [initials] |
| | 8/6/18 | | Visited both Bgdes RFA near LACHY. Routine work | [initials] |
| MONDEMONT. | 9/6/18 | | D.H.Q. moved to MONDEMONT. Visited 150 I. Bgde at BROYES. Capt H. Newton AVC despatched to Base after handing command of M.V.S. to Capt W. H. Jackson AVC. Capt. Woods newly arrived attached to Infantry Bgdes. for duty. | [initials] |

D. D. & L., London, E.C.
(A10266) Wt W5300/P713 750,000 2/18 Sch. 52 Forms/C2118/16

Instructions regarding War Diaries and Intelligence Summaries are contained in F. S. Regs., Part II. and the Staff Manual respectively. Title pages will be prepared in manuscript.

# WAR DIARY
or
~~INTELLIGENCE SUMMARY.~~
(Erase heading not required.)

DADVS 50' Div

Army Form C. 2118.

| Place | Date | Hour | Summary of Events and Information | Remarks and references to Appendices |
|---|---|---|---|---|
| MONDEMONT | 10/6/18 | | Checked the no. of humane cattle killers in Division and made sure that each V.O. was equipped with one. | |
| | | | Inspected 13 animals at M.V.S. before evacuation - 1 was a stray animal | E.H. |
| | 11/6/18 | | S/Sgt D.B. Douglas AVC despatched from M.V.S. for duty with No. 9 Veterinary Evacuating Station. | |
| | | | Visited and inspected 149 Inf Bgde at BROYES | E.H. |
| | 12/6/18 | | Inspected all animals of 251 Bgde R.F.A. & No. 1 Coy ASC at LACHY. | E.H. |
| | 13/6/18 | | Inspected all animals in 151 Inf Bgde. BROYES. | E.H. |
| | 14/6/18 | | Informed A.D.V.S Corps of the rare cases of Tetanus in Division. Proposed to observe any case without the administration of anti-tetanic serum. Reports will be furnished later. | E.H. |
| | 15/6/18 | | Attended conference at CORPS HQrs. | |
| | | | Inspected Vety. equipment of smaller units. | |
| | | | Visited & inspected animals of 149 Bgde + 2nd N.F.A.mbce. | E.H. |
| | 16/6/18 | | Visited 251 Bgde R.F.A. to examine feet & shoeing. Recommended the issue of a Field Forge for B. Battery 251 Bgde. | |
| | | | Reported a shortage of horse shoes, especially of the larger sizes to Q. | E.H. |

D. D. & L., London, E.C.
(A10266) Wt W5300/P713 750,000 2/18 Sch. 52 Forms/C2118/16

Instructions regarding War Diaries and Intelligence Summaries are contained in F. S. Regs., Part II. and the Staff Manual respectively. Title pages will be prepared in manuscript.

# WAR DIARY
~~or~~
~~INTELLIGENCE~~ SUMMARY.
(Erase heading not required.)

D.A.D.V.S., 50th Division

Army Form C. 2118.

| Place | Date | Hour | Summary of Events and Information | Remarks and references to Appendices |
|---|---|---|---|---|
| LA NOUE | 17/6/18 | | Division moves to LA NOUE. | |
| | | | Moves M.V.S. to BEAUVAIS la NOUE. | |
| | | | Accompanied A.D.V.S Corps on his inspection of animals of D.A.C. & Artillery Bdes. | Est |
| | 18/6/18 | | Inspected 3 Field Coys. RE. | Est |
| | 19/6/18 | | Examined 8 animals in M.V.S before their evacuation to Base. 1 horse believed to belong to French gendarmes found and evacuated through V.E.S. | |
| | | | Inspected 2 Coys. ASC. | Est |
| | 20/6/18 | | Inspected animals of D.H.Q. & Sig. Coy. RE. | |
| | | | Visited No. 4 Coy. ASC. | Est |
| | 21/6/18 | | Issued to units of Division 4 of the M.V.S. riders which had become surplus on reduction of establishment. | |
| | | | Visited 150 Inf. Bgde. | Est |
| | 22/6/18 | | Attended conference of D.A.D.V.S at Office of A.D.V.S IX Corps. | |
| | | | Inspected 60 animals which were being transferred from 25 Div. to 50th. | Est |
| | 23/6/18 | | Visited units of 25th Composite Inf Bgde. | Est |
| | 24/6/18 | | Posted an officer A.V.C. + one Sgt A.V.C for duty with 25th Comp. Bgde. | |
| | | | Inspected 75 animals before their evacuation to Base. | Est |
| | 25/6/18 | | Inspected 99 animals surplus to Division going down to Base on 28th. Selected from remaining surplus 26 for Art. 17 HD for ASC 6 Riders for CRE. | Est |

D. D. & L., London, E.C.
(A10266) Wt W5300/P713 750,000 2/18 Sch. 52 Forms/C2118/16

Instructions regarding War Diaries and Intelligence Summaries are contained in F. S. Regs., Part II. and the Staff Manual respectively. Title pages will be prepared in manuscript.

# WAR DIARY
~~or~~
~~INTELLIGENCE SUMMARY.~~
*(Erase heading not required.)*

D.A.D.V.S, 50th Div

Army Form C. 2118.

| Place | Date | Hour | Summary of Events and Information | Remarks and references to Appendices |
|---|---|---|---|---|
| | 26/6/18 | | Inspected animals of Fd. Ambces & M.G. Battn.<br>Visited all Corps. A.S.C. | E.L.T. |
| | 27/6/18 | | Inspected 19 animals before their evacuation to Base & evacuated 1 French horse found.<br>Again inspected Inf. transport animals of the 2 Composite Bgdes. Infantry. | E.L.T. |
| | 28/6/18 | | Attended at the entraining of animals I inspected on 25th inst.<br>Visited & inspected DAC animals. | E.L.T. |
| | 29/6/18 | | Attended Corps - Conference of D.A.D.V.S at office of A.D.V.S.<br>Inspected 20 animals sent for issue to units of this Division by A.D.V.S. IX Corps. | E.L.T. |
| | 30/6/18 | | Visited M.V.S. & had 2 carcases sold to a local horse butcher for 500 francs.<br>Inspected animals of D.H.Q. & Div. Sig. Coy. R.E. and M.G. Battn.<br>Instructed M.V.S. to collect from French Vety. Hospital at PONT sur SEINE 4 British horses - authority to collect given by A.D.V.S. IX Corps | E.L.T. |

E. L. Taine [signature] Maj AVC
D.A.D.V.S, 50th Div

D. D. & L., London, E.C.
(A10266) W.W5300/P713 750,000 2/18 Sch. 52 Forms/C2118/16

CONFIDENTIAL.

# WAR DIARY

OF

D.A.D.V.S, 50TH DIVISION

FROM 1ST JULY to 31ST JULY 1918

VOLUME XXXIV

Vol. XXXIV 17

Instructions regarding War Diaries and Intelligence Summaries are contained in F. S. Regs., Part II. and the Staff Manual respectively. Title pages will be prepared in manuscript.

# WAR DIARY
~~or~~
~~INTELLIGENCE SUMMARY.~~
(Erase heading not required.)

D.A.D.V.S
50th Division

Army Form C. 2118.

WR 37

| Place | Date | Hour | Summary of Events and Information | Remarks and references to Appendices |
|---|---|---|---|---|
| LA NOUE | 1/7/18 | | Division preparing to move by rail from FERE-en-CHAMPENOISE to PONT REMY - was present at railhead - | E.H. |
| | 2/7/18 | | FERE en CHAMPENOISE for two days superintending entraining of animals of Division | E.H. |
| | 3/7/18 | | En route by rail for PONT REMY superintended | E.H. |
| PONT REMY & HUPPY | 4/7/18 | | Arrived PONT REMY and ~~[illegible]~~ detraining. | E.H. |
| | 5/7/18 | | DHQ located HUPPY. Selected site for M.V.S and inspected transport animals after train journey. | E.H. |
| | 6/7/18 | | Reported arrival to ADVS 22nd Corps, and inspected standings of A.S.C. | E.H. |
| | 7/7/18 | | Inspected animals of 50th Battn. M.G. Corps. Reported on inefficiency of Sgt A.V.C attached that unit & has been replaced. | E.H. |
| | 8/7/18 | | Visited ADVS XXII Corps. | |
| | | | Inspected 30 animals (L.D.H) arriving for Division from H.T. Depot ABBEVILLE | |
| | | | Visited 4 cases left behind by units and arranged with D.D.V.S. Army for their collection by motor ambulance - a distance too far for horse float which was at that time not serviceable enough to undertake their collection. Inspected 6 animals in M.V.S before their evacuation. | E.H. |
| | 9/7/18 | | Accompanied DDR 4th Army on his inspection of Artillery horses. Selected 138 poor animals for replacement and reported this to D.D.V.S 4 Army & Q. | |
| | | | Recommended "Q" that AIRAINES be put out of bounds for animals of Division on account of reported contagious disease amongst civilian's horses. Detailed a V.O. to investigate & report on steps taken by civil authorities to combat this disease. | E.H. |
| | 10/7/18 | | Inspected 24 D.D.R. cases from 50th D.A. before their evacuation. | |
| | | | Made a redistribution of work for V.Os. to avoid unnecessary journeys & to avoid overlapping. | E.H. |
| GAMACHES | 11/7/18 | | Div. moved by road to GAMACHES. Inspected 22 animals before their evacuation in M.V.S | |
| | | | Detailed V.O. to visit VERGIES & vicinity & report on foot & mouth ~~[illegible]~~ disease amongst animals of civilians. | E.H. |
| MARTIN EGLISE | 12/7/18 | | Div. moved on to MARTIN EGLISE. & M.V.S went to SERQUEUX | E.H. |
| | 13/7/18 | | Made arrangements for Veterinary attendance on animals of troops in ABANCOURT & SERQUEUX areas. | E.H. |

(A7092). Wt. W12839/M1293. 750,000. 1/17. D. D. & L., Ltd. Forms/C.2118/14.

Army Form C. 2118.

# WAR DIARY
~~or~~
~~INTELLIGENCE~~ ~~SUMMARY.~~ D.A.D.V.S., 50 Div

(Erase heading not required.)

Instructions regarding War Diaries and Intelligence Summaries are contained in F. S. Regs., Part II. and the Staff Manual respectively. Title pages will be prepared in manuscript.

| Place | Date | Hour | Summary of Events and Information | Remarks and references to Appendices |
|---|---|---|---|---|
| MARTIN EGLISE | 14.7.18 | | Division taking over fresh troops in training in MARTIN EGLISE area. Inspected their existing transport & lines. | Est |
| | 15.7.18 | | On further inspection of transport of Inf. selected 8 cases for immediate evacuation, and despatched them direct to No. 9 V.H. DIEPPE. | Est |
| GRÈGES | 16.7.18 | | D.H.Q. moved to GRÈGES and I reported to D.D.V.S. (Southern L. of C.) On account of having to detail 2 V.Os for duty in ABANCOURT & SERQUEUX areas the attendance of all animals in MARTIN EGLISE area devolved on myself. Doubtful cases discovered by Sgts A.V.C. with Bgdes. were paraded each morning for my inspection & those I considered ought to be evacuated were sent to DIEPPE - No. 9 V.H. Two other V.Os were left behind at ALLERY in 9th Corps area with the Artillery. Not satisfied with horse management of 5th Royal Irish Regt. & made suggestions to T.O. for its improvement. | Est |
| | 17.7.18 | | Visited R.E. units & A.S.C. Coy at MARTIN EGLISE and evacuated 1 to Base. | Est |
| | 18.7.18 | | Inspected all units with transport in MARTIN EGLISE area to accelerate shoeing which was not satisfactory. Evacuated 1 animal to Base. | Est |
| | 19.7.18 | | Visited all animals of troops in SERQUEUX & ABANCOURT areas with AA.&Q.M.G. and evacuated 1 animal direct to Base. Saw 4 others in M.V.S. at SERQUEUX before their evacuation. | Est |
| | 20.7.18 | | ~~Motored to Grandcourt & had an~~ inspection of M.G. Battn. Submitted written report to Q on the stable management &c. of the 4 Coys. comprising the Battalion. Visited D.D.V.S. (Southern L. of C.) Destroyed 1 rider suffering from Tetanus - (f. u. n.) | Est. |
| | 21.7.18 | | Visited Inf. horse lines in Camps at MARTIN EGLISE. Attended Staff Conference. Notified D.D.V. 4th Army what precautions had been taken with regard to outbreak of Foot & Mouth disease in VERGIES & immediate area. Suggested a proportion of animals with defective vision could be used effectively in water carts & forage wagons. | Est. |

(A7092). Wt. W12839/M1293. 750,000. 1/17. D. D. & L., Ltd. Forms/C.2118/14.

Instructions regarding War Diaries and Intelligence Summaries are contained in F. S. Regs., Part II. and the Staff Manual respectively. Title pages will be prepared in manuscript.

# WAR DIARY ~~or~~ ~~INTELLIGENCE SUMMARY.~~

(Erase heading not required.)

D.A.D.V.S. 50 Division

Army Form C. 2118.

| Place | Date | Hour | Summary of Events and Information | Remarks and references to Appendices |
|---|---|---|---|---|
| GRÈGES | 22 7/18 | | Again visited Inf. transport lines in MARTIN EGLISE and made a thorough inspection of animals of 5th Royal Irish Regt. (Pioneers) and reported on poor horse management. Grooming was very indifferent – animals feet appeared to be very rarely examined and the fitting of harness needed more attention. | |
| | | | Inspected 12 animals belonging to other formations before their evacuation by M.V.S. to Base | Est |
| | 23 7/18 | | Again visited Pioneer Regt. and 3 Fd Coy. R.E. | Est |
| | 24 7/18 | | Evacuated 5 animals from Inf Bgde & R.E.S. direct to Base Hospital DIEPPE | |
| | | | Inspected M.G. Batt. & Div'l Wing. | Est |
| | | | M.V.S. arrived in this area from SERQUEUX and I selected a site within convenient distance of the units having the bigger majority of horses. | |
| | 25 7/18 | | Inspected animals of 149 Bgde. | |
| | | | Sent G.O.C's rider to Hospital at DIEPPE and visited O.C. there to arrange a minor operation on an animal of No. 4 Coy A.S.C. | Est |
| | 26 7/18 | | Inspected animals of 150th Bgde. & found shoeing not at all satisfactory – especially in 7th Wilts. Regt. | |
| | | | Drew attention of O.C. 4 Coy A.S.C. to waste of forage – hay especially – through paucity of haynets. | Est |
| | 27 7/18 | | Attended office of D.D.V.S. (Southern) | |
| | | | Inspected 8 animals at M.V.S. before their evacuation to Base. | Est |
| | 28 7/18 | | Visited transport lines of 1/3 N.F. Ambce & horses of 1/1 N.F.A. | Est |
| | 29 7/18 | | Inspected 6 animals at M.V.S. before their evacuation to Base | |
| | | | Visited 3 Coy. A.S.C. at MARTIN EGLISE | Est |

(A7092). Wt. W12839/M1293. 750,000. 1/17. D. D. & L., Ltd. Forms/C.2118/14.

Instructions regarding War Diaries and Intelligence Summaries are contained in F. S. Regs., Part II. and the Staff Manual respectively. Title pages will be prepared in manuscript.

# WAR DIARY

or

INTELLIGENCE SUMMARY.

(Erase heading not required.)

D.A.D.V.S. 50th Div

Army Form C. 2118.

| Place | Date | Hour | Summary of Events and Information | Remarks and references to Appendices |
|---|---|---|---|---|
| GRÈGES | 30/7/18 | | D.A.D.V.S. proceeded on leave today. Capt. W. M. Jackson A.V.C. O.C. 1/1 N.M.V.S. acting D.A.D.V.S. Division. Informed A.D.V.S. III Corps of move of M. G. Battalion into area of troops administered by him. | WMJ |
| | 31/7/18 | | Attended Staff conference | WMJ |
| | | | Visited 3 Fld. Coy. R.E., and attended draught horse on D.H.Q. | |
| | | | F.A.P. 1.8.18. W M Jackson Capt A.V.C for D.A.D.V.S. 50 Div. | |

(A7092). Wt. W12839/M1293. 750,000. 1/17. D. D. & L., Ltd. Forms/C.2118/14.

CONFIDENTIAL

# WAR DIARY

OF

D.A.D.V.S. 50th DIVISION.

FROM 1st AUGT. 1918 to 31st AUGT. 1918.

VOLUME XXXV

Vol XXXV

Instructions regarding ~~War Diaries~~ and Intelligence Summaries are contained in F. S. Regs., Part II. and the Staff Manual respectively. Title pages will be prepared in manuscript.

# WAR DIARY
~~or~~
# ~~INTELLIGENCE SUMMARY.~~
*(Erase heading not required.)*

Army Form C. 2118.

DADVS 50th Division

Vol 38

| Place | Date | Hour | Summary of Events and Information | Remarks and references to Appendices |
|---|---|---|---|---|
| GRÈGES | 1/8/18 | | Capt. W. M. Jackson AVC O.C. 1/1 N'bn. M.V.S. acting D.A.D.V.S. Division from 31st July to 15th Augt. Forwarded to "Q" a report submitted by V.O. i/c Infantry Details on the absence of a shoeing smith and indifferent stable management in that formation. | EH |
| | 2/8/18 | | Issued instructions as laid down in G.R.Os. to V.Os not to condemn "bad" oats by giving certificates to that effect to units, but to instruct that they be returned to Base for treatment. | EH |
| | 3/8/18 | | Visited D.D.V.S. (Southern) with weekly returns for Division. Again reported to 'Q' on the unsatisfactory conditions existing in transport lines of Dn'. details | EH |
| | 4/8/18 | | Visited and inspected animals of 1/3 N.F. Ambce. Issued 2 H.D. to 1/3 N.F. Ambce. Informed 'Q' of the number of L.D. convalescent in M.V.S. and practically fit for reissue. | EH |
| | 5/8/18 | | Issued mule to 447 Fd. Coy. R.E. Returned to Base Vety. Stores Vouchers forwarded to 66th Dn. for drugs issued to units which had now been absorbed into that Divn. | EH |
| | 6/8/18 | | Issued 2 L.D. - one to 446 Fd. Coy, 1 to 6th N.F. | EH |
| | 7/8/18 | | Routine Work. | EH |
| | 8/8/18 | | Visited civilian farms in village occupied by D.H.Q. to investigate cases of Foot + Mouth disease reported by French Mission. Warning notices were placed on farms, & gates of fields where disease existed. Arranged with "Q" to remove the 447 Fd. Coys' horse lines which were too near the Princess as the latter unit has a few cases of mange. Wrote O.C. Machine Gun Battn. informing him of correct procedure to obtain Sgt AVC to replace the one evacuated sick. | EH |

(A7092). Wt. W12839/M1293. 750,000. 1/17. D. D. & L., Ltd. Forms/C.2118/14.

Instructions regarding War Diaries and Intelligence Summaries are contained in F. S. Regs., Part II. and the Staff Manual respectively. Title pages will be prepared in manuscript.

# WAR DIARY

or

~~INTELLIGENCE SUMMARY.~~ D.A.D.V.S, 50th Div

(Erase heading not required.)

Army Form C. 2118.

| Place | Date | Hour | Summary of Events and Information | Remarks and references to Appendices |
|---|---|---|---|---|
| GRÈGES | 9/8/18 | | Brought to notice of "Q" the shortage of grooming kit, haynets, shoes, nosebags at Ordnance and recommended that delivery of nosebags be hastened, as it was essential that individual nosebags be used in view of recent mange cases. Again wrote "Q" to hasten delivery of new horse float. | E.H. |
| | 10/8/18 | | Visited D.D.V.S. (Southern) with returns for Division. Wrote O.C. Pioneers informing him of my endeavours to have animals in unit under his command put through dipping bath. | E.H. |
| | 11/8/18 | | Visited 1/3 N'bn F. Ambce. and submitted a written report to O.C. on the unsatisfactory condition of horse lines and irregularity of stable hours. | E.H. |
| | 12/8/18 | | Attended Staff Conference at D.H.Q. Gave "Q" a detailed state of animal wastage for past week both for their information and to enable a remount demand to be compiled for their replacement. | E.H. |
| | 13/8/18 | | Routine Work. | E.H. |
| | 14/8/18 | | Routine Work and return of D.A.D.V.S to duty from leave | E.H. |
| | 15/8/18 | | Examined animals of Div. Details previous to their transfer to Base to join another Division. Inspected 6 animals in M.V.S. before their evacuation. | E.H. |
| | 16/8/18 | | Visited Vety. Hosp. DIEPPE to make further arrangements for the dipping of animals of 5/R.I.R (Pioneers) and instructed V.O. of unit to attend at the dipping on 19th inst. | E.H. |

(A7092). Wt. W12839/M1293. 750,000. 1/17. D. D. & L., Ltd. Forms/C.2118/14.

Instructions regarding War Diaries and Intelligence Summaries are contained in F. S. Regs., Part II. and the Staff Manual respectively. Title pages will be prepared in manuscript.

# WAR DIARY
or
# ~~INTELLIGENCE SUMMARY.~~
(Erase heading not required.)

D.A.D.V.S., 50 Div

Army Form C. 2118.

| Place | Date | Hour | Summary of Events and Information | Remarks and references to Appendices |
|---|---|---|---|---|
| GREGES | 17/8/18 | | At HQ. D.D.V.S (Southern) with weekly returns. | |
| | | | Visited 150 Bgde. Div. Sig. Coy. RE. and DHQ. horse lines. Reported on unsatisfactory work of Shoeing Smith on DHQ. to Camp Commandant & recommended his removal. | |
| | 18/8/18 | | Divisional Horse Show | |
| | 19/8/18 | | Inspected horses & standings of 1/3 N.F.A. to see what improvements had taken place since last adverse report. | |
| | | | Reapplied to D.D.V.S.(S) for a Sgt. A.V.C. for duty with 150 Bgde vice one reduced & returned to Base for inefficiency. | |
| | | | Arranged to inspect 2 unsuitable animals in Signal Sec. with 150 I Bgde | |
| | 20/8/18 | | Visited 3 Fd Coy. RE. Pioneers. 6 Inniskilling Drs. & 1st KOYLI. Found cases of ringworm in last named unit, and had officers animals brought out of dirty stables & picketed in open. Instructed that one animal be taken to "dip" on 24th inst. from this unit. | |
| | 21/8/18 | | Inspected animals of 151 Bgde HQrs. & 4th K.R.R. Corps | |
| | | | Examined at 1/1 N.M.V.S 10 animals prior to their evacuation to Base. | |
| | | | Visited horse lines of Div. Sig. Coy. RE. | |
| | | | At 9 Vety. Hospital. | |
| | | | Made arrangements with 'Q' to collect G.O.C's charger, which had been despatched from Hospital to Remounts. | |

(A7092). Wt. W12839/M1293. 750,000. 1/17. D. D. & L., Ltd. Forms/C.2118/14.

Instructions regarding War Diaries and Intelligence Summaries are contained in F. S. Regs., Part II. and the Staff Manual respectively. Title pages will be prepared in manuscript.

# WAR DIARY
or
~~INTELLIGENCE SUMMARY.~~
(Erase heading not required.)

Army Form C. 2118.

D.A.D.V.S., 50 Division

| Place | Date | Hour | Summary of Events and Information | Remarks and references to Appendices |
|---|---|---|---|---|
| GRÈGES | 22/8/18 | | Visited and inspected 1/3 N. Fd. Ambce. | |
| | | | At Vet. Hosp. DIEPPE made arrangements to have animals of Pioneer Battn. re-dipped – informed O.C. unit & V.O. concerned. | JH |
| | 23/8/18 | | Inspected 6 animals at M.V.S. before their evacuation to Base. | |
| | | | Again visited horse lines of 1/2 N.F.A. and drew attention of O.C. to scarcity of haynets & nosebags. This resulted in an urgent demand being made on Ordnance. | JH |
| | 24/8/18 | | Inspected 1/1 N.F.A. and 13th Black Watch. In latter unit shoeing was not up to date and grooming was poorly done. Reported state of shoeing to Q. and am visiting this unit again soon to ascertain what progress, if any, has been made. | JH |
| | 25/8/18 | | Inspected animals of 7th Wilts. DHQ & Sig. Coy. R.E. 1/1 N.F. Ambce & 3rd Royal Fusiliers | JH |
| | 26/8 & 27/8 | | Visited Artillery in forward area – only saw about half animals as some of the batteries were changing positions & moving forward. | JH |
| | | | Made redistribution of work for V.Os. | |
| | 28/8/18 | | Inspected 5 animals at M.V.S. before their evacuation, and instructed 1/3 N.F.A. to send a H.D. to M.V.S. | |
| | | | Visited watering points and inspected watering arrangements – recommended alteration of system to save time. | JH |
| | | | Inspected lines of 447 Fd. Coy. R.E. and 3rd R. Fusiliers. Former short of haynets and the latter deficient in nosebags. Impressed on both units the importance & utility of these articles. | |
| | 29/8/18 | | With C.R.E. and inspected 3 Fd. Coys. R.E. & Div. Sig. Coy. R.E. | JH |
| | | | Submitted detailed report to Q on condition in which I found animals of Artillery on 26th inst. | |

(A7092). Wt. W12839/M1293. 750,000. 1/17. D. D. & L., Ltd. Forms/C.2118/14.

Instructions regarding War Diaries and Intelligence Summaries are contained in F. S. Regs., Part II. and the Staff Manual respectively. Title pages will be prepared in manuscript.

# WAR DIARY
*or*
~~INTELLIGENCE SUMMARY.~~
*(Erase heading not required.)*

Army Form C. 2118.

D.A.D.V.S, 50th Division

| Place | Date | Hour | Summary of Events and Information | Remarks and references to Appendices |
|---|---|---|---|---|
| GREGES | 30/8/18 | | Inspected 6 animals at M.V.S before their evacuation to Base. | |
| | | | Visited & inspected all units transport animals in 151 Inf. Bgde. | E.H. |
| | 31/8/18 | | Reported to A.D.M.S on my visit to 1/3 N.F.A & suggested he applied to have some of the H.D. returned which were detached for duty with A.S.C. to relieve the pressure on the remainders who were being heavily taxed in present area. | |
| | | | Inspected farms & animals in GREGES reported, as being infected with Foot & Mouth disease. All precautions were taken to safeguard the health of the troops billetted in village area. | E.H. |

D.H.Q.
1.9.18

[signature] Maj A.V.C
D.A.D.V.S, 50th Division

(A7092). Wt. W12839/M1293. 750,000. 1/17. D. D. & L., Ltd. Forms/C.2118/14.

Confidential

WD39

# WAR DIARY

OF.

# D.A.D.V.S. 50TH DIVISION

FROM. 1ST SEPTR 1918 TO 30TH SEPTR 1918.

VOLUME XXXVI

31

Vol 36

Instructions regarding War Diaries and Intelligence Summaries are contained in F. S. Regs., Part II. and the Staff Manual respectively. Title pages will be prepared in manuscript.

# WAR DIARY
*or*
~~INTELLIGENCE SUMMARY.~~
*(Erase heading not required.)*

Army Form C. 2118.

D.A.D.V.S. 50th Division

| Place | Date | Hour | Summary of Events and Information | Remarks and references to Appendices |
|---|---|---|---|---|
| GREGES | 1/9/18 | | Inspected No. 274 Coy. A.S.C. and examined 2 Riders of D.H.Q. both foot cases. | |
| | | | Submitted Veterinary Inspection Reports for month of August to D.D.V.S. (L of C). | |
| | | | Reported Shoeing-Smith Pruslin with M.V.S. to D.D.V.S. for inefficiency and requested that he be replaced. | [initials] |
| | 2/9/18 | | Gave Vety. authority for 7th Fd. Coy. R.E. to apply to Div. Train for 2 lbs. linseed per day. | |
| | | | Inspected shoeing in 13th Black Watch, and reported improvement to Q. | |
| | | | Inspected forage of several units, & in many cases "heated" oats were found. Gave orders for these to be returned to Supplies and replaced. | |
| | | | Visited & inspected 446th, 447th Fd. Coys. R.E. and 151 Bgde. H.Qrs. | [initials] |
| | | | Examined Pioneer animals – grooming needed more attention. | |
| | 3/9/18 | | Inspected 1/3 N.F.A. mainly to examine feet of animals. | [initials] |
| | | | Visited lines of 150 I Bgde. 2nd N.F. 7 Wilts. 2nd Royal Munster Fusiliers. | |
| | 4/9/18 | | Took Route march for Inf. Units. & R.E.s. with their 1st line Transport. Detailed necessary A.V.C. personnel to accompany troops. Visited M.V.S. and saw lines of units as left by horses when they set off on march. | |
| | | | Interviewed new A.V.C. Sgt. for 150 I Bgde. Inspected 5 animals before their evacuation to Base. | |
| | | | Detailed O.C. M.V.S. to sit on examining board at No 4 Coy. on 4th inst. for purpose of testing cold shoers as shoeing smiths. Informed O.C. Train which officer had been selected. | [initials] |
| | 5/9/18 | | Inspected 150 I Bgde. 7th, 446th Fd. Coys. R.E. and Pioneers. | |
| | | | Visited lines of 1/1 N.F. Ambce. Reported 2nd N.F. to Bgde. H.Qrs. for bad shoeing. There were also too many kicks in this unit & recommended stricter action on part of stable guards & line orderlies | [initials] |

(A7092). Wt. W12839/M1293. 750,000. 1/17. D. D. & L., Ltd. Forms/C.2118/14.

Instructions regarding War Diaries and Intelligence Summaries are contained in F. S. Regs., Part II. and the Staff Manual respectively. Title pages will be prepared in manuscript.

# WAR DIARY
*or*
# ~~INTELLIGENCE SUMMARY.~~ D.A.D.V.S. 50th Division

*(Erase heading not required.)*

Army Form C. 2118.

| Place | Date | Hour | Summary of Events and Information | Remarks and references to Appendices |
|---|---|---|---|---|
| GRÈGES | 6/9/18 | | Inspected No 2 & 3 Coy. ASC of 50th Div. Train ASC, 2nd Dublin Fus. 13th Blk Watch and 3rd Royal Fusiliers. A marked improvement was noticed in stable management of Inf. units. | Est. |
| | 7/9/18 | | Visited D.D.V.S. (Lof C) and 149 Bgde. transport lines. No transport officer in attendance and I propose visiting these units again on 9th inst. | Est. |
| | 8/9/18 | | Routine work and visited Remount Depot. Inspected 4 animals before their evacuation to Base. | Est. |
| | 9/9/18 | | Inspected 50th Batt. M.G. Corps after their detachment from forward area. Evacuated 12 to M.V.S. Reported on my inspection of these animals to Q. Again visited lines of 149 I. Bgde. Formulated a scheme for dealing with casualties in animals & forwarded it to Q. It is proposed to put the scheme into execution during coming manoeuvres of Division. | Est. |
| | 10/9/18 | | Visited and inspected animals of 150. Inf Bgde. Submitted to Q a scheme of veterinary arrangements such as would be carried out in the case of an advance. Inspected 21 animals at M.V.S. before their evacuation. | Est. |
| | 11/9/18 | | Examined animals of 151 I Bgde & M.G. Battn. At M.V.S. and gave instructions to O.C. on part M.V.S. were to play in manoeuvres on 12th. | Est. |
| | 12/9/18 | | Attended manoeuvres. Established an advanced collecting post on line of upward moving traffic, and selected new sites as advance progressed. Gave M.V.S. conducting parties & dressers plenty of practice in roles they would have to fill in a real attack. Inspected 12 animals at M.V.S. before their evacuation. Reported to Q on condition of animals of M.G. Battn. Brought to notice of Q the widespread misuse of horse shoe nails for improper purposes, and had matter brought to notice of Unit Commanders. | Est. |

Instructions regarding War Diaries and Intelligence Summaries are contained in F. S. Regs., Part II. and the Staff Manual respectively. Title pages will be prepared in manuscript.

# WAR DIARY
*or*
# ~~INTELLIGENCE SUMMARY.~~
*(Erase heading not required.)*

D.A.D.V.S, 50 Div.

Army Form C. 2118.

| Place | Date | Hour | Summary of Events and Information | Remarks and references to Appendices |
|---|---|---|---|---|
| GRÈGES | 13/9/18 | | Made a thorough inspection of M.G. Battn. animals with G.O.C Division. Some of animals in low condition – having only rejoined Division from forward area on 9th inst. | E.H. |
| | 14/9/18 | | Visited M.V.S. & inspected 9 animals before their evacuation. Distributed 6 Humane Cattle Killers to Officers & Sergeants A.V.C. Inspected all animals & standings of 149 I. Bgde. | E.H. |
| GRÈGES/ LUCHEUX | 15/9/18 | | Division entraining at ROUXMESNIL for DOULLENS area. | E.H. |
| | 16/9/18 | | DHQ entrained and office opened at LUCHEUX. | E.H. |
| LUCHEUX | 17/9/18 | | Visited A.D.V.S. XVII Corps and reported arrival of Division in Corps area – gave him also location of M.V.S. Again inspected M.G. Battn. animals and those of Pioneers. | E.H. |
| | 18/9/18 | | Inspected site of M.V.S. – poor one but best available in area. Despatched an officer to Artillery to relieve one going on leave to U.K. Visited and inspected animals of 151 I. Bgde. Some of units short of [illegible] so brought this matter to notice of Transport Officers. | |
| | 19/9/18 | | Again visited M.G. Battn. 149 Bgde HQrs 151 Bgde HQrs 13th Black Watch and 4th K.R.R.Corps. At Corps HQrs. and made arrangements with ADVS for the evacuation of sick from this area to the Corps Evacuating Station at BOISLEUX au Mont. Informed OC MVS of the arrangements. | E.H. E.H. |
| | 20/9/18 | | Inspected S.A.A. Sec. D.A.C. 1/3 & 2/3 Nthn Fd. Ambces. Arranged with S.S.O. for a supply of linseed for veterinary purposes to M.G.C. Pioneers 446 & 447 Fd Coy. | E.H. |
| | 21/9/18 | | Inspected animals of M.G. Pioneers. 446 Fd Coy. 150 Bgde HQrs. 2 N.F. 7 Wilts. & No 3 Coy ASC. | E.H. |
| | 22/9/18 | | At M.V.S. Examined a foot case of a mule with Reinforcement camp. Animal was on loan from S.A.A. D.A.C. & was returned to its unit for treatment & replaced. Informed A.D.V.S. XVII Corps of death of a horse from exhaustion & old age in III Army Aux H.T. Coy ASC. | E.H. |

Instructions regarding War Diaries and Intelligence Summaries are contained in F. S. Regs., Part II. and the Staff Manual respectively. Title pages will be prepared in manuscript.

# WAR DIARY
*or*
# ~~INTELLIGENCE SUMMARY.~~
(*Erase heading not required.*)

DADVS 50 Div

Army Form C. 2118.

| Place | Date | Hour | Summary of Events and Information | Remarks and references to Appendices |
|---|---|---|---|---|
| LUCHEUX | 23.9.18 | | Visited and inspected 7th Fld Coy RE, 2 R.D.F., 3 RF, 446 Fld Coy RE. + M.G. Corps. Advised OC of latter unit to arrange to give small proportion of hay at midday feed. | E.S.H. |
| | 24.9.18 | | At M.V.S. + inspected 8 animals before evacuation (1 belonging to unit of some other formation) | |
| | | | Requested ADC to issue sack of bran to M.G.C. for veterinary reasons. | |
| | | | Inspected animals of 446 Fld Coy RE, Div Sigs. 4 Coy ASC + Pioneers. | E.S.H. |
| | 25.9.18 | | Examined all animals of SAA DAC and sent 2 to M.V.S. | E.S.H. |
| MONTIGNY | 26.9.18 | | Div. moved by road to MONTIGNY – FRICOURT area. | |
| | | | Accompanied GOC + inspected Transport on the march. Greater care appears to be now given re loading transport. | |
| | | | Saw M.V.S. at BEAUCOURT – 2 animals of 151 Bgde. to M.V.S. | E.S.H. |
| | 27.9.18 | | Div. moved to FRICOURT – MEAULTE area | E.S.H. |
| COMBLES | 28.9.18 | | Div. moved to COMBLES. MOISLAINS, NURLU area. M.V.S. at MOISLAINS | E.S.H. |
| | 29.9.18 | | Inspected DHQ. Sigs. M.M.P., 3 ASC, SAA DAC, 446 Fld Coy + 150 Bgde H.Qrs. | E.S.H. |
| | 30.9.18 | | Visited DDVS III Corps. Attended animal of M.M.P. | |
| | | | Again inspected S.A.A. Sec. DAC before they left for new area on 1st prox. | E.S.H. |
| | | | Inspected Div. Sig. Coy on march. | |

D.H.Q. 30.9.18

E S Hearne Maj. AVC
DADVS, 50 Div

(A7092). Wt. W12839/M1293. 750,000. 1/17. D. D. & L., Ltd. Forms/C.2118/14.

Confidential

# WAR DIARY
OF
D.A.D.V.S. 50TH DIVISION

FROM 1. 10. 18 TO 31. 10. 18.

VOLUME XXXVII

Vol 41

Instructions regarding War Diaries and Intelligence Summaries are contained in F. S. Regs., Part II. and the Staff Manual respectively. Title pages will be prepared in manuscript.

Vol 37

# WAR DIARY
*or*
# ~~INTELLIGENCE~~ SUMMARY.
(*Erase heading not required.*)

Army Form C. 2118.

DADVS 50 Dw.

| Place | Date | Hour | Summary of Events and Information | Remarks and references to Appendices |
|---|---|---|---|---|
| LIERAMONT | 1/10/18 | | Moved from COMBLES to LIERAMONT. Selected a site and established M.V.S at MOISLAINS. Inspected [illegible] Fd Ambce. Saw "C" Squadron Northumberland Hussars treating one animal for colic and sending one with gunshot wound into M.V.S. | [initials] |
| | 2/10/18 | | Visited transports of 149 and 150 Inf Bgdes. and moved M.V.S further forward to LIERAMONT. Reported to ADVS XIII Corps on the subject of the withdrawal of one VO from Divisions in July 1917 when warfare was stationary & suggested how useful his services would be now during more mobile operations. | [initials] |
| | 3/10/18 | | Fixed an advanced veterinary collecting post at St. EMILIE in the most forward area of Division's upward moving transport. Inspected at M.V.S 5 animals of Divn. and 75 belonging other formations prior to their evacuation. Visited and inspected 446 [illegible] Fd. Coy RE | [initials] |
| | 4/10/18 | | Saw 3 animals of Division and 11 belonging other formations at M.V.S before their evacuation. Inspected animals of DHQ & Sig. Coy. RE and SAA. Secn. DAC. Wrote CRA to return Capt AVC doing duty during absence of VO attached Art. Bgdes. on leave on return of latter, for posting with Inf Bgdes & REs. | [initials] |
| EPÉHY | 5/10/18 | | Instructed OC M.V.S to submit detailed report of all cases of gas poisoning admitted into M.V.S. Inspected 151 Inf. Bgdes. and 3 Fd. Ambces. Moved to EPÉHY. Saw 3 animals of Div. and 23 belonging to other formations at M.V.S before their evacuation. | [initials] |
| | 6/10/18 | | Moved M.V.S. to St. EMILIE and withdrew Advanced Collecting Post. Visited 150 Inf Bgde - units of which had 3 mules killed by shell. Instructed M.V.S to collect a float case left by Sig. Coy. RE at RONSSOY. Saw all animals of SAA. Secn. DAC. and 6 animals in M.V.S (2 of Div. & 4 belonging to other formations) before their evacuation to Base. | [initials] |

(A7092). Wt. W12839/M1293. 750,000. 1/17. D. D. & L., Ltd. Forms/C.2118/14.

Instructions regarding War Diaries and Intelligence Summaries are contained in F. S. Regs., Part II. and the Staff Manual respectively. Title pages will be prepared in manuscript.

# WAR DIARY
*or*
# ~~INTELLIGENCE SUMMARY.~~
*(Erase heading not required.)*

DA.D.V.S 50 Div.

Army Form C. 2118.

| Place | Date | Hour | Summary of Events and Information | Remarks and references to Appendices |
|---|---|---|---|---|
| EPEHY | 7/10/18 | | Visited and provided Vety. attendance for 2 sections No. 21 Army Aux. H.T. Coy. at RONSSOY. Sent to 151 Inf. Bgde. 2 riders from M.V.S to replace 2 riders killed by shell. Inspected animals of 50 Battn. M.G.C. Instructed Officers AVC & Sgts. AVC. with Field units to avoid all stables and standings marked with the notice "RAUDE" (MANGE) and to notify me of locations of any they saw in order that necessary action could be taken. Instructed Sgts. AVC with Field Units to submit daily casualty returns for animals killed or wounded by hostile bombs or shells as battle casualties were reported to A.D.V.S. Corps bi-weekly. M.V.S. instructed to collect L.D.H of Pioneers – gunshot (shell) casualty. Saw at M.V.S. 4 animals of D.W. and 12 of other formations before their evacuation. Issued a cured L.D. to 7th Wilts. | E.H. |
| | 8/10/18 | | At M.V.S. and ordered destruction of a L.D. Mule of M.G.C. with shell wounds. Saw 1 animal of Division and 19 of other formations before their evacuation. Inspected 2 Coy ASC and 151 Inf. Bgde animals & sent 1 Pack Mule to M.V.S. with shellwounds. | E.H. |
| | 9/10/18 | | Saw 2 animals of D.W. and 6 of other formations at M.V.S. before their evacuation. Examined all animals of Pioneer Battn. and 1 Coy A.S.C. | E.H. |
| GUISANCOURT FARM | 10/10/18 | | D.H.Q. moved to GUISANCOURT FARM and I moved M.V.S forward to MACQUINCOURT FARM near GOUY. Inspected D.H.Q. & Sig. Coy RE & 1 Coy A.S.C. animals. | E.H. |
| | 11/10/18 | | With O.C. M.V.S to fix new site for M.V.S. further forward. Inspected animals of 3 Fd. Ambces. | E.H. |
| LE TROIS AUX SOLDATS | 12/10/18 | | D.H.Q. moved to LE TROIS AUX SOLDATS and I moved M.V.S. to MARETZ site selected on 11th inst. Instructed 149 Bgde to obtain assistance of nearest V.O. for a serious colic case. Received notification from A.D.V.S Corps of LE TROIS AUX SOLDATS having been a German mange isolation Camp. Informed Q and issued orders for animals to be picketted in open until stables were disinfected and declared harmless. | E.H. |

(A7092). Wt. W12839/M1293. 750,000. 1/17. D. D. & L., Ltd. Forms/C.2118/14.

Instructions regarding War Diaries and Intelligence Summaries are contained in F. S. Regs., Part II. and the Staff Manual respectively. Title pages will be prepared in manuscript.

# WAR DIARY

*or*

~~INTELLIGENCE SUMMARY.~~

*(Erase heading not required.)*

D.A.D.V.S. 50 Div

Army Form C. 2118.

| Place | Date | Hour | Summary of Events and Information | Remarks and references to Appendices |
|---|---|---|---|---|
| LE TRON AUX SOLDATS | 13/10/18 | | Visited M.V.S. and inspected before evacuation 5 animals of Div. and 75 of other Formations. | |
| | | | Inspected 149 + 150 Inf. Transport lines & animals, as well as those of 7th Fld Coy RE. | E.H. |
| | 14/10/18 | | Attended at Corps HQ. | |
| | | | Visited 151 Inf Bde HQrs. and 2 Corps RE. | |
| | | | Examined at M.V.S. 10 animals of other Formations [illegible] before evacuation. | |
| | | | Wrote A.D.V.S. Corps for his instructions regarding 6 wounded animals left behind by Canadian M.V.S. - two were only fit for destruction, and there being no opportunity to sell carcases it was suggested they be given to French civilians in the captured villages in the vicinity. Authority obtained from Corps. | E.H. |
| | | | Inspected at M.V.S. 2 animals of Division and 62 of other Formations before their evacuation. | |
| | 15/10/18 | | Visited and Examined animals of 2 Fld Coys RE. | |
| | | | Replied to D.V.S. letter to A.D.V.S. Corps stating that in my opinion animals having to proceed to forward Dumps ought to be provided with horse respirators. | E.H. |
| | 16/10/18 | | Again visited the 6 animals left behind by Canadian M.V.S. seen on the 14th and evacuated 4 to Base and destroyed 2 giving the carcases to civilians for food on authority of Corps arrangements with French Mission. | |
| | | | Arrangements made with A.D.V.S. Corps for personnel from Corps Evacuating Station to meet animals being evacuated by M.V.S. halfway as the distance was so great, and M.V.S. was working under heavy pressure at the time. | E.H. |
| | 17/10/18 | | Inspected at M.V.S. 4 animals of Division and 31 of other formations before their evacuation to Base. One other animal belonging to 86 Army Bde R.F.A was destroyed at M.V.S. and carcase given to civilians for food. | E.H. |
| | | | Visited and Examined animals of Pioneer + M.G. Battalion. | |
| | 18/10/18 | | Instructed M.V.S. to collect a wounded horse of Northumberland Hussars by float. | |
| | | | Inspected on instructions of A.D.V.S. Corps 12th Royal Lancers. | |
| | | | Visited and inspected animals of the 3 Fld Ambces. | E.H. |

(A7092). Wt. W12839/M1293. 750,000. 1/17. D. D. & L., Ltd. Forms/C.2118/14.

Instructions regarding War Diaries and Intelligence Summaries are contained in F. S. Regs., Part II. and the Staff Manual respectively. Title pages will be prepared in manuscript.

# WAR DIARY
*or*
# ~~INTELLIGENCE SUMMARY.~~

*(Erase heading not required.)*

Army Form C. 2118.

D.A.D.V.S. 50 Div

| Place | Date | Hour | Summary of Events and Information | Remarks and references to Appendices |
|---|---|---|---|---|
| LeTRON aux SOLDATS | 19/10/18 | | Attended A.D.V.S. Office Corps H.Q.<br>Inspected at M.V.S. 5 animals of Div. and 12 of other formations before their evacuation to Base<br>Inspected 18 German (captured) horses. 10 riders of L.D.H. sent into M.V.S. by 1/8 Worcester Regt. and had them malleined. Informed A.D.V.S. Corps of action taken. | S.H. |
| | 20/10/18 | | Inspected all D.H.Q. riders and Div. Signal Coy R.E. and 151 Inf Bgde animals. | S.H. |
| | 21/10/18 | | Examined at M.V.S. before their evacuation 5 animals of Div. 12 of other formations and 9 of the German horses captured on 19th inst. None of these latter reacted to mallein test.<br>Attended Conference of G.O.C.<br>Inspected all transport of 50 Batt. M.G.C. and 149 Inf Bgde.<br>Arranged to test on 22nd inst a cold shoer of 3rd Royal Fusiliers for classification as shoeing smith at forge of No. 2 Coy A.S.C.<br>Forwarded veterinary certificate to S.S.O. for supply of linseed for 1/3 N'h'n Fd. Ambce. | S.H. |
| | 22/10/18 | | Tested cold shoer at No 2 Coy. A.S.C. horse lines. Inspected animals of this Coy.<br>A.D.V.S. called to make arrangements for inspecting the Artillery.<br>With horse master of D.A. & inspected animals of the 2 Bgdes. Reported to "Q" & A.D.V.S. on poor condition of about 100 animals many of which were quite young. Suggested their withdrawal for about 3 mos. and replacement by hard conditioned remounts. | S.H. |
| | | | Inspected animals of M.G. Batt. deficient of haynets. Drew attention of Q to this matter. | S.H. |
| | 23/10/18 | | Examined animals of 150 Inf Bgde. & "C" squadron Northumberland Hussars.<br>Saw 9 animals of Div. and 29 of other formations at M.V.S. prior to their evacuation. | |
| | 24/10/18 | | At M.V.S. issued 4 of captured German horses to M.G. Batt. Inspected 6 animals of Div. 29 of other formations & one German horse before their evacuation.<br>Inspected 151 & 149 Inf Bgdes. | S.H. |

(A7092). Wt. W12839/M1293 750,000. 1/17. D. D. & L. Ltd. Forms/C.2118/14.

Army Form C. 2118.

Instructions regarding War Diaries and Intelligence Summaries are contained in F. S. Regs., Part II. and the Staff Manual respectively. Title pages will be prepared in manuscript.

# WAR DIARY
*or*
# ~~INTELLIGENCE~~ SUMMARY.
*(Erase heading not required.)*

D.A.D.V.S. 50 Div

| Place | Date | Hour | Summary of Events and Information | Remarks and references to Appendices |
|---|---|---|---|---|
| Le TROU aux SOLDATS | 25/10/18 | | Visited & examined animals of M.G. Batt. & 1/3 Fld. Ambce. | |
| | | | Saw 1 animal of Div and 33 of other Formations before their evacuation to the Base. | |
| | | | Informed A.D.V.S. Corps of buildings in AVELU which had been used as mange case standings by the enemy. Had place put "out of bounds". Issued German Rider to 446 Fd. Coy. R.E. | E.H. |
| | 26/10/18 | | With A.D.V.S. Corps visited 150. 151. Inf Bgde & 1/1 N.F. Ambce. | |
| | | | Wrote requesting Australian units to collect several animals from M.V.S. now fit to return to duty. | E.H. |
| | 27/10/18 | | Inspected at M.V.S. 13 animals of Div. and 4 of other formations before their evacuation to Base | |
| | | | Examined animals of 3 Corps A.S.C. and Machine Gun Battalion. | E.H. |
| | 28/10/18 | | Visited lines of 151 Inf Bgde units. 1/3 N. Fd Ambce. and Pioneers. | E.H. |
| | 29/10/18 | | Met A.D.V.S. Corps at M.V.S. and arranged a site for M.V.S. when it moves forward on 30th. | |
| | | | Saw Infantry Transport on line of march. | |
| | | | Issued 3 remaining German Riders in M.V.S. to D.H.Q. – 2 for Officers 1 for M.M.P. | |
| | | | Inspected before their evacuation to Base 12 animals of Division & 3 of other Formations. | |
| | | | Arranged with D.A.D.O.S. as to issue of first supply of horse rugs to units with biggest percentage of clipped animals in Div. | E.H. |
| Le CATEAU | 30/10/18 | | D.H.Q. moved to Le CATEAU | |
| | | | Had M.V.S. moved to Les ESSARTS FARM | E.H. |

Instructions regarding War Diaries and Intelligence Summaries are contained in F. S. Regs., Part II. and the Staff Manual respectively. Title pages will be prepared in manuscript.

# WAR DIARY
*or*
~~INTELLIGENCE~~ SUMMARY.
(*Erase heading not required.*)

Army Form C. 2118.

DADVS, 50th Div

| Place | Date | Hour | Summary of Events and Information | Remarks and references to Appendices |
|---|---|---|---|---|
| le Cateau | 31.10.18 | | Veterinary arrangements made for attendance on various units in neighbourhood of le CATEAU - a re-distribution of work amongst VOs made. Conference of VOs. | |
| | | | DHQ 31.X.18. A. Kearne Maj. DADVS. 50 Div. | |

(A7092). Wt. W12839/M1293. 750,000. 1/17. D. D. & L., Ltd. Forms/C.2118/14.

Vol 42

CONFIDENTIAL.

# WAR DIARY

OF.

## D.A.D.V.S., 50TH. DIVISION

From 1st. Novr to 30th November 1918.

VOLUME XXXVIII

10

Army Form C. 2118.

Instructions regarding War Diaries and Intelligence Summaries are contained in F. S. Regs., Part II. and the Staff Manual respectively. Title pages will be prepared in manuscript.

# WAR DIARY
*or*
# ~~INTELLIGENCE SUMMARY.~~
*(Erase heading not required.)*

D.A.D.V.S., 50 Division

Vol 38

| Place | Date | Hour | Summary of Events and Information | Remarks and references to Appendices |
|---|---|---|---|---|
| Le CATEAU | 1/XI/18 | | My office still at Le CATEAU M.V.S was brought forward to Les ESSARTS FARM Q14d 6.8/57B. | |
| | | | Submitted to Division 'Q' a draft of veterinary arrangements for prospective advance of Division. | |
| | | | Arranged to establish an Advanced Collecting Post at K30 b 9.2 in close proximity to Art^y wagon lines & infantry transport in forward positions whilst M.V.S remained with A.S.C and H.Q. Coys R.E. | |
| | | | Inspected before evacuation from M.V.S. 20 animals of Div. and 2 unknown animals. | |
| | | | Visited lines of S.A.A. Sec D.A.C and examined 2 L.D.M wounded by shellfire, 2 others being killed. | E.S.A. |
| | 2/XI/18 | | Instructed M.V.S. to collect 5 float cases and 8 walking cases belonging to 86 (Army) Bgde R.F.A. which unit was moving out to take up battle positions. | |
| | | | Inspected 149 Bgde (Infantry) animals and directed treatment of 5 wounded by shell. | E.S.A. |
| | 3/XI/18 | | Examined at M.V.S. before their evacuation 15 animals of Division and 14 of other Formations, and ordered the destruction of a L.D. of 86 (Army) Bgde R.F.A in M.V.S suffering from shell wounds. | |
| | | | Inspected 151 Inf Bgde and M.G. Battalion both formations having several animals killed or wounded by hostile shell. | E.S.A. |
| | 4/XI/18 | | At M.V.S. and despatched two float cases to V.E.S. in float borrowed from another Division. | |
| | | | Examined a stray mule sent into M.V.S and returned to a unit of Division. | |
| | | | Despatched 2 other cases to V.E.S from M.V.S by motor ambulance. | |
| | | | Again visited M.G. Battalion 4 mules had been hit by shrapnel, sent 2 of worst cases to M.V.S. | E.S.A. |

Army Form C. 2118.

Instructions regarding War Diaries and Intelligence Summaries are contained in F. S. Regs., Part II. and the Staff Manual respectively. Title pages will be prepared in manuscript.

# WAR DIARY
*or*
# ~~INTELLIGENCE SUMMARY.~~
(*Erase heading not required.*)

D.A.D.V.S., 50 Division

| Place | Date | Hour | Summary of Events and Information | Remarks and references to Appendices |
|---|---|---|---|---|
| LANNOY | 5.XI.18 | | Hy Office at LANNOY.<br>Moved M.V.S. to I.25 a.5.8 and established Advanced Collecting Post at FONTAINE au BOIS.<br>Inspected at M.V.S before evacuation 8 animals of Div. and 8 of other Formations<br>Sent into M.V.S. to be malleined from 2 Roy. Dublin Fus. which unit had captured them 4 R. 6 LD. 1 R was immediately evacuated to V.E.S. gunshot (shell) wds. Remainder were kept in M.V.S under observation. | [illegible] |
| | 6.XI.18 | | Visited 3 Coy. ASC and ordered destruction of H D. - old age and paralysis.<br>Inspected animals of Pioneer Battalion: and 2 mules animals of M.G. Battn. wounded by shell. | [illegible] |
| NOYELLES | 7.XI.18 | | Hy Office and M.V.S to NOYELLES<br>Inspected at M.V.S before their evacuation 7 animals of Div. 29 other Formations and 1 German Rider.<br>Destroyed HD in 2NF - fractured tibia<br>Examined animals of 151 Inf. Bgde & 2nd section DAC.<br>Shell wounds during wk. ending 7.XI.18. - 36 LDM and 20 Horses. | [illegible] |
| MONCEAU ST WAAST | 8.XI.18 | | Hy Office at MONCEAU ST WAAST. Left M.V.S at NOYELLES<br>Ordered destruction in M.V.S of LD. of 104 (Army) Bgde RFA shell wds.<br>Inspected all animals of 150 Inf. Bgde. | [illegible] |
| | 9.XI.18 | | Made veterinary arrangements for working with the selected forces sent forward to LA SAVATE<br>Inspected 3 Fld Coys RE, and 3 Fld. Ambulances | [illegible] |
| | 10.XI.18 | | Moved M.V.S from NOYELLES to MONCEAU ST WAAST area C 28 d. 4.4. Party left behind in old billet to bring on a few sick animals had to leave 2 with another Div. M.V.S unable to travel.<br>On receipt of information from French Mission that SEMOUSIES a village in forward recaptured territory had been a mange Camp used by the enemy, all buildings were immediately put "out of bounds" until declared fit for use by a V.O.<br>Inspected animals of 251 Bde RFA | [illegible] |

Army Form C. 2118.

Instructions regarding War Diaries and Intelligence Summaries are contained in F. S. Regs., Part II. and the Staff Manual respectively. Title pages will be prepared in manuscript.

# WAR DIARY
or
~~INTELLIGENCE SUMMARY.~~
(Erase heading not required.)

DADVS, 50 Div

| Place | Date | Hour | Summary of Events and Information | Remarks and references to Appendices |
|---|---|---|---|---|
| DOURLERS | 11/11/18 | | DHQ moved to DOURLERS. | |
| | | | Inspected animals of 250 Bgde RFA. Enquired into reasons for deficiency of haynets and nosebags in Art Bgdes. and took matter up with DADOS | |
| | | | Vety arrangements made for M.V.S to evacuate sick from forward area to rear M.V.Ss and thence to VES. | Ent |
| | 12/11/18 | | Examined animals of D.A.C and 2 Field Ambulances. | Ent |
| | | | Made redistribution of work for V.Os as Div was concentrated in new area. | |
| | 13/11/18 | | Inspected DHQ & Sig. Coy RE animals. Sent 2 of latter unit to M.V.S | |
| | | | Examined at M.V.S before their evacuation 47 animals of Div. 3 German horses & 1 from 104 (Army) Bgde RFA | Ent |
| | | | Visited lines of 149 Inf. Bgde. 17 more captured animals sent to M.V.S from 149 Bgde for mallein test. | |
| | 14/11/18 | | Inspected 150 & 151 Inf Bgdes & 2/2 Fd Ambce. | Ent |
| | 15/11/18 | | Assumed tempy. duty as A.D.V.S. 13 Corps. OC M.V.S acting DADVS during my absence. | Ewing |
| | | | Informed DADVS 18th Div of having destroyed a L D of 92 Fd Coy. with fracture | |
| | 16/11/18 | | Capt GOERTON AVC reported for temporary duty with Division. | |
| | | | Instructed M.V.S to collect 2 float-cases from 66 Div. (SARS POTERIE) and a mule 66 DAC. left behind with an inhabitant at MARBAIX. | Ewing |
| | | | Selected 83 horses from Div for 32 Division and certified them free from disease & fit for immediate duty. | |
| | 17/11/18 | | Submitted to ADVS Corps mallein chart for German animals malleined in M.V.S | |
| | | | Inspected before their evacuation to Base 12 animals of Div. 2 of other formations & 3 captured Riders | Ewing |
| | | | Instructed M.V.S to collect 2 float cases from 1/1 East Lancs M.V.S. | |

(A7092). Wt. W12839/M1293. 750,000. 1/17. D. D. & L., Ltd. Forms/C.2118/14.

Instructions regarding War Diaries and Intelligence Summaries are contained in F. S. Regs., Part II. and the Staff Manual respectively. Title pages will be prepared in manuscript.

# WAR DIARY
*or*
# ~~INTELLIGENCE SUMMARY.~~
*(Erase heading not required.)*

D.A.D.V.S. 50 Division

Army Form C. 2118.

| Place | Date | Hour | Summary of Events and Information | Remarks and references to Appendices |
|---|---|---|---|---|
| DOURLERS | 18.XI.18 | | Selected from units of Division 105 animals for a Division proceeding into enemy territory. | |
| | | | Instructed M.V.S. to collect from an inhabitant a mule of 66 Division left on line of march, and to evacuate it to V.E.S. | |
| | | | On receipt of orders from Corps. M.V.S were also instructed to collect 37 animals from IX Corps V.E.S. and to evacuate 52 animals for other Divisions. | WMJ |
| | 19.XI.18 | | Wrote D.A.D.O.S on the inexpediency of providing rugs for all horses, as in my opinion only those partially or wholly clipped were in need of them, and it would be a tax on transport if rugs were issued for all animals. | WMJ |
| | | | Inspected before their evacuation from M.V.S 7 animals of Division and 3 of other Formations. | |
| | | | Ordered the destruction in M.V.S of a L.D. of 6th Division - shell wds. | |
| | 20.XI.18 | | Inspected animals of DHQ and evacuated 1 to M.V.S suffering from Grease. | WMJ |
| | | | Informed Q for the information of D.D.R. as to the disposal of all captured horses. | |
| | | | Examined before their evacuation 2 animals of Divn + 2 of other Formations. | |
| | 21.XI.18 | | Instructed M.V.S to collect from inhabitant an animal left by B/331 Bgde. 66th Divn. | |
| | | | Visited & inspected animals of M.M.P. and sent 1 to M.V.S | WMJ |
| | | | Requested Corps to assist in evacuating by collecting 3 foot cases with motor ambulance | |
| | 22.XI.18 | | Examined before evacuation 8 of Division and 8 of other Formations. | WMJ |
| | | | Ordered destruction in M.V.S of H.D. No 3 A.S.C. suffering from P.U.N. and Septicaemia. | |
| | 23.XI.18 | | Returns for Corps and Routine Work. | WMJ |
| | | | Issued a stray mule in M.V.S. to D.A.C. | |

(A7092). Wt. W12839/M1293. 750,000. 1/17. D. D. & L., Ltd. Forms/C.2118/14.

Instructions regarding War Diaries and Intelligence Summaries are contained in F. S. Regs., Part II. and the Staff Manual respectively. Title pages will be prepared in manuscript.

# WAR DIARY
*or*
~~INTELLIGENCE SUMMARY.~~
(*Erase heading not required.*)

Army Form C. 2118.

D.A.D.V.S., 50 Div

| Place | Date | Hour | Summary of Events and Information | Remarks and references to Appendices |
|---|---|---|---|---|
| DOURLERS | 24.xi.18 | | Detailed V.O. to inspect previous to their issue to Division 80 animals to replace those withdrawn from Div. for other Divisions proceeding to RHINE. | |
| | | | Visited M.V.S on my return from Corps. on completion of temporary duty and released OC M.V.S. to go on leave. | [illegible] |
| | 25.xi.18 | | Appointed Capt Woods to act temporarily as OC M.V.S | |
| | | | Inspected animals of 151 Inf Bgde. Pioneers, and attended cases amongst civilian animals. | |
| | | | Ordered destruction in M.V.S of animal of 1st Siege Bty. RGA Septic wound coronet. | |
| | | | Instructed OC M.V.S to inspect stables at HUGEMONT before their occupation by HQrs Corps Heavy Artillery. | [illegible] |
| | 26.xi.18 | | Submitted to A.D.V.S. Corps report on state of these stables declared fit for occupation | |
| | | | Visited and inspected M.G. Battn + 446 Fd Coy. RE animals. Instructed M.G. Battn. to treat their standings with lime. | |
| | | | Detailed a V.O. to attend 2 Heavy Batteries in neighbourhood. | [illegible] |
| | 27.xi.18 | | At M.V.S and examined 6 animals of Div and 5 of other formations before their evacuation | |
| | | | Visited and inspected Hq Bgde. 2/2 + 1/3 Fd Ambces. 7th + 447 Fd Coys RE. | [illegible] |
| | 28.xi.18 | | Inspected animals of 1/1 N.F. Ambce and 150 Inf Bgde | |
| | | | Submitted to 'G' arrangements made under the Education Scheme to instruct at M.V.S a few men each week in treatment of minor ailments and animal management. | [illegible] |

(A7092). Wt. W12839/M1293. 750,000. 1/17. D. D. & L., Ltd. Forms/C.2118/14.

Instructions regarding War Diaries and Intelligence Summaries are contained in F. S. Regs., Part II. and the Staff Manual respectively. Title pages will be prepared in manuscript.

# WAR DIARY
*or*
~~INTELLIGENCE~~ SUMMARY.
*(Erase heading not required.)*

Army Form C. 2118.

D.A.D.V.S., 50' Division

| Place | Date | Hour | Summary of Events and Information | Remarks and references to Appendices |
|---|---|---|---|---|
| DOURLERS | 29/XI/18 | | Conference with V.Os. | |
| | | | Visited and inspected all animals of 251 Bgde R.F.A. | |
| | | | Sent animal of 1/1 N.F. Ambce to M.V.S. - cystitis | |
| | 30/XI/18 | | Inspected animals of D.A.C. and also of M.V.S. | [illegible] |
| | | | Visited A.D.V.S. XIII Corps. | |
| | | | Total casualties during month: Died & destroyed (shellfire) 39; Evac. for other reasons 149 | [illegible] |
| | | | D.M.S. 30.XI.18. | |
| | | | [signature] Maj. A.V.C. D.A.D.V.S., 50 Division | |

7

CONFIDENTIAL.

V843

WAR = DIARY

OF

D. A D. V. S., 50TH. DIVISION.

FROM. DEC 1St. to DEC 31st.

VOL. XXXIX.

Vol 39

Instructions regarding War Diaries and Intelligence Summaries are contained in F. S. Regs., Part II. and the Staff Manual respectively. Title pages will be prepared in manuscript.

# WAR DIARY
~~or~~
~~INTELLIGENCE~~ SUMMARY.
(Erase heading not required.)

D.A.D.V.S. 50th Division

Army Form C. 2118.

| Place | Date | Hour | Summary of Events and Information | Remarks and references to Appendices |
|---|---|---|---|---|
| DOURLERS | 1 XI/18 | | Inspected animals of 250 Bgde R.F.A., 149 I. Bgde H.Q., Div. Sig Coy RE, and D.H.Q sending animal into M.V.S from last named unit with contused jaw. | [initials] |
| | 2 XI/18 | | Examined animals of 3rd R. Fus. and 7th Fd. Coy R.E. Discovered a big shed capable of holding 500 animals, & of being easily disinfected. Would have made a good reception hospital if required. Informed A.D.V.S. Corps of its location. | [initials] |
| | 3 XI/18 | | Corps Troops Units being scattered over a wide area it was found impossible for V.O. i/c to visit all units. Instructed V.Os under my administration to attend therefore to any Corps troops they encountered on their daily rounds. Saw 1 L.D. from Art. at M.V.S before its evacuation to Base. Made small change in distribution of Riders to Chaplains. | [initials] |
| | 4 XI/18 | | Inspected 11 animals at M.V.S before their evacuation to Base. On receipt of wire from A.D.V.S XIII Corps visited 115 Labour Coy at BAVAY and found animal left by 146 Labour Coy had died of twist as revealed by P.M. Made arrangements under Education Scheme for short classes to be held at M.V.S in First Aid to Animals & Stable management. Duration of class not to exceed 6 days & max. no. of students 10. O.R. Suggested to A.D.V.S Corps that on account of lack of soyers' stoves and insufficient transport for same an issue of 2 cwt. of linseed cake (of foreign manufacture) per day would be quite ample. | [initials] |
| | 5 XI/18 | | Visited and inspected M.V.S, 2/2 Nbn. Fd. Ambce. and 50 Battn. M.G.C. | [initials] |

(A7092). Wt. W 2839/M1293. 750,000. 1/17. D. D. & L., Ltd. Forms/C.2118/14.

Army Form C. 2118.

Instructions regarding War Diaries and Intelligence Summaries are contained in F. S. Regs., Part II. and the Staff Manual respectively. Title pages will be prepared in manuscript.

# WAR DIARY
~~or~~
# ~~INTELLIGENCE SUMMARY.~~
(Erase heading not required.)

D.A.D.V.S, 50 Division

| Place | Date | Hour | Summary of Events and Information | Remarks and references to Appendices |
|---|---|---|---|---|
| DOURLERS | 6 XII 18 | | 1 animal to Base from M.V.S. Conference with V.O.S. Inspected all Batteries of 150 (Army) Bgde F.A attached to Division. | E.J.H. |
| | 7 XII 18 | | Reported on my visit to 150 (A) Bgde F.A to A.D.V.S. Corps informing him of shortage of nosebags and grooming kit and the difficulty unit was having to obtain supply of this equipment. Animals of "C" Batty. were in poor condition. Inspected again animals of Div. Sig. Coy R.E. and sent 2 to M.V.S. | E.J.H. |
| | 8 XII 18 | | Units having moved it was found expedient to make a fresh distribution of work for V.Os. Visited and inspected animals of S.A.A. & 2nd sec D.A.C. A mule was found in latter unit suffering from lockjaw and I ordered it to be kept quiet and left in a loose box. This animal continues to improve. | E.J.H. |
| | 9 XII 18 | | Inspected at M.V.S before evacuation 8 animals of Div and 17 of Other Formations. | E.J.H. |
| | 10 XII 18 | | Visited 50 Battn. M.G.C, 3rd Roy. Fus. 2nd Royal Munster Fus. 1st/2 N.F. Ambce. Again examined animals of D.A.C and evacuated to M.V.S 1 with broken knees, inspected also animals of Pioneer Battn, 446 and 447 Fd. Coy R.E. | E.J.H. |
| | 11 XII 18 | | On being informed by Corps of location of 3 (R.H.G) M.G.C. I arranged for one of my V.Os to provide them with necessary vety aids and to attend to them regularly. | E.J.H. |
| | 12 XII 18 / 13 XII 18 | | Selected from all Riders & L.Ds in Bgde Art & D.A.C. most suitable mares for breeding purposes. Selected from all other units of Div. most suitable mares for breeding purposes of Rider & L.D type and examined again all those that had been previously selected in the earlier part of the year. | E.J.H. / E.J.H. |

Instructions regarding War Diaries and Intelligence Summaries are contained in F. S. Regs., Part II. and the Staff Manual respectively. Title pages will be prepared in manuscript.

# WAR DIARY
*or*
# ~~INTELLIGENCE~~ SUMMARY.
*(Erase heading not required.)*

D.A.D.V.S., 50th Div.

Army Form C. 2118.

| Place | Date | Hour | Summary of Events and Information | Remarks and references to Appendices |
|---|---|---|---|---|
| BOURLERS | 14 XII 18 | | Inspected at M.V.S before their evacuation 7 animals of Div. and 1 belonging to unit of other Formation.<br>Visited new area to select a convenient site for M.V.S.<br>Forwarded to Corps all correspondence relating to supply of grooming kit and nosebags to 150(A) Bgde R.F.A. showing what difficulty this unit was having to obtain these from Ordnance. | E.H. |
| | 15 XII 18 | | Routine Work<br>Inspected animals of Sig Coy. R.E. M.M.P. and D.H.Q. In latter unit treated G.O.C's rider suffering from suppurating corn.<br>Issued instructions to M.V.S for their move on 18th. to new area.<br>Advertised in Routine Orders 3 stray mules at present in M.V.S. | E.H. |
| | 16 XII 18 | | Instructed 150 I. Bgde to collect L.D. from M.V.S (on loan) for the move.<br>Acting on instructions received, went to Leval area to meet Corps Selection Committee to [illegible] show horses [illegible] selected on 11, 12 & 13th. inst. – inspection was postponed.<br>Advertised R. & D. 'stray' animals at present in M.V.S. | E.H. |
| | 17 XII 18 | | Visited and inspected Pioneer Battn. 50th Battn. M.G.C. Sent animal into M.V.S from latter and issued to same unit 2 stray animals.<br>Inspected at M.V.S 4 animals before their evacuation to Base. | E.H. |
| | 18 XII 18 | | Instructed M.V.S to proceed to RAMPONEAU today.<br>Inspected S.A.A. D.A.C and a mule left behind by 2/D.A.C suffering from Tetanus. | E.H. |
| LE QUESNOY | 19 XII 18 | | D.H.Q. to LE QUESNOY. Instructed M.V.S to collect mule with Tetanus and another animal of 63 Fd. Coy. R.E. at LOUVIGNIES with P.U.N.<br>Arranged Veterinary attendance for 2 units of other Formations in Div. Area & informed A.D.V.S Corps of action taken. | E.H. |

(A7092). Wt. W12839/M1293. 750,000. 1/17. D. D. & L., Ltd. Forms/C.2118/14.

Instructions regarding War Diaries and Intelligence Summaries are contained in F. S. Regs., Part II. and the Staff Manual respectively. Title pages will be prepared in manuscript.

# WAR DIARY
*or*
# INTELLIGENCE SUMMARY.
*(Erase heading not required.)*

D.A.D.V.S., 50 Div

Army Form C. 2118.

| Place | Date | Hour | Summary of Events and Information | Remarks and references to Appendices |
|---|---|---|---|---|
| LE QUESNOY | 20 XII 18 | | DADVS goes on leave. O.C. M.V.S (Capt. W.M. Jackson) Acting DADVS. | WMJ. |
| | 21 XII 18 | | Routine Work. | WMJ. |
| | 22 XII 18 | | Asked Corps for nearest reception post for sick animals. Visited and inspected animals of DHQ., Signal Coy RE. + 1/1 N.F. Ambce. | WMJ. |
| | 23 XII 18 | | Made redistribution of work for VOs now that units had got settled for a while. On receipt of instructions from ADVS Corps arranged vety. attendance for an (?) Aux. H.T. Coy in BAVAY area. | WMJ. |
| | 24 XII 18 | | Visited + inspected 3 Corps A.S.C. | WMJ. |
| | 25 XII 18 | | I (?) reminded Q of the issue, possibly in the near future, of foreign manufactured linseed cake and asked that it be published in DROs that this cake be thoroughly boiled before being fed. | WMJ. |
| | 26 XII 18 | | Visited 50th D.A.C & inspected animals | WMJ. |
| | 27 XII 18 | | M.V.S. + evacuated 27 sick animals to XIII Corps V.E.S. | WMJ. |
| | 28 XII 18 | | Made arrangements with 149 Inf. Bde to have all animals paraded in LE QUESNOY for inspection by Veterinary Board. Sent my opinion into "Q" with regard to R.A.V.C with Division. | WMJ. |

(A7092). Wt. W12839/M1293. 750,000. 1/17. D. D. & L., Ltd. Forms/C.2118/14.

Instructions regarding War Diaries and Intelligence Summaries are contained in F. S. Regs., Part II. and the Staff Manual respectively. Title pages will be prepared in manuscript.

# WAR DIARY
*or*
# INTELLIGENCE SUMMARY.
*(Erase heading not required.)*

Army Form C. 2118.

| Place | Date | Hour | Summary of Events and Information | Remarks and references to Appendices |
|---|---|---|---|---|
| LE QUESNOY | 29/XII/18 | | at M.V.S, inspected animals for evacuation. Made preparations for the Board of Veterinary Officers, re classifying of horses. | WMJ |
| | 30/XII/18 | | Attended Veterinary board & examined the animals of 3rd Royal Fus, 13th (S.H) Black Watch, & 149 Bde H.Q.s. Visited 50th D.A.C. after receiving notification of 22 mules being drowned, the result of a dam bursting. Notified A.D.V.S XIII Corps of the fact. | WMJ |
| | 31/XII/18 | | Veterinary board. Inspection of 2nd Dublin Fus. animals, 50th Divisional Signals, & CRE, 7th Field Coy R.E. 1/1st N.F.A & 2/2 N.F.A also M.M.P. 50 Div. Notified A.D.V.S XIII Corps No of Butcher cases in M.V.S. for evacuation. Sent instructions to units, whose horses had been before Veterinary Board to send their animals grouped D. into M.V.S.<br><br>WmJackson<br>Capt R.A.V.C<br>A/D.A.D.V.S.<br>50th Division | WMJ |

9

CONFIDENTIAL 50

VA 44

# WAR DIARY
OF
# D.A.D.V.S 50TH DIVISION

FROM 1st JANY to 31st JANY
1919

VOL. 40

Vol 40

Instructions regarding War Diaries and Intelligence Summaries are contained in F. S. Regs., Part II. and the Staff Manual respectively. Title pages will be prepared in manuscript.

# WAR DIARY

~~or~~

~~INTELLIGENCE SUMMARY.~~

(Erase heading not required.)

Army Form C. 2118.

D.A.D.V.S., 50th Division

| Place | Date | Hour | Summary of Events and Information | Remarks and references to Appendices |
|---|---|---|---|---|
| LE QUESNOY | 1/1/19 | | Made arrangements for Veterinary Board to inspect 150 Infantry Bgde + 446 Field Co RE. Evacuated 36 animals to 13 V.E.S. | WWJ. |
| | 2/1/19 | | Veterinary Board assembled at 150 Bde H.Q. inspected all animals, also 446 Field Co RE. Made arrangements to inspect M.G Bn. animals on 3rd inst. | WWJ. |
| | 3/1/19 | | Veterinary Board inspected M.G. Bn. animals in SAULTAIN area. Conference of V.Os at D.A.D.V.S Office. | WWJ. |
| | 4/1/19 | | Veterinary Board inspected & classified the animals of 250 Bgde RFA. Informed A.D.V.S XIII Corps the number of animals by classes, classified since commencement of Board. I return from leave to England. | WWJ. |
| | 5/1/19 | | Made arrangements with CRA to parade animals of DAC for inspection by Veterinary Board. Visited M.V.S & inspected animals for evacuation. | Wt. |
| | 6/1/19 | | Veterinary Board examined & classified animals of 50 D.A.C. Evacuated 31 animals from M.V.S to No 13 V.E.S. | Wt. |
| | 7/1/19 | | Veterinary Board examined & classified animals No 1 & 3 Coys R.A.S.C. | Wt. |
| | 8/1/19 | | Visited 151 Bgde group. Veterinary Board examined animals of 151 Bgde, 1/3 Northumbrian Field Ambce, + 447 Field Co R.E, also 14th Aux. Horse Transport Coy. | Wt. |
| | 9/1/19 | | Made arrangements with C.R.A 50th Division to parade animals of 251 Brigade R.F.A. for examination by Veterinary Board. Inspected animals in M.V.S. Veterinary Board inspected & classified D.H.Q. horses. | Wt. |

(A7092). Wt. W12839/M1293. 750,000. 1/17. D. D. & L., Ltd. Forms/C.2118/14.

Army Form C. 2118.

Instructions regarding War Diaries and Intelligence Summaries are contained in F. S. Regs., Part II. and the Staff Manual respectively. Title Pages will be prepared in manuscript.

# WAR DIARY
or
~~INTELLIGENCE SUMMARY~~
*(Erase heading not required.)*

| Place | Date | Hour | Summary of Events and Information | Remarks and references to Appendices |
|---|---|---|---|---|
| LE QUESNOY | 10 1/19 | | Inspected animals for evacuation, M.V.S.<br>V.Os Conference at D.A.D.V.S Office.<br>Veterinary Board examined animals No 2 Coy, 50th Divisional Train. | Ejt |
| | 11 1/19 | | Veterinary Board examined animals of 251 Bde RFA.<br>Evacuated 35 animals to 13 V.E.S. | Ejt |
| | 12 1/19 | | Veterinary Board examined animals which were not classified when their respective units were paraded. | Ejt |
| | 13 1/19 | | Veterinary Board examined remainder of 151 Infantry Bgde, Pioneer Batt., 14 animals from D.A.C. & No 4 Co. R.A.S.C.<br>Sent V.Os. instructions to proceed with the malleining of animals classified Y + Z | Ejt |
| | 14 1/19 | | A.D.V.S XIII Corps called.<br>Visited M.V.S + made arrangements with a local butcher to purchase a horse for meat. | Ejt |
| | 15 1/19 | | Veterinary Board examined the few remaining animals of the Div. not classified.<br>Sold horse to local butcher for destruction | Ejt |
| | 16 1/19 | | Paid over to XIII Corps Field Cashier 300 francs, obtained by selling horse to local butcher<br>Visited M.V.S + inspected sick animals<br>Inspected D.H.Q. horses. | Ejt |
| | 17 1/19 | | V.Os Conference at D.A.D.V.S. Office<br>Made arrangements for V.O to mallein Y+Z animals of 150 Bde.<br>Evacuated 8 sick animals and 5 "D" cases to 13 V.E.S. | Ejt |
| | 18 1/19 | | Visited M.V.S + inspected animals<br>Classified animals at M.G. Bn., also visited 330 R.C.C., RE ST WAAST & classified animals | Ejt |

2449 Wt. W14957/M90 750,000 1/16 J.B.C. & A. Forms/C.2118/12.

Instructions regarding War Diaries and Intelligence Summaries are contained in F. S. Regs., Part II. and the Staff Manual respectively. Title pages will be prepared in manuscript.

Army Form C. 2118.

# WAR DIARY
*or*
# INTELLIGENCE SUMMARY.
*(Erase heading not required.)*

| Place | Date | Hour | Summary of Events and Information | Remarks and references to Appendices |
|---|---|---|---|---|
| LE QUESNOY | 19/1/19 | | Routine work | Est. |
| | 20/1/19 | | Visited M.V.S and evacuated 16 animals to 13 V.E.S. | Est |
| | 21/1/19 | | Visited 330 R.C.C, RE at ST WAAST and examined animals which had been malleined, sent record of Testing to A.D.V.S.<br>Examined 33 horses class "C", being transferred to 13 V.E.S from Divisional Artillery, sent record of Mallein Test to A.D.V.S. | Est. |
| | 22/1/19 | | With Veterinary Board classifying animals belonging, 177 Tunnelling Coy RE., 178 Tunnelling Coy R.E. at MAUBEUGE and 324 Quarrying Co, R.E. at BETTRICHIES also 335 R.C.C. Coy R.E. | Est |
| | 23/1/19 | | Demobilization of horses | Est |
| | 24/1/19 | | V.Os conference at D.A.D.V.S office.<br>Visited No 1 Coy 50 Divl Train | Est. |
| | 25/1/19 | | Visited units in 149 Inf. Bgde. | Est. |
| | 26/1/19 | | Routine Work. | Est |
| | 27/1/19 | | Met C.R.A. at GOMMEGNIES, and examined 263 animals before despatching to Animal Collecting Camp. | Est |

D. D. & L., London, E.C.
(A8001) Wt. W1771/M2031 750,000 5/17 Sch. 52 Forms/C2118/14

Instructions regarding War Diaries and Intelligence Summaries are contained in F. S. Regs., Part II. and the Staff Manual respectively. Title pages will be prepared in manuscript.

# WAR DIARY
*or*
# INTELLIGENCE SUMMARY.
*(Erase heading not required.)*

Army Form C. 2118.

| Place | Date | Hour | Summary of Events and Information | Remarks and references to Appendices |
|---|---|---|---|---|
| LE QUESNOY | 27/1/19 | | Inspected animals at No 2 Coy, 50th Divisional Train | E.S.H. |
| | 28/1/19 | | Investigated the conditions of which British animals, sold to French civilians, were being treated, & Notified A.A.Q.M.G of the state, animals were in. A.P.M asked to inform gendarmes to see that the conditions under which these animals were sold were carried out. | E.S.H. |
| | 29/1/19 | | Examined 25 class 'Y' animals at GOMMEGNIES before transfer to 13 Corps Animals Collecting Camp. Reclassification of Animals at 50th Divisional Train Companies. | E.S.H. |
| | 30/1/19 | | Inspected all animals classified 'Y' in 150 Bde, 5th R. I. Pioneers 1/3 N.F.A, 2/2 N.F.A | E.S.H. |
| | 31/1/19 | | V.O's conference at DA.D.V.S's Office. Routine work. | E.S.H. |

E S Hearne Major D.A.D.V.S
50th Division

D. D. & L., London, E.C.
(A8001) Wt. W1771/M2031 750,000 5/17 Sch. 52 Forms/C2118/14

Confidential

45

# WAR DIARY

OF

D.A.D.V.S., 50th DIVISION

FROM 1st FEBRUARY 1919 TO 28TH FEBRUARY 1919

VOLUME XLI

9

Army Form C. 2118.

Instructions regarding War Diaries and Intelligence Summaries are contained in F. S. Regs., Part II. and the Staff Manual respectively. Title pages will be prepared in manuscript.

Vol 41

# WAR DIARY
*or*
# INTELLIGENCE SUMMARY.
*(Erase heading not required.)*

D.A.D.V.S., 50th Division

| Place | Date | Hour | Summary of Events and Information | Remarks and references to Appendices |
|---|---|---|---|---|
| LEQUESNOY | 1 2/19 | | Examined 200 "Y" animals, before despatch to 13th Corps. Visited M.V.S. and paid men in absence of O.C. who was sick in C.C.S. | Est |
| | 2 2/19 | | Inspected 7th + 447th Fld. Coys. R.E. Notified 'Q' of animals in M.V.S. fit for reissue. | Est |
| | 3 2/19 | | Examined at M.V.S. 21 animals before their evacuation. (19 of Division + 2 of other Formations) Saw animals of 335 Road Construction Coy. which had been malleined, and forwarded chart to A.D.V.S. Corps. | Est |
| | 4 2/19 | | Informed A.D.V.S. Corps that no V.Os. in Division desired appointments in Africa. Wired all Field units of Div. having Vety. Sgts. attached, to notify me their ages, dates of attestation, + civil employment. | Est |
| | 5 2/19 | | Visited A.D.V.S. XIII Corps. Inspected at M.V.S. 16 animals before their evacuation. (15 of Divn. + 1 of other Formation) | Est |
| | 6 2/19 | | Visited and Examined animals of 169 Labour Coy. and sent 3 into M.V.S. Forwarded service particulars of officers R.A.V.C. to A.D.V.S. Corps. | Est |
| | 7 2/19 | | Received from 13th Corps H.A. 150 animals to replace 150 leaving Division and made personal examination of them. Six were sent into M.V.S and 30 others were affected with lice. Issued to 169 Labour Coy. 3 animals to replace those 3 evacuated on 6th inst | Est |

D. D. & L., London, E.C. (A8001) Wt. W1771/M2031 750,000 5/17 Sch. 52 Forms/C2118/14

Instructions regarding War Diaries and Intelligence Summaries are contained in F. S. Regs., Part II. and the Staff Manual respectively. Title pages will be prepared in manuscript.

# WAR DIARY
*or*
# INTELLIGENCE SUMMARY.
*(Erase heading not required.)*

Army Form C. 2118.

D.A.D.V.S. 50. Div

| Place | Date | Hour | Summary of Events and Information | Remarks and references to Appendices |
|---|---|---|---|---|
| Le QUESNOY | 8/2/19 | | Inspected at M.V.S. 18 animals before their evacuation. (11 of Division & 7 of other Formations)<br>Visited 2nd Royal Dublin Fusiliers.<br>Examined before despatch to BEAUVOIS XIII Corps 147 "Y" animals. | EH. |
| | 9/2/19 | | Called at "Q" to try to arrange horse sales at Le QUESNOY and BERLAIMONT and informed A.D.V.S. Corps what steps were being taken to hold these auctions. | EH. |
| | 10/2/19 | | Examined 24 "Z" animals before despatch for sale to French. | EH. |
| | 11/2/19 | | Visited 1. 3 & 4 Corp A.S.C.<br>Saw Maire of Le QUESNOY on the forage supply in neighbourhood for sustenance of animals if sold. Informed A.D.V.S. Corps that Maire stated hay to be insufficient but that he was willing to purchase it from British Army if possible.<br>Inspected at M.V.S. 14 animals before their evacuation. (11 of Division & 3 of other formations) | EH. |
| | 12/2/19 | | On instructions received from D.D.V.S Army, wired to Base for 2 N.C.O's for M.V.S.<br>Routine Work. | EH |
| | 13/2/19 | | Inspected all animals of D.H.Q. & Div. Sig. Coy R.E. & ordered destruction of L.D.H in Artillery - fractured tibia.<br>Visited M.G. Battn. and sent 1 Rider into M.V.S. suffering from Ulcerative Cellulitis to be destroyed & buried - unfit for food.<br>Issued L.D.H & L.D.M. to Div. Sig. Coy. R.E. and 1 L.D.M. to D.A.C. | EH |

Instructions regarding War Diaries and Intelligence Summaries are contained in F. S. Regs., Part II. and the Staff Manual respectively. Title pages will be prepared in manuscript.

# WAR DIARY
*or*
# INTELLIGENCE SUMMARY.

(*Erase heading not required.*)

Army Form C. 2118.

DADVS, 50 Div.

| Place | Date | Hour | Summary of Events and Information | Remarks and references to Appendices |
|---|---|---|---|---|
| Le QUESNOY | 14/2/19 | | Conference with V.Os<br>Inspected 12 animals at M.V.S. before their evacuation (9 of Div. and 3 of other Formations) | [illegible] |
| | 15/2/19 | | Visited MAIRE of BERLAIMONT to arrange sale. He was unable to give me any idea of forage supply in that and neighbouring communes until 18th.<br>Inspected animals of 1/1 N.F.A., Div. Sig. Coy. RE. 3rd Royal Fusiliers & 2nd Royal Dublin Fus. | [illegible] |
| | 16/2/19 | | Inspected all animals of S.A.A., D.A.C.<br>Saw 20 animals at M.V.S before evacuation (16 of Division and 4 of other formations)<br>Despatched remaining Sergeant R.A.V.C with M.V.S. to Base for demobilisation. | [illegible] |
| | 17/2/19 | | Examined animals of 1/1 NFA, Div. Sig. Coy. RE, Pioneers & 330 Road Construction Coy.<br>30 (Z) animals despatched to Paris for sale. 10 Riders 14 L.D.H. 6 H.D.<br>Ordered destruction of L.D.H. from 446 Fd. Coy. RE in M.V.S suffering from Chronic Debility | [illegible] |
| | 18/2/19 | | Visited Maire of BERLAIMONT and arranged sale of 100 animals ("Z" surplus) to take place 22nd.<br>Informed A.D.V.S Corps of above arrangements.<br>Inspected animals of 447 Fd. Coy. RE, 151 Inf. Bgde and Pioneer Battn.<br>Instructed V.O. 251 Bgde RFA to attend animal of 151 I. Bgde – colic case. | [illegible] |

D. D. & L., London, E.C.
(A8001) Wt. W1771/M2031 750,000 5/17 Sch. 52 Forms/C2118/14

Instructions regarding War Diaries and Intelligence Summaries are contained in F. S. Regs., Par. II. and the Staff Manual respectively. Title pages will be prepared in manuscript.

# WAR DIARY
*or*
# INTELLIGENCE SUMMARY.
*(Erase heading not required.)*

DADVS, 50 Div.

Army Form C. 2118.

| Place | Date | Hour | Summary of Events and Information | Remarks and references to Appendices |
|---|---|---|---|---|
| Le QUESNOY. | 19/2/19 | | Saw Maire of Le QUESNOY and arranged sale of 100 'Z' Surplus animals for 26th inst<br>Inspected animals of S.A.A. Secn. 50th D.A.C. | [illegible] |
| | 20/2/19 | | Instructed M.V.S to collect animal left with civilian at BEAUDIGNIES<br>Inspected all D.H.Q. animals<br>Examined 16 animals at M.V.S before their evacuation - 16 includes 4 of other Formations<br>Instructed V.O. 251 Bgde R.F.A. to inspect all animals of 151 Bgde H.Q. | [illegible] |
| | 21/2/19 | | Selected the 100 animals for sale on 22nd from various units of Division<br>Conference with V.Os. | [illegible] |
| | 22/2/19 | | Attended sale of 100 animals at BERLAIMONT.<br>Instructed V.O. to inspect animal of civilian who was claiming damages for an accident unavoidably caused to it by a runaway team + to report the extent of its injuries. | [illegible] |
| | 23/2/19 | | Deposited proceeds of sale on previous day with Field Cashier at Corps H.Q.<br>Visited A.D.V.S. XIII Corps.<br>Issued L.D. Mule - stray animal - to 50th Batt. M.G.C | [illegible] |
| | 24/2/19 | | Went to BAVAY to try to arrange a sale - unsuccessful for time being<br>Examined 22 animals of Div. and 4 of other Formations before their evacuation to Base from M.V.S. | [illegible] |

D. D. & L., London, E.C.
(A10266) Wt W5300/P713 750,000 2/18 Sch. 52 Forms/C2118/16.

Instructions regarding War Diaries and Intelligence Summaries are contained in F. S. Regs., Part II. and the Staff Manual respectively. Title pages will be prepared in manuscript.

# WAR DIARY
*or*
# INTELLIGENCE SUMMARY.
*(Erase heading not required.)*

Army Form C. 2118.

D.A.D.V.S., 50 Div

| Place | Date | Hour | Summary of Events and Information | Remarks and references to Appendices |
|---|---|---|---|---|
| Le QUESNOY | 25-2/19 | | Inspected 43 Y animals before despatch to Base through Corps Collecting Camp BEAUVOIS<br>Selected from various units 100 Z surplus animals for sale on 26th inst. | E.H. |
| | 26 2/19 | | Inspected 43 Z animals before despatch to Paris for sale<br>Attended at sale of Z animals in Le QUESNOY - 98 sold to civilian farmers<br>Detailed OC. M.V.S. to be member of a Board held on 28th. for testing of cold shoers to be shoeing smiths. | E.H. |
| | 27 2/19 | | Inspected 12 Riders selected from units of Division for shipment to England as Infantry Officers Chargers. | E.H. |
| | 28 2/19 | | Conference of V.Os.<br>Arranged for two sales each of 100 animals at Le QUESNOY on 5th & 8th March, and informed A.D.V.S. Corps of arrangements.<br>Examined stabling & men's accommodation at M.V.S. | E.H. |

1. 3. 19

Estienne Maj. RAVC
D.A.D.V.S. 50 Division

D. D. & L., London, E.C.
(A10266) Wt W5300/P713 750,000 2/18 Sch. 52 Forms/C2118/16.

CONFIDENTIAL.

Vol 46

# WAR DIARY

OF.

# D.A.D.V.S., 50TH DIVISION

FROM 1ST MARCH 1919 TO 31ST MARCH 1919.

VOL. XLII

14

42

Vol XLII

Instructions regarding War Diaries and Intelligence Summaries are contained in F. S. Regs., Part II. and the Staff Manual respectively. Title pages will be prepared in manuscript.

# WAR DIARY
*or*
# INTELLIGENCE SUMMARY.
*(Erase heading not required.)*

Army Form C. 2118.

D.A.D.V.S., 50th Division

| Place | Date | Hour | Summary of Events and Information | Remarks and references to Appendices |
|---|---|---|---|---|
| Le Quesnoy | 1/3/19 | | Instructed V.Os. to give certificates to units for disinfected harness before its return to Ordnance. | |
| | | | Inspected 50 'Z' animals before their despatch to ABBEVILLE. | |
| | | | Examined 31 animals at M.V.S. before their evacuation to Base V.H. 24 belonged to Division and 7 to other formations. | |
| | | | Kept A.D.V.S. Corps informed of all sales of 'Z' animals arranged locally. | Est. |
| | 2/3/19 | | Saw stray mule with 17th Labour Group and ordered its evacuation to M.V.S. | |
| | | | Sent 1 man R.A.V.C. from M.V.S. for demobilisation. | |
| | | | Visited several local villages, and neighbouring communes to advertise sales of 'Z' animals | Est. |
| | 3/3/19 | | Inspected 50 'Z' animals before their despatch to ABBEVILLE. | |
| | | | " 100 Z " " " " CANDAS. | Est. |
| | 4/3/19 | | Selected 100 animals for sale on 5th. – accompanied by Officer i/c Sales. | |
| | | | Submitted to A.D.V.S. Corps Rolls of R.A.V.C. personnel selected for retention as part of machinery of demobilisation. | Est. |
| | 5/3/19 | | Sale of 96 'Z' animals Le QUESNOY. | |
| | | | Saw 2 animals of 335 Road Construction Coy. R.E. and ordered them to M.V.S. | Est. |

D. D. & L., London, E.C.
(A10266) Wt W5300/P713 750,000 2/18 Sch. 52 Forms/C2118/16.

Instructions regarding War Diaries and Intelligence Summaries are contained in F. S. Regs., Part II. and the Staff Manual respectively. Title pages will be prepared in manuscript.

# WAR DIARY
*or*
# INTELLIGENCE SUMMARY.
*(Erase heading not required.)*

Army Form C. 2118.

D.A.D.V.S., 50 Div

| Place | Date | Hour | Summary of Events and Information | Remarks and references to Appendices |
|---|---|---|---|---|
| LeQUESNOY | 6 3/19 | | Arranged sale of 'Z' animals at BERLAIMONT for 12th inst.<br>Saw DAC mules attached 13th Black Watch and gave Transport Officer a written report on their favourable condition. | Est |
| | 7 3/19 | | Selected with Officer i/c Sales, 100 'Z' animals for sale on 8th inst.<br>Examined 18 animals before their evacuation to Base. 11 of Division & 7 of other Formations.<br>Inspected 100 'X' animals before their despatch to Dieppe – withdrew 3<br>Reported to Corps on progress made in malleining in Division. | Est |
| | 8 3/19 | | Sold 99 Z animals at LeQuesnoy – one withdrawn. | Est |
| | 9 3/19 | | Kept ADVS Corps informed of nos. of A B & C classes of animals still in Division to date<br>Took proceeds of sale on 8th to Field Cashier at Corps HQ.<br>Conversation with Maire LeQUESNOY re forage possessed by prospective buyers of Army horses and their ability to feed them sufficiently well. Went into the question with him of civilians obtaining of ^or repayment supplies of hay oats from British Army, and reported results of conversation to ADVS Corps. | Est |
| | 10 3/19 | | Inspected 200 'Z' mules from Artillery before their despatch to ABBEVILLE – 3 were withdrawn and replaced by others from surplus with Pioneer Battn.<br>Routine Work. | Est |

D. D. & L., London, E.C.
(A10266) Wt W5300/P713 750,000 2/18 Sch. 52 Forms/C2118/16

Instructions regarding War Diaries and Intelligence Summaries are contained in F. S. Regs., Part II. and the Staff Manual respectively. Title pages will be prepared in manuscript.

# WAR DIARY
*or*
# INTELLIGENCE SUMMARY.
*(Erase heading not required.)*

Army Form C. 2118.

D.A.D.V.S., 50th Div

| Place | Date | Hour | Summary of Events and Information | Remarks and references to Appendices |
|---|---|---|---|---|
| Le Quesnoy | 11/3/19 | | Inspected 25 'T' riders before their despatch to DIEPPE. | |
| | | | " 200 Z animals " " " Abbeville - 1 was withdrawn & replaced. | |
| | | | Selected with Officer i/c sales 100 'Z' animals for sale BERLAIMONT on 12th inst. | Est |
| | 12/3/19 | | Sale of 100 Z animals BERLAIMONT. | |
| | | | Inspected 65 'X' H.D. horses for DIEPPE. | |
| | | | Gave instructions for 1 Sgt. R.A.V.C. with Artillery to be demobilised. | Est |
| | 13/3/19 | | Examined 31 animals before their evacuation (15 of Div. & 16 of Other Formations) | Est |
| | | | Routine Work | |
| | 14/3/19 | | Examined 50 'Z' Riders for ABBEVILLE | |
| | | | Selected with Officer i/c sales. 100 'Z' animals for sale Le Quesnoy 15th inst. | Est |
| | 15/3/19 | | Sale of 100 'Z' animals Le Quesnoy. | |
| | | | Inspected 50 'Z' Riders for ABBEVILLE - withdrew 1 | |
| | | | " 12 'X' L D horses withdrawn from 7 H/Cy. reduced to Cadre 'A' | |
| | | | " 54 'favourite' animals going to Base for repatriation & sale | Est |
| | 16/3/19 | | Examined 37 animals before their despatch to Base. 19 of Div & 18 of Other Formations. | Est |

D. D. & L., London, E.C.
(A10266) Wt W. 5300/P713 750,000 2/18 Sch. 52 Forms/C2118/16

Instructions regarding War Diaries and Intelligence Summaries are contained in F. S. Regs., Part II. and the Staff Manual respectively. Title pages will be prepared in manuscript.

# WAR DIARY
*or*
# INTELLIGENCE SUMMARY.
*(Erase heading not required.)*

Army Form C. 2118.

D.A.D.V.S., 50 Div.

| Place | Date | Hour | Summary of Events and Information | Remarks and references to Appendices |
|---|---|---|---|---|
| Le Quesnoy | 17/3/19 | | Selected 45 'Z' animals to be sent same day to ABBEVILLE. | |
| | | | Submitted claim of Capt T. Woods R.A.V.C. for repatriation to Brazil to A.D.V.S. XIII Corps. | Ent |
| | 18/3/19 | | Capt Austin R.A.V.C. left for demobilisation. | |
| | | | Inspected 100 'Y' Riders before despatch to Base. | |
| | | | " 50 Z animals sent to ABBEVILLE. | Ent |
| | 19/3/19 | | Examined 21 animals before their evacuation to Base V.H. (16 of Division & 5 of Other formations.) | |
| | | | Selected and examined 43 'Z' animals before their despatch to ABBEVILLE. | Ent |
| | 20/3/19 | | Routine Work | |
| | | | Examined all animals of Inf. Bgdes & R.E.S. | Ent |
| | 21/3/19 | | Conference with V.Os. | |
| | | | Inspected 75 R. and 49 L.D.M. selected from Artillery for despatch to Army of Occupation. | Ent |
| | 22/3/19 | | Examined animals remaining with D.A.C. and Art. Bgdes | |
| | | | Submitted to Corps a roll of Officers available for reposting | |
| | | | Applied to Q for a shoeing smith to be attached to M.V.S in place of the regular one sick in Hospital or leave. | Ent |

D. D. & L., London, E.C.
(A10266) Wt W. 5300/P713 750,000 2/18 Sch. 52 Forms/C2118/16

Instructions regarding War Diaries and Intelligence Summaries are contained in F. S. Regs., Part II. and the Staff Manual respectively. Title pages will be prepared in manuscript.

# WAR DIARY
*or*
# INTELLIGENCE SUMMARY. D.A.D.V.S. 50 Div.
*(Erase heading not required.)*

Army Form C. 2118.

| Place | Date | Hour | Summary of Events and Information | Remarks and references to Appendices |
|---|---|---|---|---|
| LE QUESNOY | 23 3/19 | | Routine Work<br>Inspected all remaining animals of Fd. Coys. R.E. and Ambulances | E.H. |
| | 24 3/19 | | Visited A.D.V.S. XIII Corps. to report on progress made in demobilisation of animals of Div. | E.H. |
| | 25 3/19 | | Inspected 29 Y. animals before their despatch to CANDAS<br>" 10 X L.D. from 7th Fd. Coy. R.E. before their despatch to CANDAS<br>Another Sgt. R.A.V.C. attached Artillery demobilised | E.H. |
| | | | Inspected at M.V.S. 15 animals before their evacuation to Base. 9 of Div. + 6 of other formations. | E.H. |
| | 26 3/19 | | Routine Work.<br>Inspected animals of R.A.S.C. | E.H. |
| | 27 3/19 | | Routine Work<br>Inspected animals of Inf. and R.E.s | |
| | 28 3/19 | | Inspected animals selected to complete M.G. Battn to CADRE 'B' establishment<br>Again wired Corps numbers of releasable R.A.V.C. personnel | E.H. |
| | 29 3/19 | | Inspected 4 R. and 373 L.D.m before their despatch to COLOGNE. In addition to these 5 Riders from Corps H.Q. were also entrained. Was present at the entraining | |

Instructions regarding War Diaries and Intelligence Summaries are contained in F. S. Regs., Part II. and the Staff Manual respectively. Title pages will be prepared in manuscript.

# WAR DIARY
*or*
# INTELLIGENCE SUMMARY.
(*Erase heading not required.*)

D.A.D.V.S. 50th Div.

Army Form C. 2118.

| Place | Date | Hour | Summary of Events and Information | Remarks and references to Appendices |
| --- | --- | --- | --- | --- |
| le Quesnoy | 30/3/19 | | Inspected 9 animals at M.V.S. before evacuation to Vet Hospital 5 belonged to Division and 4 to units of other formations. | T.H. |
| | | | D.A.D.V.S left for IRELAND - special leave of 14 days. | |
| | 31/3/19 | | Capt E.R. Staples RAVC left Division for Corps Concentration Camp pending demobilisation | T.H. |
| | | | 3 Sergeants RAVC. left Division for Corps Concentration Camp pending demobilisation. | |
| | | | OC. M.V.S instructed by Div. Q to wind up affairs at M.V.S. and proceed at earliest for duty at 14. Vet Hospital. | |

T Woods, Capt. for
D.A.D.V.S., 50th Division

D.H.Q.
31. 3. 19

D. D. & L., London, E.C.
(A10266) Wt W 5300/P713 750,000 2/18 Sch. 52 Forms/C2118/16

www.ingramcontent.com/pod-product-compliance
Lightning Source LLC
Chambersburg PA
CBHW080854010526
44117CB00014B/2251
* 9 7 8 1 4 7 4 5 2 7 6 6 8 *